THE CANARY ROOM

A Novel

EDWIN F. CASEBEER AND LINDA CASEBEER

SEREALITIES PRESS
www.serealities.com

All characters appearing in The Canary Room are fictitious. Any resemblance to real persons, living or dead, is purely coincidental.

Copyright

ISBN: 1494423766
ISBN 13: 9781494423766

Library of Congress Control Number: 2013922942
CreateSpace Independent Publishing Platform
North Charleston, South Carolina

Table of Contents

One

A thousand songs. A thousand birds. Silver sun and universal morning song piercing the rose of the morning sky.

Herman started from his long dream. **Canaries.** At the foot of his cot, canaries boxed and hutched, cages shaped in minarets and domes, wood, rusty iron, gold, silver. Cages and cages glowed in the Idaho sun filtering through the gnarled black tangle of climbing brown rose cane clawing the dusty windows of the porch. **Canaries. Look at that.** Cages of canaries, coral, orange, white, yellow wings striped tar black, flutter and hop, flap and clatter, peck and sip, warble and warble and warble until song ached.

Herman threw back the blue flannel sheets, then froze in an upward arc. **My arm's numb! Ohmygod. Not again.** Outside the door and down the hall he heard dim metal kitchen clatter, heavy thump of boot leather on the hall's wooden floor. *Outside the door he hears the clatter of high heels on the hall wood.* **She'll make me exercise.** No._Mom. Don't. I can't. I can't move it that high. Mom!* Fear knotted his belly. He grabbed his crotch. He turned and swiveled his feet to the cold linoleum. He scowled. **Moron. You can't get polio twice. Your arm's just asleep. Yella belly. Mom's in Georgia. Dad lives in a basement. And Karl and Howie burned out Tank's eyes. And Tom...and Uncle Cory are not here.** He stood in his baggy long johns, thin, tall, twelve.

How could Dad do this? Who are these people he left me with? I've never seen them. I don't know them. He stooped and picked up a shoe. **She**

bought this for me. Out of her first paycheck from Sears. Three months after Dad left the first time. When he tried to get into the O.S.S. He sat back down on the bed and turned to the tan plaid lumberjack shirt hanging on a bedstead knob. And this. He brought the heavy wool shirt to his face, covered his eyes. He trembled. Mom. Oh, Mom. Pain glowed, sliced, rode in, seized gut and crotch, climbed and split shoulder blades, rose, spun behind his eyes.

Never. Never. It'll never end. Herman watched himself rising from the bed, dressing, eating, leaving the house, walking to school, and always, the same, always alone, always taking the next step, always under a cloud, in the shadow, in a cold, cold valley. One step after the other. Alone. Raising his head, he looked at the shirt again. This damn war. If it wasn't for the war…He punched his pillow. What're all these canaries doing here? Who are these people? These crazy Williams people? Who in the hell? He punched his pillow again. War. I'll give you war! And again he punched. Take that, Tojo! The canaries began to dart in their cages, flashing yellow against moss green walls, wings humming and flapping. He punched the pillow harder. Damn Nazis. The birds crashed against their cages, but he wouldn't stop. No sir. Tears blurred canaries into clouds, yellow, orange, white.

"Herman. What's all that ruckus about? What's all that flapping for? Herman! Come out here! Breakfast!" He stopped punching. Bird flutter. "Herman, do you hear me?" A feather floated in the air.

"Coming, Mrs. Williams!" Coming, Ma. HenRY, Henry Aldrich!!! "Coming, Ma," he muttered as he pulled a horizontally striped pullover over his long john tops. Well, poor little Hermy. All alone. Just walking all alone. He smiled and saluted. Left, left, yir left-right-left. He laughed. Ya hadda good son and ya left. YIR RIGHT. Ya hadda good son and ya left. YIR RIGHT. SOUND OFF. ONE, two. He stopped, his fine brown hair falling over his face, and pulled a heavy cardboard suitcase from under the cot.

"Herman! Get out here! It's time to go to school!"

"Yes, Mrs. Williams." **Four times I've packed this damn cardboard suitcase this year. Walla Walla. Cashmere. Seattle. Now Boise. And three times in Boise. The ballpark. The Schultzes. These damn Williams and their canaries. Well, to hell with it. To HELL with this damn suitcase. Who ever heard of a cardboard suitcase anyway?**

He stooped to close the suitcase and then saw a book on top of the clothing. Lassie Come Home.

"Here's some money. You know where the Book Nook is?" Herman nods.

"Go buy yourself Lassie Come Home. *I know they've got it...it just came out a couple of years ago."*

"Gee, Dad. Thanks." Thank you. **He loves me. Herman grins.** *Far off the crash of the newspaper's presses, here in his nostrils the keen bite of rubber glue.* **I love all this. I love him. Then why did he put me here? Karl had it coming.**

"Herman! Don't make me come out there!"

"Yes, Mrs. Williams. I'm coming." He pulled out a pair of tan trousers and slipped into them, tugging the broad waistband up under his ribs and cinching the belt tightly. He stuffed his hands into the deep pockets. **The good old twills Mom got at Sears. Cavalry cut.** He slipped on his shoes, picked up his lumberjack shirt and a Dodgers baseball cap off the headboard, walked out into a hall to turn left into the bathroom. "Be right there, Mrs. Williams!"

At the toilet, he unzipped.

"Don't splash. Hit the bowl." **O.K., Dad. They won't hear me pissing. Peeing. Something.** Zipping up, he turned to the washbasin and rolled up his sleeves. On his left arm in the crook of an elbow was a small, delicately etched tattoo of a snake. He straightened out the arm. The snake stretched. **Hi there.**

He touched the tattoo and then saw himself, smeared, on the steamy mirror in a drop of water condensing, rainbow in its bulge, the sun suddenly pressing behind him and now exploding into flash in glass. He closed his eyes into shattered purple. He rubbed them and saw ruby, then emerald.

Herman washed his hands. He looked for a towel and found one on the floor, wet and stained. **Somebody's had a bath. Probably Mr. Williams. No. He'd fold it up. Max? Charlie? That little kid—what's his name? Sonny?** He dried his hands on his pants, pulled out a comb, wet it, and pulled it through his hair, shaping a pompadour. A strand of hair arched out from his temple. **I look like Dagwood.** He jammed the baseball cap backwards on his head. **Now I look like Sandy.** He left the bathroom and entered the dark hall. **One step at a time.** At its end, he saw a round dining room table to his left and then peered into the dim living room beyond. "Mrs. Williams?"

"In here," alto from the right. "We eat breakfast in here." Herman stepped into the kitchen's light. Large and cluttered, a sink full of dishes on the wall opposite, a wood-burning stove to his left, the kitchen smelled of wood smoke, coffee, bacon, and burnt toast. Enormous with wild carrot-orange hair, lids heavy over dim and drowsing brown eyes, Gladys Williams sprawled at the large rectangular table. A pale green canary perched on her shoulder. She followed Herman's gaze. "This here's Shamrock. Say 'hello,' Shamrock." The bird pecked at her ear. "Help yourself." Burnt toast, a Mason jar of strawberry jam, its paraffin lid sticky side down on the shiny oilcloth, partially concealing a little red Mexican boy taking a siesta against a lime cactus, his face concealed by a huge sombrero. "Better hurry." Herman hung his lumberjack shirt on the back of the chair. "You take your cap off at this table." He removed his cap, then looked for a knife and the toast.

They stand together in the night. Dad knocks again. The door opens. Yellow light frames the woman's bulk, illuminates the orange halo of hair. Her face is in shadow. "Gladys?"

"Jake. That Herman?"

"Yes. Shake hands, Herman." He does.

"Let me put that suitcase right here." In the room beyond, a lean man and two adolescent boys sit in a pool of light around a floor model radio from which comes the discordant whine of a violin and the lines, "I didn't expect to find you in the orchestra." Herman smiles. **It's the Jack Benny Show. Bing Crosby is supposed to be on tonight.**

Although the boys don't look up, the man stands. He is a head taller than Jake. He extends his hand. "It's been a long time. Good to see you again, Jake."

"Same here, Andy."

"I hear you're running the Bond drive this year."

"Yes. For the whole state. The paper's given me leave to do the job." Andrew nods and smiles. Gladys turns to Jake. "Let's talk in the kitchen."

Sitting at the kitchen table, his hands around a mug of coffee, Jake explains. "You know that Hope and I finally divorced." Gladys nods. "Herman needs some kind of a home life and my brother Frank said…" He looks up at the boy, who still stands and then turns to Gladys. "Could he sit in the living room while we talk?"

Gladys nods. "Do you like Jack Benny, Herman?" He nods and leaves to sit on the davenport. He watches the others at the radio. Static squalls. Andrew leans forward from the purple and green of an afghan coverlet and adjusts a dial.

"I can't understand it. I've never played so poorly." The audience laughs but Andrew and the two boys remain unsmiling, intent.

"Oh, cheer up, Jack. Sure you have." The audience laughs louder. Andrew smiles now.

"I even washed my fingers in Duz. If Duz doesn't do it…" The radio squeals again. Andrew frowns and patiently begins to turn dials.

*Herman hears a woman's voice speaking from the radio. "Well, Mary Livingstone!"
Applause. He looks at the lamp about Andrew's head. Small orange balls hang from its rim.
"What do all the women see in Bing Crosby? Look at him. He's got blue eyes like mine…"*

*Mary cuts Jack off: "Stop right here, brother!" Andrew and the boys laugh. Herman
scratches at a shiny spot on the davenport's arm. **Some kind of food.***

*Jake's voice rises from the kitchen. "…busy with the Seventh War Loan Drive. Frankly,
I think that Herman needs to know who's boss. With the Schultz family and me living under
the same roof, he got confused. He got into a fight with one of their boys. Karl, a good enough
kid…" On a coffee table before Herman are two framed photographs. He examines the larger
one, the Williams' wedding photograph, framed by a heavy silver metal worked into small roses
and irises. **Iris. I wonder if I will ever see my cousin again.** In the photograph, she is
a slender girl with a round and pretty face, Andrew even leaner, clearly uneasy in suit and tie.
Next to the wedding photograph in a plain bronze frame is a sepia print of a girl in uniform,
a WAC. Her dark curls tumble about her face. **She is beautiful. Even more than Iris.***

*Looking up from the photograph, Herman sees that one of the boys has been watching him
but now glances away. Smaller and slimmer than the other boy, he has a neat crewcut, very short,
his skull gleaming at the crown beneath black hair that comes to a widow's peak in the center of
his pimpled forehead. His shirt is black, closely-fitted, its long sleeves neatly rolled one turn up,
revealing on his left wrist a watch with a heavy silver band. He sits cross-legged before the radio
in clean, faded denims, a highly polished loafer visible under one knee, a silver dime glinting in
the horizontal slot on its tongue. **It looks like his clothes were made for him.** The other
boy is larger, thicker, wearing a white t-shirt, its sleeves rolled up to expose sun-tanned biceps
and shoulder muscles. He also sits cross-legged, bare-footed, in dirty tan corduroys. He now runs
his hand through an overgrown blond crewcut. The smaller boy laughs and looks up at Andrew,
who smiles back. The boy stops smiling and looks away.*

*"Sixty a month is very reasonable." Gladys and Jake emerge from the kitchen and stop
next to Herman, who rises. "I have to go now, son. I'll see you next weekend." He puts out his
hand. Herman takes it. Jake looks over at Andrew and smiles.*

Gladys leads Jake to the door. While they stand there talking, Andrew gestures from his chair. "Good night, Jake. Come on over here, boy. I didn't catch the name."

"Herman. Auerbach."

"Meet the boys, Herman. This is my son, Max. Max? Get up off your duff and shake Herman's hand." Scowling, grunting, the blond boy heaves himself to a standing position and squeezes Herman's hand. Herman winces. Max grins. "And this is Charlie. Charlie Como. You know, like Perry Como. He boards here with us. His mother is a nurse. Used to be attached to the Air Force at Gowan Field. In Los Angeles now. Right Charlie?" The smaller boy rises and nods at Herman but refuses his extended hand. Herman blushes. "My youngest, Sonny, is sound asleep—he's just eight. You'll share a room with him—and one or two hundred canaries Gladys is raising for fun and profit. Helen—that's the one you were looking at over there—she's an officer in the WAC's." He looked down at the afghan, then up. "And we lost a son in the war."

"Goodnight, Hermy." Jake waves from the doorway. Herman takes a step toward his father. The door closes. Gladys walks over, carrying the suitcase. "Here's your stuff. Let me show you to your room." Gladys leads him down the long hall to the porch at the end of the hall. "The room on the left here belongs to Max and Charlie. The little room on the right's my sewing room and the nesting room. I raise canaries. If you need me, Mr. Williams and I sleep in the room off the living room at the front of the house. And this is the bathroom. Here's the porch. Don't turn on the light. I don't want Sonny to wake up." When she closes the door behind herself, Herman undresses in the dark, slips between the cold flannel sheets and listens to the peep and flutter of birds resettling as the thick cloth warms about his bare legs.

Gladys put down her newspaper. Shamrock fluttered. "Herman, your breakfast's cold. Hurry up and eat or you're going to be late for school. Sonny's gone already." She disappeared behind her newspaper again. Herman picked up a piece of toast. It was thick, charred homemade bread. He saw the loaf now, lying on the tablecloth, a serrated knife beside it. He couldn't see a toaster. Sighing, he reached for oleomargarine to spread on the toast. The spread was still white and studded with black crumbs. In front of him was a bowl of sugar, brown and flaking. He put down the toast and, reaching for a spoon, looked at the sugar bowl. **Just like Auntie Ide's.**

The sugar is stained tan by coffee dripping from spoons and caked into crusts around the inside of the cut crystal bowl, jagged, and toward the bottom, thicker and solid, too hard to chip away. **Like a volcano filled with snow.** *Herman lifts the bowl, holds it over his Cream of Wheat and carefully drops heaping teaspoonsful, one, two, three—lucky number—in overlapping circles that form a triangle. He watches the steamy milk seep up through the cereal and darken the white sugar.*

Gladys rattled the paper and coughed. She looked over its top at Herman. He stopped chopping at the sugar and put the spoon down. She returned to her reading. With his forefinger, he touched the oatmeal. It was firm and cold.

And then he digs deeply into the center of the triangle and puts the first warm, sweet bite into his mouth. He feels the last crunchy sugar grains melt into liquid as he holds the bite in his mouth and then slowly, softly chews, and swallows. He swallows once more and clears his throat. "Auntie Ide?"

"Yes?"

"If Iris is a twin, what happened to her brother? Did he die because he fell from the apple tree?"

"Not the tree. Apples. It was apples that Thomas puked up and choked on."

"I thought the fall killed him."

"No, honey, the damn apples. He couldn't wait and went out and stuffed himself sick with green apples. Sure, Thomas fell. But he just broke his arm. He died choking on green apples at the hospital when they gave him the ether. Never had another son. Always wanted one. That's

why it's so nice to have a boy around the house again. Same age as Iris. Takes me back, it does, havin you here." She pats his hand.

Herman looked up again at Gladys when she turned a page, her arms spreading wide and closing again before her, the flesh at her triceps swaying. **Like fins. Whale fins.** He looked at the captions. They were blurred. He dug into the plaid shirt pocket, pulled out a scarred metal glasses case, clicked it open, and put on gold-framed glasses. Then he removed the glasses and polished them on his pullover. He picked up the newspaper.

<u>RUSSIANS</u>

War news. I hate news. He leaned forward. **Huh. A young woman killed over a hundred Nazis.** He began humming. **Sniper. Watching and waiting. Picking them off. And she says that she is going to go back and get herself some more. The Russians are heroes.** Herman hummed louder. Words came. **Through meadowlands we are marching and our guns are blazing. When we march back through our dear Me-eh-eh-dow LANDS. Then people's cows'll be grazing. I think.**

Gladys looked up. "Herman."

"Huh?"

"Would you stop makin that noise? I've been up since five makin breakfast and I want some peace." Gladys stared at him. "What is that song, anyway?"

"The Russian Infantry's Marching Song. 'Meadowlands'."

"Herman, that's Communist."

"But they're on our side."

"They weren't. Till Hitler stabbed them in the back. We're better off without the Reds. They're just using us. And now that we've beat the Germans, they're pushin right in there. Herman, I won't…" Gladys suddenly leaned toward him. "Herman, what's that on your neck?" Herman took off his glasses. "Is that a wound? I'm not being nosey, boy, you at the age you are and all—I see you blushin—but when I take in a new youngen I always look them over real close. I got to know what's happened to them before they came here. That way your father don't blame me for somethin that's already done to you."

"I got shot." Gladys started. "My father knows about it. It was right after the divorce. Even before I moved to Boise. I was spending the summer outside Cashmere on my aunt's apple orchard while my mother was getting settled." Herman snapped the case on the glasses and returned it to his shirt pocket.

"I knew Hope. And her sister Ide, too, when the Marshalls lived in Cashmere. I thinned apples with them a couple of summers." The woman and the boy watched one another. "So did you accidentally set off a gun? Boys been known to do that time and again if you don't watch them."

"No." Herman looked down at the oilcloth. "It was Uncle Cory, Auntie Ide's husband. He shot me. And he shot Gypsy. My rat that the gypsy lady gave me. I forgot about rats and chickens. He was drunk. Auntie Ide took me to the bus and…and." **And Tom.**

"Hold on, boy. That's enough. I know what I have to know. I know Willy Pillton, too. Well enough not to want to know anymore."

"Willy?"

"That's what they called your uncle before the Japs caught him at Corregidor." Her lips pressed tightly together, Gladys turned back to her paper. "Eat your breakfast." Shamrock fluttered down to the table, pecked at a toast crumb.

Herman took a spoonful of oatmeal and pulled a section of the newspaper around so that he could look at it.

RAINBOW RUNS!

...reports that the hunter thought that they finally had trapped Rainbow when he led the herd into the box canyon. But when they awoke this morning, the stallion had once again escaped. They found...

"Mrs. Williams?"

"Hmmh?"

"Rainbow got away again."

"Good for him. Now eat your breakfast."

Herman tipped his chair back and examined Gladys. **She's bigger than Auntie Ide.** He rocked backward and peered under the table. Her small feet were buried in large fuzzy pink slippers. Veins, some delicate, some swollen, laced her legs under stockings rolled down below her knees. He rocked forward again. Gladys' dress was faded green cotton. **Like Shamrock.** *He takes another bite of Cream of Wheat now and looks at Auntie Ide. He likes her dress with the red Hawaiian flowers. It's so big. And the bigger Auntie Ide, the better because she is so good and comfortable and strong even if she is messy with the sugar.*

"Auntie Ide?"

"Yes, honey?"

"What happened to Uncle Ralph?"

"Honey, after our son died, your Uncle Ralph hit the bottle as hard as Joe Lewis hit Max Schmelling. He didn't even come up for air, didn't look nohow at Iris. Maybe he couldn't stand seeing

Thomas' face on Iris' shoulders. Fishin and drinkin, drinkin and fishin, that's all that man did till the end of his life. The only living thing he ever touched was Blacky, that old Labrador of his. Did you know, Ralph died six months to the day after Thomas. It must have even been the same time of day."

"How'd he die, Auntie Ide? Do you think he did away with himself?"

"No, it was like everybody said. Must have been twenty people bathing on the beach. The boat tipped while he was moving from the back to the front with a big brown bottle in his hand. He tripped over old Blacky. Everybody said he yelled for help. But he went down once, twice, and then just before young Mark Southesby reached him, he went down for the third time. The bottle floated there in the lake to mark the spot. And that was that." He looks at arcs of sunlight trembling on the linoleum. **I hate being under the water. You choke. When Dad threw me in, I thought I was a goner.**

"When did it happen?"

"It was a long time ago. I've been married to Cory Pillton these last seven years."

"What happened to Blacky, Auntie Ide?"

"Oh, he swam back with Mark." Ide suddenly holds out her arms to Herman. He stiffens as she hugs him. Ide mutters, "God I miss him." She pushes Herman back at arms' length and looks into his eyes.

Gladys was sprawled on the table, drowsing. Her head bobbed. Herman looked again at the brown oatmeal. **What a mess.** He pushed back from the table, pulled his lumberjack shirt over his pullover and clapped on his cap backwards. Seeing a doorway opening from the kitchen onto a shallow stairwell, he headed that direction. As he swung back the screen door, the squeal of its springs roused Gladys. "Herman."

"Yes."

"Don't forget your lunch." Shamrock began to warble.

Two

After school, Herman rode his bicycle to the white clapboard house where his father lived. Leaning the Schwinn against an elm tree, he entered the back door and descended the basement staircase. He unbuttoned his lumberjack shirt and fumbled out from under the collar of his pullover a plastic necklace, flesh-colored and tooth-marked. Strung on it were two keys. He stooped and, forehead pressed against wood, he opened the door. The odor of cold and ancient cigarette smoke laced the musty air of the concrete basement. Before him was a single room, lit only by a small window at the ceiling to his left. Facing him in the dim light was a bed, sheets tangling with an orange and brown-striped Indian blanket. **Their honeymoon blanket. Crater Lake.** Switching on the overhead light bulb, he moved to a bookcase on his left. **One hundred and nine books now, with the ones in my suitcase. My library.** He drew from the third shelf a small volume, its back broken, <u>Velvet Paws and Shiny Eyes</u>. **Good buy. Lowell Grade School should hold more book fairs.** He turned to the dresser on the opposite wall. On it was a litter of coins, cigarettes, Kleenex, paper clips, a brown rectangular gum eraser, pencils blue on one end and red on the other. And a small square package with a note taped to it. He put on his glasses and read. At the top was some advertising copy neatly printed in soft carbon pencil on pulp paper:

7TH MIGHTY WAR LOAN DRIVE

Below were sentences in his father's neat handwriting:

Hermy,

Sorry. Can't make it today. Big Deadline all day. See you next Sunday. This box came for you in the mail.

Dad

The mouse! Tipping his Dodgers cap back, he pressed the box to his ear. He could hear light scratching inside. **THE WALTZING MOUSE. Yeah. From <u>Whiz</u>. I won't open it here. It could get away.** Jamming his glasses in a shirt pocket, he ran out of the apartment and up the stairs. Halfway up, he stopped, ran down again, and locked the apartment door.

Outside he put the box into the front basket hanging from his Schwinn's handlebars, mounted and pumped down the sidewalk and off the curb with a bump onto the wet tar street. Although it was cold, he didn't button up his lumberjack shirt and its tan checkered sides flapped out behind him like wings as the bicycle tires hissed on the soft black tar street carved flat and straight under a thick roof of black tree branches edged with emerald buds. Then he swung right, leaning into the turn. **Just like Sandy did on the motorcycle.** He could feel the tattoo stir in the crook of his left arm.

"You still sure you want to go through with this tattoo business?" Herman nods. "Well, if you want out, just say so. I got to go over and pay him some money anyway. Okay. Hold still. I'm getting on now."

Sandy turns on the ignition and kicks the starter. The machine roars. Herman jumps. "Put your arms around me, Hermy. And hold on tight. These Seattle hills are steep. It's a little wet out today and we got a couple skids comin. Don't let loose and you'll be okay. Look, I'm gonna make a turn pretty soon. I'll do it slow. And you'll feel the bike lean into it. Don't pull away. Lean into it, too. You won't fall. Now I'm gonna go slow until you get used to it. You got any problems, you just shout 'Sandy.' Here. I'm gonna gun the motor real loud and you should try yelling louder. Okay?" The motor roars.

"Sandy!!"

"I got you, kid. Let's get on the road." Sandy reverses his Dodgers cap and wheels down the alley in a slow roll. "Better hold on." Herman gingerly puts his hand on Sandy's ribs. "No! Hold on. Wrap your arms around me. Hell, I ain't gonna bite, kid. Squeeze!" Just then, the motorcycle hits a chuckhole and Herman bounces on the seat. When he comes down, he squeezes. They are out of the alley, onto the street, turning right up a steep grade. Herman feels himself sliding backwards and squeezes tighter.

When the machine finally struggles up the grade of the next cross street, Sandy takes a turn, skidding slightly on the wet pavement, and begins to pick up speed on level pavement. With motor exhaust dense and bitter in his nostrils, Herman watches Seattle's central business district passing by—bars, pawnshops, decaying theaters, trolley cars clacking and sparking at the end of the leashes linking them to the wires above, grocery and liquor stores, a gas station, the occasional intent dog, an old woman with a headscarf and a light coat protecting her from Seattle drizzle, and homes perching about on the sides of hills at first bare, then studded dark green by rock gardens, and a flash of forsythia gold.

Herman can smell all aroma more intensely, flowers, food, garbage, the mist of the ocean fog. He feels new cold hard in the sudden wind rush and draws even closer to the warmth and wall of Sandy's back carving through the hush. He can smell the leather of the man's jacket, the faint sweet trace of Brill Cream. **A little dab'll do ya.** *The thick black tires hiss on the highway shining wet and black.* **It's like wading in Auntie Ide's cow pool. I can feel hot and cold. The air's thick as water.** *Grinning, Herman begins to feel the surge and build of energy in spine, in heart and chest. "Faster! Sandy! Faster!" Sandy guns the machine and Herman feels the surge pull him back and laughs. Sandy gives a cowboy whoop. "Yahoo!!!" He begins to weave shallow curves from side to side.*

Herman leaned into another curve, straightened, balanced, threw his arms up and yelled "Yahoo!!" The shout echoed in the empty street under the black, bare elms. Steering the bicycle with body and knees, he lifted the box from the carrier. **Hi, mouse. Little honey. You're going to love it here.**

Now the road begins to go downhill, turns from pavement to dirt. They are jolted by the ripples of washboard road. They move under pine trees and through sharp pine perfume, into darker shadow and duller cold. Sandy rounds a bend and swings the machine into stop. The motor stutters into silence. "End of the trail, Hermy. We're at the Home of the Tattoo Man!"

At the Williams' house, Herman found Gladys ironing shirts, humming "As Time Goes By." Her heavily-lidded eyes were fixed on a spot at the kitchen window. **Casablanca, I bet. Casablanca, Idaho.** Herman smiled. "Uh, Mrs. Williams?"

"Yes."

"I got a package at my Dad's today." He held the box up. "It's a mouse. A pet. Can I keep it?"

"Mouse?" Gladys paused, looking down at him. He cleared his throat and shifted the box to his other hand. "Oh, I guess so. But not upstairs. Look down in the basement by the furnace. There is an old canary cage there. Put the mouse in it—and keep it down there. I don't want mice in with my birds. And take Sonny with you." **Uh-huh. She's gonna turn me into a baby sitter. He's gonna start talking to me on the playground.** "Well, Herman?"

Herman sighed. Then he shouted, "Sonny!"

"You're gonna deafen me! He's out in the back yard feeding the rabbits."

Herman walked through the backyard to the garage housing the rabbits that his father had told him Andrew Williams raised to supplement the meat rations. Sonny was standing on his tiptoes, slowly reaching into the wall-mounted hutch with a tray of green pellets for the huge buck, the father of the garage's community. Sonny's little dog Kelly, a half-breed terrier cur, stopped sniffing among the rabbit droppings to look at Herman, barked once, looked again.

Sonny turned around. Dressed in jeans and a sized-down soldier's fatigue shirt, he wore a fatigue cap pulled to the back of his head so far that the bill was vertical. Kelly exploded into another bark, his stiff white and tan spotted legs bouncing on the dirt garage floor, his white tail wagging.

"Shut up, Kelly." The boy casually glanced at the terrier. He looked back at Herman. His eyes were like his mother's, sad and drowsy.

"You about finished?"

"Un-huh."

"That big buck rabbit dangerous?"

"Sure is."

"What's his name?"

"Dad won't let us name them. Says they're meat, not pets."

Kelly approached Herman to sniff gingerly at the leg of his twills. "Knock it off, Kelly!" Sonny grabbed at Kelly's collar but the little dog darted out of the garage.

"Why do you call him Kelly?"

"I named him after Colin Kelly."

"The guy who flew into the Jap smokestack?"

"Yeah."

"That's a good name."

"Uh-huh."

The boys fell silent. Herman cleared his throat. "You want to see my new pet?"

"What kind of pet you got?"

"I got a mouse." He held up the box.

"So have we." Sonny pointed to the burlap sacks stacked under the garden tools neatly hanging from nails at the back of the garage. "They're back there right now. Trying to get into that rabbit food." He stooped to pick up a small rock that he threw into the pile of sacks. A tiny shadow flickered.

"Mice eat rabbit food?"

"Yeah."

"Great. Bring some along. You're going to like this mouse. He dances."

"Dances? Geez. Who taught him?"

"I don't know. They advertised him in Whiz. Wanta see?"

"Sure!"

The boys went back to the house and down into the basement where they found the rusty cage that Gladys had said he could use. Herman blew on its floor to clear it of coal dust while Sonny ran upstairs to get a newspaper to line it. He came back slowly, the tip of his tongue sticking from between his pressed lips, the newspaper folded under one arm and a jar lid full of water. "I have another lid for his food," he said, carefully setting the water lid beside the cage. He stuck his hand in his pocket and pulled out a wad of grass. "This is for his bed."

"Great. Look let's make this—no, this corner the bedroom. I'll put the water and food right next to the door here. Now I'm going to open the box in the cage so the mouse won't get away."

"Why don't you put the grass in the box after the mouse is out? That'll make him a good bedroom."

"Good idea, Sonny. Okay. Now. Um. These knots are tight. There. Okay."

Herman withdrew his hand and closed the cage door. Soon a tiny black snout pushed at the lid, whiskers sprung out, then one white ear. Then the mouse flowed into the cage. "It's spotted black and white, Sonny." Both grinned. The mouse had found the water and was lapping it daintily and steadily. It sniffed at the food but didn't eat. Suddenly, it spun around. The boys stared at one another. Sonny breathed heavily through an open mouth, his outsized adult front teeth gleaming above a drooping lower lip. They looked back at the mouse. It sat quietly. And then it spun again. And again and again. Herman and Sonny erupted into laughter. Herman nudged Sonny. "Did you see that?"

"I don't believe it," whispered Sonny. "It's really dancin!" They both lay flat on the concrete floor, their chins in their hands and their faces close to the cage.

They watched the mouse dance.

"What are you gonna name him, Herman?"

"Call me Hermy. I don't know. Got any ideas?"

"Yeah, I got a good idea."

"Well?"

"Fred. Like Fred Astaire."

"Hey, I like that. Hi, Fred."

The boys continued to watch the mouse spin in dizzying patterns—to the left one/two/three—to the right one/two/three—always arching tightly toward its bent tail. Then Herman heard Sonny clearing his throat and turned to find that the boy was watching him. "What?"

"I was wonderin…"

"Wondering what?"

"Well. Well, where's your mother? Even Charlie has a mother. Everybody I know has one. Except orphans. Are you an orphan?"

"I do have a mother, stupid. She's in Georgia."

"So how come you're here?"

"I live with my dad, not my mom. But I got in a fight with some boys my dad and I lived with. They killed my turtle, burned his eyes out with a magnifying glass. The turtle Mom gave me."

"Burned his eyes out?"

"Yeah."

"Gosh."

"Sonny!" Gladys shouted. "Get up here and peel these potatoes."

"Okay, Ma!" Sonny turned to Herman. "I'm sorry about your turtle." He waggled a finger at the cage. "So long, Fred. See you after dinner." He ran upstairs. Herman stood and looked around the musty basement. The walls were lined with glass jars of vegetables Gladys had canned from her Victory Garden. **Doing her part for the war effort.** Next to the stairs were fishing poles and a woman's straw hat with a lure tucked into the ribbon. On the floor were several tackle boxes. **Never seen so much fishing equipment.** A metallic glitter caught his eye. **Rifles. In a rack. Mr. Williams said they were going pheasant hunting this week. To get off rabbit meat for a while.** Herman walked over to the rifle rack.

When the boy reaches the bank, he begins to run toward the rocks. Herman shouts, "Wait!" and follows him but he suddenly disappears. A bush moves. Herman circles it and looks in from the other side. "Why did you run? Are we playing hide and seek?" The boy jumps and turns.

"Do you live around here?"

He slowly shakes his head. "Neither do I. I'm just here for a visit with my aunt, Ide Pillton."

"Hey, that's a neat looking BB gun! Is it a Red Ryder?"

Herman returned to the mouse's cage. Black spots dappled the creature's white fur. "You're just like Little Beaver's pinto." He picked up a pellet of rabbit food and, smiling, held it against the cage's bars. "Aren't you hungry after that trip? All the way from New York?" The mouse spun. "You know I used to have a rat. Except she was all white. And lots bigger than you." Herman stopped smiling. "She was some rat." He sighed. "She got shot." He looked into the dark shadow behind the furnace. "She's dead."

Out of the neon lights of the midway, in a dimly lit patch of the carnival, before a tent striped red and white and blue, he sees a heavy woman sitting at an oval table across from a stocky man with a baseball shirt stuffed into his jeans. She wears something white on her shoulder. **No, it's a rat! A white rat! Will you look at that?** *"Cory! Look over there. That's a white rat! I saw one in a pet shop in Seattle."*

"That's not all, boy." Hitching up his overalls, Cory smiles at a young woman standing near the table. She wears a blue polished cotton dress with a sailor collar piped in white. "Now will you look at that. You think that's for sale, boy?"

"The rat?"

But by this time Pillton has reached the young woman. "Ahoy, there, sailor! Permission to board?" The young woman smiles but doesn't reply. Herman watches the rat.

The woman bends over the stocky man's palm. "And this line, the line of your occupation is interrupted by the small line here. Probably an ending. What is your work?"

"I'm a baseball player. A catcher."

Herman smiled. **Sandy.** He held out his finger to the mouse. "Have you ever known a baseball player, Fred?" The mouse stopped spinning and sniffed the finger. "Well, I have. Look. He helped me get this. He rolled up his shirtsleeve and displayed the snake tattoo. Maybe you'll meet him some day." Herman could hear the gypsy as clearly as if she were in the basement.

"The lifeline. See?" Herman watches the rat. **Boy, I wish I had one.** *"Cory!" At the sound of the young woman's voice, Herman jumps. Pillton and the girl have pulled back into the shadows. Sandy stands and hands the gypsy a coin. He smiles at Herman and then moves into the bright midway.*

"Son?" The gypsy touches Herman. "Let me read your fortune in the cards. No. No money. Your friend will pay my daughter." Herman watches her deal cards into a cross. The

motion bares her left arm. **Look at that tattoo. That's a snake! Winds right around her arm. And some kind of flowers. Roses.** *She indicates the cards.* **House falling down. A man hanging by his foot. Uh, oh. There's a skeleton.** *"A river flows within. Mine is close now, so I hear yours. Listen."* **I hear something. Like a shell. She's right. Or is it just my ears hissing? Is that a river?** *"You shall soon hear your river clearly, son. And there will be an end."* *They gypsy frowns, then smiles. "I think you like Miranda. Would you like to hold her?" Herman nods. She lays her hand on his shoulder. The rat inches toward him, stopping to sniff his direction. Finally, she arrives. He feels the brush of her whiskers on his cheek and grins.*

"Will she bite?"

"No."

"Oh, she's great. Does she know any tricks?"

"I just started training her. She was born this year."

Miranda lightly nibbles Herman's ear. "I can feel her little teeth. How much does a rat like this cost?"

"Do you want her?"

"Oh, yes."

"Keep her. A gift. I have many of her sisters and brothers in the tent. Her mother is my pet. Now that lady does tricks!"

"This is great. Thank you. Thank you. Boy, wait till the guys see this."

"You ready, Herman?" Pillton stands behind him, yawning.

"Look what I got!"

"Where'd that come from?"

"She gave it to me. For free."

"Keep it out of the henhouse. Come on. I got to milk cows tomorrow."

Herman stretched. His knees ached. "You would have liked her, Fred. Miranda was a real lady."

"Herman! I've called you twice now. Are you deaf?"

"What, Mrs. Williams?"

"Get up here and wash that mouse off your hands. Dinner's ready."

Three

While the family talked, Herman and Sonny sat side by side, looking down at their food. Herman lifted a spoonful of mashed potatoes, looked at them. *Herman smells something new in the steamy kitchen.* **We're going to eat this?** *He examines the gaunt woman, her hair wrapped in a towel stained an odd red. Before her on the stove, cabbage and onions boil in a cast iron pot. She pours in a cup of apple vinegar. She removes her wire-rimmed spectacles and polishes them on a corner of a full apron studded by huge black polka dots, meanwhile squinting at him.* "Wash your hands, Herman. Supper's in a half hour." **Dinner. Mom calls it dinner.**

"Eat your meat, Herman."

"Yes, Mrs. Williams." Herman looked at the two slices of meat, dark brown, shining where the gravy gathered and slowly, slowly flowed into the plate. Sonny arranged four of his green beans into a square.

"Sonny."

"Yes, Ma."

"Eat."

Herman sits at the dinner table. He looks down at the pale ham, the cabbage, the apples from the tree in the back yard. He smells vinegar and onion. He looks up. Jake looks at him steadily and shakes his head. Herman begins to eat. In the long pauses between bites, he examines the family gathered around him. Mrs. Schultz, her cheeks bright red in her pale, moist face, the left cheekbone mounted by a bright purple mole; her small husband whose curly blond hair is a tight golden cap on his skull; the two boys—Karl and Peter, both red-haired, Karl a large and heavy junior high school student with his mother's flushed cheeks, Peter a thin and pale six-year-old.

Andrew and Gladys Williams sat, respectively, at the head and foot of the table, listening to Charlie. "I don't think so, Max. I can handle it."

"California isn't Idaho, Charlie. Have you ever heard of Hell's Canyon?"

Andrew frowned. "Max's right, Charlie. The Snake River can get dangerous. It's too far. We will never have enough gas to get that far and back. I've done some fishing up there but it was before the war. Why not the Boise River?"

"I can handle the Snake. No sweat. I've paddled rough water. Lots of times."

"Well, maybe the Plain." Andrew looked over at Max. "Have you boys thought about the Plain?"

"What's that?"

"The Snake River Plain. You go west to…"

"Today I read in the <u>Statesman</u> that the government in its deepest wisdom has seen fit to bless each American housewife with rations for an extra pound of sugar every year for each person in her home—for canning, for jams and fruit." Mr. Schultz clears his throat. "What I would like very much to know is where I am going to find the sugar to sell this fine lady. Can someone tell me?" Mrs. Schultz shakes her head slightly and then delicately places a small piece of ham between her lips. Karl sighs sharply, exasperated. Peter looks to the right and left and then giggles.

Jake leans forward, his expression intent, serious. "You're right again, Christian. This is a mess. The war should have been over months ago. Now if Governor Dewey had won…" Herman eats another bite of ham. He hasn't begun the cabbage yet. Or the apples.

"What kind of meat is this, Mrs. Williams?"

"Venison, Hermy. Sonny. Sonny! Stop playin with your food!"

"What's venison?"

"Deer meat." Andrew smiled. "I potted him in the Rockies at the end of the season. He's a little tough and a little gamey but he'll grow on you." He laughed. "Or you'll grow on him. Get it?" Herman nodded. "We'll be eating trout pretty soon. You like fish, Hermy?"

"I didn't used to. I like it now."

Max tapped his father on the shoulder. "Do we know anyone who has a canoe?"

"Jeff."

Herman follows Sandy down the steep sidewalk. He smells fish. He looks past the traffic light into the night above the Sound. Sandy breaks the silence. "We're gettin there. This cafeteria's one of the oldest in downtown Seattle. I washed dishes there one winter. They opened it up Christmas, 1922, and threw away the key. Never been closed since. Not for a minute. You can get most anything to eat there and I know a guy there who'll give us some free grub. Then we'll try ringing your aunt again. Hold it." Sandy places his hand on Herman's shoulder and sniffs the night air. "Smell that?" The boy nods. "Dead fish. That's the public market. Great place. Built right on the side of this hill and has all kinds of different stores. You like fish?" Herman shakes his head. "You don't know what's good, kid. I'll get you some fish and chips when we get to the cafeteria. Look. You can see it from here. Over there. No, to the left."

"They dropped 2,000 tons of bombs and didn't lose a Superfortress! Look—hand me the <u>Statesman,</u> Charlie. Over there on the buffet. Yeah. Here. On the front page. Colonel Carl Storey says, 'We laid our bombs right down the main street of the city and that town must sure be burning tonight.'"

"Son, you know that we agreed…"

The cafeteria doors swing open onto a narrow aisle bordered on the right by a row of tables, on the left by a long steam table. Sandy leads Herman down the aisle into a cavernous dining room. He points to a corner table. "Sit there. I'll be right back. I gotta talk to the cook and get us some grub." At the table Herman looks around. The cafeteria is nearly empty. Four tables away, two sailors sit, silently eating. An elderly man reading a paper is in a booth on the opposite wall. A door next to him swings open. Sandy gestures.

"Hermy, I want you to meet my buddy." Sandy leads him into the steaming kitchen. To their right a tall, fat man, sweat plastering his sparse hair onto an unusually small skull lifts a clinking basket of dishes and splashes them into a tub of steaming water. "That used to be my job. Come over here." Herman sees a short man with a thin black moustache and a chef's cap standing before a grill, frying hamburger. "This is Lester. Lester. Hermy. Lester, we're gonna eat and then I got something to do so Hermy's gonna stay out front for a while by himself. Any problems?" Lester shakes his head and turns back to the grill. "What about you, Hermy?" Herman shrugs. "Let's get some grub. Oh, Les?"

"Yeah."

"Can I borrow your motorcycle?"

"If you pay for some gas."

"No problem."

Walking behind the steam table, Sandy fills two trays with food, gives one to Herman, and leads him back to his seat. "Here's your chow. Green beans. A glass of milk. And fish and chips—the way they eat fish in England. The cafeteria used to have great desserts but the sugar shortage cut that back. And there isn't a hell of a lot left this late at night." Herman looks at the plates. He eats a french fry. "Go ahead. Eat some of the fish. Hey, it's good. It doesn't even taste like fish." Herman gingerly bites into the crisp and salty crust. The delicate, tasteless fish rests warm in his mouth. It's not fishy. "Like it?" He chews, swallows, and nods.

Herman chewed venison. He pushed back from the table. "Migod this meat is tough!"

Charlie laughed, "You shoulda been here the year Max shot a bear. We ate that for a whole year. Finally even Kelly turned up his nose at it."

Max reached for the bread. "I don't have to listen to this crap, Charlie."

Bending over the table to clear dishes, Gladys rapped Max lightly on the crewcut with a fork. "Watch your language, Max! You boys be happy you got somethin to eat. Think of all those starvin Armenians."

"Gee, Auntie Glad, all those Armenians must be dead by now. They started starvin when I was Sonny's age."

"Well, I'll bet the Polish and the Chinese and the Norwegians and a lot of others'd be happy to have Max's bear or your uncle's deer. We're still sendin whole boatloads of food to the French. Besides, this is the last of the venison. The ice house's empty and we're back to rabbit and the V-garden."

Max groaned. "Those damn Japs causin me a heap of trouble. I gotta get over there and get me one. I wanta run the flame thrower and bake me a Jap. Prolly better than rabbit."

Charlie rose from the table and stretched. "Big man." He headed for the living room. "Gonna get a little shuteye." He leaped onto the davenport.

"4F!"

"Charlie, you get your shoes off if you're gonna lie on that sofa!"

Sofa. Davenport! Herman chewed more vigorously. "Max, Sonny told me you fight fires."

"Yeah."

"What was it like?"

"Lousy."

"What'd they make you do?"

"They gave me a peevee."

"What's a peevee?" asked Sonny.

"Jeez. What's with all the questions?" Max took a mouthful of mashed potatoes. "A peevee's like a hoe on one end," he mumbled, coughed, and then swallowed. "And a pick on the other."

"Max, don't talk with your mouth full." Gladys was clearing the table. "Sonny, you finish up, you hear? We want to play some cards."

"So what did you do with the peevee, Max?"

"They made me dig most of the time. Some guys'd chop down trees and then we'd dig out the brush and make a road along the fire path."

"Path? How can a fire walk?"

"Wind, jerk. The wind makes it move. And, Sonny, that fire don't walk—it runs, runs like hell."

"Watch your language, Max."

"'Hell' isn't a cuss word any longer, Ma. Anyway, there was some guys doin something at one end of the forest when the wind shifted their way. The fire just jumped from one treetop to the other. They saw it comin and had time to dig in but it wasn't enough. It baked their butts."

"Max!"

"What happened?"

"Whatta you think? Sonny? They croaked. Whatta we gonna play, Mom?"

"Hearts."

"Let's play blackjack instead. Hey, Charlie, you got any dough?"

"Count me in."

"I'm in too. Call me when you start." Max rose and walked into the hall.

Sonny mounded his potatoes, made a depression in them with the back of his spoon, and poured gravy into it. "Look, Hermy, a volcano." Herman silently chewed venison. Sonny mashed the potato mound flat. Then he pursed his lips and began blowing rhythmically. "Hermy?"

"Yeah."

"How come I can't whistle?"

"You got a funny mouth."

Sonny continued to blow. Then he tore a small piece of bread off the loaf, tipped his head back and dropped the morsel into his mouth. "Bombs away!" He chewed and swallowed. "Hermy?"

"Jeez. What's with all the questions?"

"I'm gonna give you one more minute, Sonny." Gladys reached onto the table for another plate and went into the kitchen.

"Hermy?"

"Huh?"

"Do you like President Roosevelt?"

"Nope."

"How come?" Herman chewed venison. "Dad says he did good for Idaho workers during the Depression. Dad says he wouldn't have got a college education without him. Or a job. So how come you don't like President Roosevelt?"

"My Dad doesn't like him. He worked for Governor Dewey last summer. Wrote ads for him." Sonny made a road in his potatoes. From the hall, Herman could hear the cough of a flushing toilet. **Max.**

Gladys' voice rose from the kitchen. "Listen, Andrew. I don't want that gypsy in this house. Look at all the people here already! We've even got kids sleepin in the canary room!"

"Now, Gladys, Rose doesn't care where she sleeps. And my sister's no gypsy."

"You're darn right about that. Gypsy's just a fancy name for somethin else."

"Gladys, you do this every time. First, you kick and scream about her coming." Sonny nodded his head, sighed loudly, and rolled his eyes toward the ceiling. He pulled two blue balls out of his pocket. "Then you can't wait to hear what she has to say about the future. And hang on to every word."

"Andrew…"

"I'm not criticizing you, honey. These days who doesn't want to know the future? And she's got The Knack. You've got to admit that. Look at everything she's told you. Even told you about Charlie's father, and look how much mileage you got out of that, gossiping with Mabel." Sonny was tossing the two balls from hand to hand at chest level. Herman looked over at the davenport at the top of Charlie's head. Charlie was still.

"Mabel and I don't gossip."

"And besides, she never stays for long. She drifts away about the time you're really getting interested." Sonny dropped a ball.

The conversation became inaudible again. When Herman rose and carried his plate into the sink, the couple stopped talking, and Andrew came into the living room to hunt for the playing cards. Herman rejoined Sonny at the dining room table. "You're gonna like Rose, Hermy. She's a gypsy. She tells us all kinds of stuff that happened that we never knew about or that's gonna happen. The gonna-happen stuff's the best."

"Where's she live?"

"Doesn't live anywhere. Dad has thirteen kids in his family. Rose is one of the twins. She just moves around from one family place to another. And in between, just moves. I don't know. But Hermy, you should see all the rings she has! Ma says some of them are glass. But you should see all of them."

"How do you know she's a real gypsy?"

"Oh, she just is. It's the rings and the stuff she says. She touches your wrist to find out things about you. She says she's listnin to your heart singin. Except for that, she's just my aunt. She's fat and sloppy. She has spots where she spills things."

"What's she tell you?"

"One time it was spooky. She said Gramma was gonna die in an accident. Ever since I was little, people had been tellin Grampa to stop drivin cause he couldn't hear anymore, and he drove too fast. They called him a maniac. Then she does."

"Who does? What?"

"Gramma. Dies in a car crash. Just like Rose said."

"A gypsy told my fortune once. She told me my sister would die. But I don't have a sister."

"Okay, you el shrimpos, clear off. We're playin us some blackjack. Charlie, hustle those buns over here. I said get up." Max rocked Sonny's chair back and forth.

"Stop that, Max! Max!"

"Max, stop tormenting that child!" Andrew dealing, the blackjack game began, Sonny and Herman circling the table, craning to see the players' hands. Suddenly, Max pulled his cards close to his chest. "Those doggone kids are gonna give my hand away." Max ran his fingers through his crewcut, its bristles springing back up as his hand passed over.

Charlie pulled in winnings. "Hey Max, we're playin blackjack. It don't make any difference. Dealer hits sixteen. He don't hit seventeen. Instead of your father, the dealer could be one of them robots you're always readin about in them science fiction magazines you got piled up in the bedroom." Charlie leered. "Or do you just look at the pictures? Got some lovely ladies there, Max. Huh? Lovely ladies, Max. Huh? Huh?"

Gladys looked up from her hand. "Ladies?"

"Don't mind him, Ma. Charlie, why don't you bite on a banana or something?"

"Japs got all the bananas nowadays, Max."

"Watch it, gimp."

"Max!"

"Ma, I ain't gonna take all that stuff from a 4-F like Charlie."

Andrew flipped his cards over. "Okay, boys. Read em and weep. Cowboy and his lady. Dealer pays twenty-one." Max and Gladys threw their cards in the center of the table while he scooped in their money. Charlie flipped over his down card.

"I got twenty. It's a tie."

"Push goes to the dealer in this house. And everywhere else in the United States."

"What?"

"Down, boy." Max punched Charlie's right arm. "Them's the rules." He laughed. "You know, like robots."

Charlie jumped up from the table, his chair falling to the floor. "Watch the goddam arm!"

"Did I urt the ittle baby boy? I's sowwy."

"Goddamn you, Max!" Charlie's voice was cracking.

"Charlie, you watch your language." Gladys glared. "There's little kids around."

Sonny whispered to Herman. "Charlie's a cripple."

"What?"

"He's got a crippled arm."

Herman watched the boy as he left the table for the hallway to his bedroom. Charlie was holding his right arm stiffly out from his side, the elbow akimbo. **Like me.** When the family resumed the game, Herman got up from the table and sat down in front of the radio. He pulled a <u>Liberty</u> out of the magazine rack by Andrew's chair and began thumbing through it. He put it back and picked up a <u>Saturday Evening Post</u>. He looked for cartoons. He stopped at a story about the Nisei infantry battalions that had been fighting in Germany.

"I hunt for my food. Gotta magpie yesterday."

"You ate a magpie?"

"Well, after I took the feathers off and the head and the feet and I cooked it."

"What did it taste like?"

"It was okay."

"Who gave you the BB gun?"

"My Dad. It was the only one he didn't throw in the river the night the roundeyes came up to the farm."

"What are the roundeyes?"

"You're a roundeye."

"I am not."

"You are too. Your eyes are rounder than mine."

"I guess you're right."

The boys look at one another. "What's your name?" Herman asks.

"Tom. Tom Ohashi."

"Hi. Mine's Herman."

"Hermy."

"What, Sonny?"

"Can we play somethin? They won't let me sit at the table with them."

"Just a minute. I'm reading something."

"What?"

"About American Japanese soldiers fighting the Nazis."

"The Japs are our enemy."

"What if they're Americans?"

"The Japs stabbed us in the back."

"When I lived in Walla Walla before the war, the guys in the neighborhood would all go out together on Saturdays and everybody would spend his allowance. Norman, Clarence, Sonny—one of them was named Sonny, too—would go to the movies..."

"You had a friend named Sonny?"

"Yeah, that's what his Mom called him. His real name was George. His Dad was killed in North Africa. Well, anyway, after we went to the matinee at the Roxy, we'd go down to the Book Nook and buy comics—different ones so that we could trade—and we'd go to this little grocery store and get some penny candy. It was this little store that this old Japanese couple ran. They had stuff you could buy for just a penny. I remember buying some rocks there that I'd put into water in my goldfish bowl and they'd turn into flowers."

"Rocks that turned into flowers?"

"Yeah. It was just a little tiny shop but it had this one table down the center and tables and shelves along the walls—all packed with all kinds of things, little Japanese dolls, whistles, bamboo flutes, fans, chopsticks..."

"Chopsticks?"

"Yeah, the Japanese eat with sticks. And they had tea sets and games and incense. That's a perfume that they burn. They always burned it in the shop in these little metal bowls. It had all kinds of smells. I liked it."

"It sounds neat."

"Yeah. Well, one Saturday pretty soon after Pearl Harbor, we all went down there as usual and the shop was closed. Later on, Clarence told me that they'd sent the old man and his wife to prison—to a concentration camp."

"You know, Hermy, I'll bet they were spies."

"There's nothing to spy on in Walla Walla except pea fields and wheat fields. At least then there wasn't. Besides, they were sending all the Japanese into these concentration camps. Some people said all these white farmers got the Japanese cherry orchards around Richland for next to nothing and sold them to the government when it wanted to build this big bomb factory, the Hanford Project. Well, anyway, I had this friend I met in my Aunt Ide's orchard one day—Tom Ohashi—"

"You had a Jap for a friend?"

"Come on, Sonny. See this article? An American is an American."

"You don't sound very patriotic, Hermy."

"I been buying war stamps, one every week for years now."

"That's because you want to get that .22 you told me about."

"I'll bet you can't say the Pledge of Allegiance, Sonny."

"A kid told me you're a German."

"I'm a better American than you are. My family came over here in 1742. Dad says I had seven grandfathers fighting in the Revolutionary War. And half of them were Scotch or Irish."

"Liar, liar, pants on fire. No one has seven grandfathers. Herman the German. Herman the German. Herman Gerring ate a herring."

"Forget it, Sonny. Just forget it." Herman turned back to the <u>Post</u>. Sonny began to play with radio knobs.

When Herman comes back with two ham sandwiches in a sack, his rat riding on his shoulder, he finds Tom crouching in a corner of the barn. The boy seizes the sack from him and eats quickly. Afterwards, he licks his fingers and looks at the white rat.

"What's the rat's name?"

"Gypsy."

Tom touches the rat's pink nose with the tip of this finger. When it nibbles his nail, he laughs. Herman laughs with him. "Do you have to go home soon?"

"I don't have no home."

"Hermy?"

"What?"

"Wanta play a game?"

"Wanta play a game?"

"Sure. What kind of game?"

Tom fishes a penny out of his pocket. "It's a guessing game I learned from some Indians livin up near our place. They use bones. We gotta use pennies. Got one?"

"Real Indians?"

"Yeah. You got pennies?"

Herman digs in his corduroys and pulls out three pennies and a nickel. "Uh-huh."

"I know an old Indian game."

"Indian game?"

"Yeah. It's called the 'Guessing Game.' A friend taught me. Got a penny?"

"No."

"Well, go get one." Sonny ran down the hall toward the porch.

"Don't run in the house, Sonny."

"Okay, Ma."

"Let's find a place to play." Tom looks around for a clean patch of boards. He sits down with his legs crossed. He looks up at Hermy. "Sit. No. Facing me." *Herman sits on the barn floor.*

"Here's four pennies, Hermy."

"Okay, sit down here facing me."

"Here. Make your hand like mine." Tom stiffens the fingers of his right hand and presses its edge to the clay, its back to Herman. He puts the penny behind the hand so that Herman can't see it.

"Now you gotta guess if my penny is heads or tails. Then put your penny up the same way you think mine is. Then we lift our hands and if you called it, you win. Okay?"

"Okay, Sonny. You got it?"

"That isn't much of a game."

"Wait and see."

Herman flips his penny. "No! You can't do that. You gotta guess. You gotta try to read my mind. Heads or tails?" *Hermy turns his penny over and back again while he looks at it.* **Heads or tails? Probably a head. The lucky side. But maybe he thinks I'd think that and has a tail. Tails.**

"Tails."

"No. You don't hafta say anything. Just lift your hand."

Herman and Tom simultaneously lift their hands. Tom has a head. He takes Herman's penny. "Do it again?"

"Okay." They hide their pennies with their hands again. **Will he do heads twice in a row? Or switch? He'll switch. Tails.** *"Okay." They lift their hands.* **Heads.** *Tom takes Herman's penny.*

Herman took the penny from Sonny. "Mom, can I have some pennies?"

"They don't grow on trees, Sonny. What are you boys doin over there?"

"Nothin. Just give me a couple of pennies. Please."

"No, honey. I'm savin them."

Max slapped his cards on the table and dug into his pocket. "I got some tokens that you can have if you'll just keep your yap shut."

"Thanks, Max." Sonny returned with ten tax tokens, six green plastic and two aluminum. "Here's three cents, Hermy."

"You're a token short."

"The aluminum are worth more."

"Since when, Sonny?"

"Since all the aluminum went into the bombers."

"Do you wanta play?"

"Wanta play for that nickel?"

"It's all I got. I was going to buy some candy with it when I went to town."

"Come on."

"I don't know."

"Well, I'd better get going."

"No, Tom. Sit down. I'll play."

"Okay."

"No fair, Hermy! You're takin all my money!"

"Shh, Sonny. Your mom will hear. You know what she thinks about gambling."

"Is this gambling, Hermy?"

"Sort of."

"It's no fun."

"Look, I know a way to stretch it out. Your folks got any poker chips, Sonny?"

"Uh-huh."

"Well, get them."

"I don't wanta play anymore."

"Okay with me." Herman picked up the Post again.

"Okay, I'll get them."

"But let's make it a real game, Tom. Let's get some straw and break it into pieces. Every ten pieces is a penny. So the winner has to get fifty pieces to get the nickel."

"Come on! That'd take all day."

"Five pieces."

Tom thinks. "Make it two."

"Three."

The boys sit on the clay, looking at each other. A hen ruffles feathers. Flap. Cackle. Bacaw. Tom sighs. "Okay." They rise and gather straw. When Tom returns, Herman is carefully breaking off his straws so that they are even. Tom sighs again and sits down. "Break up your straw, Tom, so it's the same size as mine."

"Here's the poker chips, Hermy. They didn't see me get them."

"What're you squirts doin?"

"Go away, Charlie. We're playin a game. Go back to sleep."

"I wanta listen to Fibber McGee and Molly. Yer playin some squirtie game, huh? Flippin coins?"

"No, Hermy says you can't flip. I'll betcha he can beat you. He beats me—all the time."

"Okay, keed, I need some laughs till Fibber McGee comes on."

"Come on. Let's play." Tom puts his hand on the floor and arranges the penny behind it. Herman looks at him for a moment, turns back to his straws and puts them into three groups of five, and then puts his hand down. **Tom won't do three in a row.** *He waits for Tom to nod his head. They lift their hands. Heads again. "Jeez, Tom!" Herman gives him a straw. The boys set up their pennies again.* **He's just going to do heads again. Must think it's luck or something. Well, two can play that game.** *He nods to Tom.* **Tails.** *He sighs and gives him another straw. "When I win, can I be the one who fixes the first penny?"*

Tom nods. "When you win." He wins four more straws with tails/heads/heads/tails.

On the fifth turn, Herman guesses tails and wins. "Okay. Now you're going to get it." He thinks for a while and then puts down tails. Tom already has his penny down. "Hey, that isn't fair! I was supposed to go first."

"I guessed what you were gonna do before you did it. Come on. Lift your hand."

"How could you do that?"

"Wanna bet two more straws that I could do it again?"

Herman counts his straws. Ten still left. "Okay, wise guy."

"Wanna make it five?"

"No. Here it is. Read it and weep! Tails!"

With a sad expression, Tom slowly lifts his hand. "Tails it is, big boy." Now he grins.

"Read it and weep, Charlie."

"Damn!"

"You watch your language, Charlie! What are you boys doin over there?"

"Nothin, Auntie Glad. It's just luck, squirt. One more penny."

Now Herman begins to play the game automatically, winning only twice more, before he loses his last straw. He hands Tom the nickel. "You earned it. You're really good. Can you teach me how to win?"

"If you think I'm good, you oughta play those Indians."

"You oughta play those Indians, Charlie."

"I'm fed up with this kid's game."

"I can't tell you how to win. You just gotta get to know the other guy. It's hard to say how. Well, uh—well, different guys just think different ways but most of them think the same way over and over again. When you learn what that way is, you got em. Just keep your eyes open. Watch."

"You squirts want me to teach you blackjack? Hey! I'm missin Fibber McGee!" Charlie reached up to turn the radio knob.

McGee: "By the time I finish readin 'Bringing up Father,' n Flash Gordon n Smokey Stover, I'm wore out." (Laughter)

Mayor: "Heh-heh. Heh-heh. Very amusing. In a pathetic sort of way." (Laughter)

"By the way, do you know where I can buy a large globe of the world for my office?"

McGee: "Why sure. La Trivia. I can get you one wholesale. How much you want to pay for a good globe?"

Mayor: "Oh, it doesn't matter much, McGee, as long as I get a good one. Things are happening so fast these days I like to keep informed."

Molly: "You want a globe with Japan on it, Mr. Mayor?"

Mayor: "Why certainly."

Molly: "Well then, you better get one quick." (Sustained laughter, applause, cheers).

Charlie turned off the radio.

"Hey, Charlie, whatta ya doin?"

"That's an old one. They did that one after the Japs burned Pearl Harbor. I heard it a lot of times."

"He's right, Sonny. That's an old one. They're probably playing it again because we got their army on the run now."

"Well, okay. I don't wanta listen to no old show." Sonny stood up. He snapped at the orange balls hanging from the lampshade. Herman picked up the Post again. "Hey, Charlie."

"You little kids better stay away from me. I'm a bad influence."

"You wanta see somethin? Hermy's got a mouse."

"Who doesn't? If that damn Max doesn't stop eating peanut butter and crackers in our room, I'll..."

"No. It's a different kind of mouse. It dances. Come down in the basement and take a look."

Charlie sighed. "What the hell?" He followed the boys downstairs. The mouse was still spinning its circle. It would stop only to spin the other way. A little of the rabbit food was on the cage floor and there were five small droppings next to the water lid. "Hey, that's one of them waltzing mice!"

"Yeah. How did you know?"

"Oh, I saw them in a pet store in L.A. You pay good money for this Hermy?"

"Yes."

"You got rooked."

"What do you mean?"

"Well, this is one of them mice they use in experiments in labs. They run them through mazes. You know, like the ones in the Sunday comics. Except they're loaded with all kinds of traps like electric shocks and stuff. Well, some of them can't take it. They go off their beans. And some of the lab assistants were selling them to pet stores for a little extra cash. A real racket. You got yourself a nutty mouse there, Herman. He's so crazy, he's chasin his tail."

Sonny's lower lip quivered. "Is he gonna die?"

"Nah. Nuts don't kill ya. Look at Max."

Charlie and Sonny went upstairs. Herman stood before the cage for a long time. He watched the mouse spin.

Four

I t's been three weeks now since he left me at the Williams. What's he doing? He can't be that busy. He's mad at me. I know he's mad at me. Under black elms, his breath steaming in the March chill, the tan plaid of his jacket collar pulled about his ears, the brim of his baseball cap slanting over his eyes in a pool of shadow, Herman stood at the street corner on traffic patrol, his chest crossed by white, his badge blinding and silver in the sunlight. He turned to the school, indistinct brown brick edged by concrete, looming through a filigree of boughs, branches and twigs.

Lay bwa. Miss Alberts says. Lay bwa. The French had been in the desert for weeks. Just sagebrush and lava rock and jackrabbit. Where'd they get water? Maybe they were following the river. Yeah. Boise River. Bwa River. And then somebody sees trees. Lay bwa, lay-bwa, lay-bwa. He points. His eyes are wide. His mouth is open under his moustache. I wonder who started calling it boy-zee? Some dumb sourdough silver miner from New York, I bet. They thought this was some kind of Garden of Eden in the middle of the desert. But it was just trees. And the river. Boise River, the Tree River.

"Hey, Hermy, gonna watch the fight?" Across the street stood a sturdy boy in a Safety Patrol harness.

"I'm still on duty, Jim."

"School's out. Your shift's up. Come on. Doug's gonna teach that spick a lesson."

"He's not a spick. Pete's Basque."

"There's a difference?"

That morning, a fight had begun between two boys on this street corner, but the school bell broke it up. Now they were going to meet in the vacant lot three blocks east of the school, a stand of trees hiding them while they fought. Herman looked at Jim's back. **I'd better go. He's a sergeant. And Doug's my Commanding Officer.** He saw small groups of boys and girls headed the same direction. **Everybody knows about this. Everybody's going to watch.**

Herman reached the small grove of evergreen trees rooted in hard red clay. Before him children in small groups stood, speaking quietly. On a small mound that raised them above the others, Jim was standing beside Doug, helping him off with his harness and jacket. Herman knew no one else well enough to talk, so he stood alone. **Where's Pete? I couldn't do this. Oh, God, I couldn't do this. If I was Pete, I'd be home by now. But then what? Everybody'd laugh. And other guys would be picking on me.** Herman's stomach knotted. **I gotta piss. Pee.** A slim, dark boy edged through the crowd and stepped onto the mound. **Pete.** Some of the children booed. The boy flushed. He began to take off his jacket. Doug's face was pale. Herman suddenly turned. **I gotta pee. I can't watch this.** He hurried away. No one spoke to him. Suddenly, he heard a shout. **It's started. Listen. All those kids. Think of sitting in school all day waiting for that fight, right from early morning through lunch. I couldn't eat lunch.** He could taste Gladys' peanut butter sandwiches. He gagged. **I gotta think about something else. Someone. Iris. Yeah. Iris doesn't mind fights. She even punched somebody in the mouth one time. Yeah. Iris. She always makes me feel better.**

Iris swims in the cow pond under sunlit trees. The freckled oval of her face twists upwards to press her tan shoulder, brown eyes staring blindly into a canopy of willows, the edges of the leaves emerald threads twisting above, snaking in the soft green mirror below. **There.** He opened his eyes. The girl and the pond and the light shimmered over muddy lawns and cracked sidewalks. **Step on a crack. Break your mother's back.**

Huff! Herman staggered forward three steps and fell to his knees. "Gotcha!" **Karl!!! Oh Jesus. It's Karl.** He twisted into a sitting position to stare at the stocky fourteen-year-old. Karl Schultz grinned at the two boys on his right, one a curly blond, the other with straight black hair. The black-haired boy was smoking. "This is little Hermy, guys. Hermy, you know Howie here." Cordially, Karl indicated the blond. "And this is Tonto." The black-haired boy grinned. "Quemo sabe."

"Him heap bad news for little candy-suckers like you. Boys, I owe this child a bad turn. Last December, the little back-stabber tried to Jap me. Just like Pearl Harbor. Right, Hermy?" He laughed. "Squirmy, Hermy?" The other boys laughed. "Now I want you guys to remember this mug and remember it well. When Four-Eyes here comes up to Junior High this fall, I'd like you to make it sorta hot for him, you know, whenever you have the time, as a personal favor to old Karl way up in high school paving the way for you boys. Let me show you. Like this!" Karl leading, the boys scrambled toward Herman, who rose, fell back again as Karl struck his face. Howie seized his right pants leg. Herman kicked down with his heel on the boy's hand. Howie yelped and toppled backward. Karl tripped over him while Tonto looked down at the pile and laughed. Herman rose and ran. He heard shouting behind him and then the drumming of their shoes on the pavement. Energy burst. His legs and lungs like iron, he ran and ran.

Coward. "Hey!" **Yellow.** He ran. "Hey! You kids!" A man's voice. "You kids!" He slowed. Herman turned. Karl and the other two boys had stopped and, panting, were watching the white-haired man. "They chasing you, son?"

"We're just playing, mister," Karl called. "We're playing tag."

"Is that right?" Herman gulped air and nodded his head.

The boys turned away. "See you later, Hermy. See you later." They walked off, talking among themselves, occasionally looking back at Herman. He turned to the man. "You okay, son?" Herman nodded and walked away. The day was darkening, the storm clouds rolling. He walked past lawns, his thoughts rolling. **Step on a crack.** He took a long step to avoid a crack. **God. Now I'm in for it. They're after me. Dad. Step on a crack. Mom. Karl.**

Jake speaks. "Understand something, Hermy. Karl is older. He's earned privileges. You don't have these privileges."

Break your mother's back.

The box contains a shell and a card:

Dear Hermy,

They have these turtles down here that are really unusual. They are called "box shell tortoises". They live in the desert so don't put him in water. They pull up their shells and hide when there is danger. Feed it liver. Hope you like it. You'll have to give it a name. I miss you.

Love,
Mom

I miss you. He picks up the shell and looks in at one end. Two small feet are visible, their toes tipped with delicate claws, a tail tucked between their heels. On the other side, through a crack between upper and lower shells, he could see slitted golden eyes. "I'm going to call you... call you Tank. You look like one."

Herman felt light press his eyes. **Thunder.** He looked up at tumbling clouds. **Thunder.**

Under the apple tree Herman plays with Tank. He puts a branch in front of him as he lumbers through the long grass. One foot up. The other. Heave. Over.

Suddenly, Herman feels his biceps gripped. "Grab his feet, Howie!" He sees a curly head bent over his legs. He kicks. Howie yells. He twists his right arm free and punches at Karl but misses. Karl grabs it again. Finally, he stops struggling under the weight of the boys. "Did he hurt you, Howie? Well, he's going to have to pay for that, isn't he? O.K. Grab his feet. Let's haul Four Eyes out to the alley." In the alley, Karl's knees pin Herman's shoulders. Karl holds his hand, palm up like a surgeon, towards Howie, who hands him a magnifying glass. He bends over Herman's face, his eye huge in its lens. "Do you know what you can do with this, Hermy? Why, you can catch the sun's rays in it." Herman feels a spot on his chin growing warm. "And focus them. And..." Herman begins to feel fire. "BURN something!" Herman begins to kick and buck. "Yahoo!! Ride'm cowboy!!!" Karl mounts Herman's shoulders with his knees. "Knock it off, Hermy. I'm not going to burn you. What kind of a person do you think I am?" Karl sighs and leans back.

"But we must punish you. You can't go around kicking your elders this way. Now, Hermy, do they ever talk about depantsing at your grade school?" Herman is silent. "That's de-pants. No? Well, over at Boise Junior High when you're a seventh grader, that's one of the first things they'll teach you. So I thought we'd show you how it all went so that you'll know how to behave when the Big Moment arrives. See, I won't be there to do The Deed myself, being a big high school freshmen and all. Right, Howie?" Howie nods, scowling at Herman. "Get his pants!" Suddenly, Howie tears at Herman's belt, slipping it open, yanking his pants, then his underwear down over his hips.

"Now look at that, will you, Howie?" Grinning, they stare at Herman's penis. "See it? It's right there. No, that's a pubic hair. The one right next to it." Howie laughs. "Just an itsy bitsy one." Karl bends over and gently touches the penis with the tip of his forefinger. He lifts up Herman's testicles. "Nary a hair on the child's body. I wonder if he will ever be a man. I know. We'll put something on it to make it grow. Hand me one of those, will you buddy?" Herman feels movement on his body. Somebody lightly brushes his penis. "Another." Movement. "More, more. This child is very fond of animals. The turtle." **They're burning me! My God!** *He screams. "Jesus! What a loud little bastard. Well, let him up."*

Karl puts his hand on Herman's shoulder. "Now you had this coming to you. You've been a bad boy. Let me give you a piece of advice. If you rat on us, you will be very, very sorry. Won't he, Howie?" Howie nods and frowns. Karl rises. Herman looks at his stomach. Red ants swarm there. Grunting in panic, he begins beating at them. One stings him. He mashes it. Karl laughs. He and Howie stand by the apple tree. Karl winks at Herman and holds up the tortoise. Then the boys enter the house.

The next morning when Herman goes out to the alley to empty the trash, he finds the tortoise on the top of the ash barrel. Its eyes are burned out. There are small black holes crusted with ash on either side.

Step on a crack. Break your mother's back. Herman steps on a crack.

The door closes. Peter Schultz walks into the kitchen. "Can I have a glass of water, Hermy? Get me a glass? Mom won't let me climb up there." Herman fills a cheese glass from the tap and gives it to the little boy. Peter sips. Suddenly, he throws water on Herman. Herman catches him at the door. Peter falls and yells. Karl appears.

"What's going on here?"

"Peter threw water on me."

"I did not."

Karl interrupts. "I'm in charge here, Peter." Peter leaves. "Now Hermy, don't fool around anymore. Finish those dishes." He stares at Herman, who looks down. After Karl leaves, he can hear the boys outside the kitchen, whispering, laughing.

Herman heard thunder. He looked up into the sky. It would rain. **I'm sure it will rain tonight. Good.**

Herman hears thunder. He looks up at the basement window near the ceiling. Rain splashes on the sidewalk outside. Karl enters. "Whew!" Herman doesn't move. "Whew!" Herman holds his breath. "These really stink. Hermy? My underwear really stink. Do you want to smell my shorts, Hermy? Check me out? You know, short arm inspection? Hermy?" Hermy turns. Against the stairwell light, he can see the boy's silhouette. Karl is nude. He steps down into the room. He nears Herman. He holds out his underwear. "They smell like shit, Hermy."

Herman jumps out of bed. He seizes Peter's little rocking chair. "Stay away!"

"Put that chair down, Hermy. Hermy! This is an order!"

"Get away. I'll kill you." Herman trembles. His voice chokes with tears. Thunder rumbles. Karl takes a step toward him and Herman swings the chair at him. Karl jumps back, his eyes wide, and then runs up the front stairway.

Outside, the rain splashes in great soft drops on Herman's bare back and shoulders. It is cold. He runs under the apple tree. Climbing, his pants' leg catches on the largest cane of the massive rose bush that grows between the tree and the garage. Soon he is on the garage roof and over its peak. On the other side, sheltered partially by the overhanging branches of the apple tree, he lies full length on the roof and looks over its edge at the house, dark except for a dim light to its left. **The kitchen.** *Lightning crackles.* **Mississippi-one. Mississippi...** *Thunder rolls. Herman feels it in his body.* **What's happening?** *He chokes. Thunder tumbles down the sky, huge, invisible within the rain.* **Oh, God.** *He touches an apple. He waits for his father.*

Herman entered the Williams' house and walked to the porch. Sonny was sprawled on Herman's cot, reading comics. "Sonny, can't you give a guy some privacy? Get off my bed and stay out of my comic books. At least until I've read them myself."

"Gee, Hermy, your shirt's all torn. Hey, look at that!" He rose to his knees and peered into Herman's face. "I'll bet you're gonna get a shiner. Who hit you?"

"Karl. The guy I used to live with."

"The one who burned your turtle's eyes out?"

"Tortoise. Box shell tortoise."

"Did you beat him up?"

"There were three of them."

"Why didn't you run?"

"Because my dad always said to stand and fight. He was a little guy when he was in school and he said the only way to make them stop is to make it hard on them every time they push you around."

"Did you?"

"Uh-huh."

"Against three of them?"

"Uh-huh."

"Gee."

Jake says, "Get up." He repeats "Get up."

"I can't." Herman begins crying again.

"You're yellow, Hermy. Get up and fight." Herman lies on the lawn and cries.

"How come, Hermy…?"

"Drop it, Sonny."

"I just…"

"Drop it." Herman sat on Sonny's bed and stared at the floor. He closed his eyes. **My eye hurts.** He turned his attention to his left arm, to its crook, to the tattoo. **The snake.**

"Son, I'm a coward right to the bone when it comes to killing or being killed. Hell, I don't even fist fight unless I can't run." Herman stares at Sandy. **A coward. Yellow. Sandy?** *"Besides, I got this finger."* He holds up his right forefinger. *"Bend it, Hermy."* The boy grabs the finger and bends. It is rigid. *"Snapped it back on a bare-handed catch one day. I just taped it to the other and it grew back this way. Well, you know what finger this is, Hermy?"* Herman shakes his head. *"Trigger finger,"* Sandy laughs. *Besides that, I caught a couple in the head here and there and they don't know what to make of that yet. But, boy, I'm alive."*

"Hell, I wouldn't make no soldier, nohow. I'm not even a good dishwasher. I'm a baseball catcher. I'll never make the majors, not even with all the competition gone, but I'm a catcher."

"Sonny?"

"Yeah?"

"Sorry. I…" Herman cleared his throat. "Some old guy broke it up. I…I was running away."

"Who wouldn't? I would. Me fight all those guys by myself? You kidding?"

"I used to live in Karl's house. Right before I came here. When Dad first brought me to Boise, we lived in the baseball park."

"Baseball park?"

"Listen, kid, I'm beat. I wouldn't make it up. Dad thought I needed some-body to cook for me and stuff. So we moved in with Karl and his brother and mother and father. After Karl killed Tank, my tortoise, he did a lot of other stuff too. So I fought back."

"I'll bet your Dad was proud of you."

"No, he got mad. That's why we moved out and that's why I'm here."

"Is that why you never get to see him?"

"I guess so. And now Karl's after me. He says I Jap-stabbed him. I didn't. I just started to defend myself and he ran away. If I'm a Jap, he's a Nazi."

"Well, you got me and Charlie. That would even it up. Boy, I'd give that Karl somethin to think about. Shazam!" Sonny stood up on Herman's cot and began shadow boxing.

"Yeah, you and Charlie. A gimp and a runt. Some gang!" Sonny kept shadow boxing. "Knock it off, Sonny! My head hurts where Karl hit me. Get on your own bed." Herman threw himself on the cot, picked up a comic book and turned towards the wall. He looked at the cover. Blackhawk. "What's this, Sonny?"

"Huh? Oh. That's Charlie's. Remember Uncle Sam?"

"I know about Blackhawk, jerk. When'd he get his own comic?"

"Charlie got that last year. Around Christmas. Haven't seen any others."

Herman turned back to the wall, rifled through the book. **Blackhawk smashes a Nazi in the mouth. Two others lie on the ground, one up against the tank. A fourth leaps from the tank on Blackhawk's back. A fifth is just coming out of the hatch. He has a Luger.** Herman looked up at the window above him. The rose cane laced the window.

Herman hears a magpie in the distance. **Tom. He's a Jap.** *"Jeez." Cory tips the wine bottle. "After a while, I didn't care. We landed on some island somewhere—still don't know* *where, and I spent years there. Didn't even ask anybody when they liberated us. Nothing ever happened on that island. Just nothing happened. That's the war for me. Nothing. Hell, that's my life. I signed up to see the seven seas and fight for our country and see strange and far away lands and Hedy Lamarr and nothing happened."*

"See those shadows? Right there?" Cory turned. "It's the apple tree." He took another drink. "There were shadows like that on the barracks wall. Used to look at them. Palm tree, though."

"What about Al?"

"Where'd you hear about Al?"

"You were telling me."

"Yeah. There were these two guys Al and Mitch that tried to escape." Cory looked at the shadows again, then slowly shook his head. "Old Al and Mitch. They were real characters, especially Al. He used to be in vaudeville or somethin and was always doin these routines. He was a ventriloquist. Like Edgar Bergen and Charlie McCarthy. Only Al had a puppet named Henry—you know, the one on the radio show?"

"Henry Aldrich?"

"Yeah. Henry Aldrich. It wasn't a real puppet. Just a palm tree branch with eyes and a mouth carved in it. Old Al and Mitch. Crazy bastards. Like decidin to escape—where the hell would they go? I mean we are on a goddamn island for Chrissakes."

"There was this guy escaped from Corregidor right at the beginning and he got away. Came back to the States and then he went back to the Pacific and he's fighting there now."

"Crazy fuck."

"What happened to Al and Mitch?"

"Oh. Yeah. Well, here they are in the front of the firing squad and they're grinning like apes. The officer lifts his sword and shouts and the squad aims. Suddenly this woman's voice comes out of the officer's mouth. "HENRY! Henry ALDRICH!!!" Cory laughs. "The god-damn firing squad turns around and looks at him, their eyes buggin out. And Al says in this teenage kid's voice, you know, crackin like Henry Aldrich's. "COMING, Mother!" And we start laughin fit to bust. Then the officer shouts and the squad shoots and Dear John, that's all she wrote. They killed him. What the hell. I was on the burial detail. I looked down at him and I said that, 'Dear John, that's all she wrote.'"

That night, Herman sat upright. **Light. White light. Wild light? Bathes me. God. Light.** Herman's eyes opened. Lost brightness flashed black against the empty night. Thunder rolled boulders. He looked out the window. Lightning shattered the sky, etched black the bare rose canes lacing the trellis outside the glass. Herman raised the blue flannel sheets, swiveled feet to floor, breathing heavily. **Silently. Like an Indian. Like the last of the Mohicans.** He rose and stood before the night shape of Sonny, dark, small, silent, intent in sleep. **There are...** Shapes of night, large and formless, shattered by light, charred into negative. Lightning unzipped the night. **Mississippi-one, Mississippi-two, Mississippi-three.** Scattered into thunder like great trees split and falling. He unlatched the porch door and stepped outside.

Five

Baseball cap pulled down to his glasses, knees up to his chest, Herman lay on his right side on the Williams' davenport, its pattern of blue and white morning glories twining with emerald and ocher leaves and vines writhing above and below his body, unnoticed, for he was deep below the sea, well off the coast and diving into the broad pages and sprawling ink drawings of Baum's The Sea Fairies, which he had just found in Gladys' odd assortment of catalogues and books on the old desk in the corner of the sewing room on a bottom shelf underneath a shattered wicker cage.

Kelly growled.

"Sonny, give me a break."

Herman looked over at Andrew who sat before his stamp collection, looking down at Sonny and his dog. Kelly was tugging on the end of one of Gladys' hand-embroidered dishtowels. "Is that your mother's towel?"

"I don't know."

"Herman...Listen to me now. Your Dad said he just couldn't make it this weekend—he has to go all the way up to Coeur d'Alene to work for the War Loan Drive. You should be proud of him. Lots of boys have to do without fathers longer than a month. Some don't have

fathers at all. The war…Matthew was, my son was…" Gladys suddenly turns and hurries down the hall.

Sonny looks up from the floor. "My big brother is a hero. He died in Italy fighting Germans. Buh-uh-uh-uh-uh-uh-uh-uh." Sonny swings his cocked finger in an arc.

"He was a machine gunner. They said he killed almost a hundred of them. We got a medal but I don't know where Mom keeps it. Hey, Hermy, let's play."

"Get Charlie to play with you."

"Charlie and Max are out on the river today. They got a job. They woke up real early. Dincha hear?"

"Enough!" Herman looked up from his book. Andrew had stood up.

"Enough is enough. Look, Sonny, take it outside, will you? I'm trying to work on my stamps and Mom is trying to take a nap." **Has he noticed the missing stamp?**

"Now look at how I am putting this in, Hermy. Bend the mounting sticker right here. Lightly lick it. Like this. Here is where you want to fix it to the stamp. See? But don't do this to mint—to unused stamps. They're more valuable than used stamps. The sticker will remove a strip of the gum and that makes the new stamp into a used stamp. Now look at these. Pitcairn Island. Have you ever heard of Nordhoff and Hall? Mutiny on the Bounty?"

Mr. Williams is a nice guy. I shouldn't have taken the stamp. What's gettin into me?

Herman stands in front of his father's dresser. He opens the top left-hand drawer, finds a three-cent stamp and an envelope. He slips them in his jacket pocket. He picks up a quarter, two nickels, a dime, three pennies. He jingles them in his hand. Then he puts them in his pocket. He takes three cigarettes out of the Lucky Strike package. He looks at himself in the mirror. **What's gettin into me?**

"There's nothing to do outside, Dad. And it's gonna rain, I'll bet you anything it's gonna."

"Sonny, it's not going to rain."

Dear Mom,

I've been living with another family now for three weeks. Dad and I didn't like living at the Schultzes' house. He's got a room closer to town, a little room in a basement. The Williams are okay, a lot better than the Schultzes. They got a little dog named Kelly and a magpie and a fishpond out in the backyard. Some other kids live here too. And their house is closer to Lowell. So I don't have to get up so early. I really miss you and

Herman heard Charlie laughing nearby. He slipped the sheet of paper into the back of the book.

He closes his eyes and lies back on the cot. **I can't see her. I can't see her face any more. She looks like Jean Arthur.** *He opens his eyes and looks at the ceiling. Then he closes his eyes again. Jean Arthur begins to cry. Charles Coburn looks guilty and Joel McCrea is angry.* **She used to take me to the movies.**

After Charlie had disappeared, Herman turned to the back of The Sea Fairies and looked at the letter to his mother.

....and no one ever hugs me. I don't see Dad at all now he's so busy with everything...

I'd better cross out that line about the hugging. Got to make this just right. Can't want it too much. Won't get it then.

"Here, I've got an idea! Remember Maggie? When I brought her back home, I split her tongue." The day after Herman had arrived, Andrew had brought home a young magpie that he had found in the scrub while out trout fishing. He built it a huge cage nailed to the trunk of the maple tree shading the north side of the lawn and overarching a goldfish pond that he had stocked with catfish. "Do you know why I did that?" Sonny shook his head. Herman clapped his book shut.

Jake's voice rose. "Hermy, we're damned lucky to get even this. There's still a housing shortage whether or not you know it and there's no way you're going to fit into that basement room of mine. Now if Gladys Williams wasn't a distant relative of your mother's, we'd be in a hell of a fix because there were three children ahead of you wanting a place with her. But I argued that you would make a good playmate for Sonny—"

"He's just a little kid! I'm not his playmate—I'm his baby sitter!"

Sonny rose. "You split her tongue?"

"Mm-hmm. You can teach them to talk then. Loosens up their tongues—so to speak." He smiled. "Get it?"

Sonny shook his head. "Get what? Maggie? Mom's not gonna like her in with the canaries."

"Forget it, son. Look, I want you to teach Maggie how to speak. You start with her name. All you have to do is say it over and over to her. Pretty soon she'll get it. One thing. Say it in a way so she can repeat it. Like this. Maaag-EEE," Andrew squawked the first syllable and squeaked up into a falsetto for the second. Sonny laughed. "You try it, Sonny."

"Maaag-EEE!"

"Perfect. Herman, can you do it, too?"

"Maaag-EEE!"

"Andrew, what's goin on out there?"

"Nothing, hon. You just go back to sleep." Andrew turned to the boys, his voice lowered to a whisper. "You're doing great. Now get to it, boys."

The boys went out the side door off the kitchen and down the walk to the tree shading the garage. On its trunk was the cage, two feet square and about a yard high. On a perch sat a black and white bird cocking her head toward them. It screeched.

Herman cleared his throat. "Maaag-EEE!"

Sonny imitated him. "Maaag-EEE!"

"Maag-EEE!"

An hour later, Herman was still at it, but Sonny was trailing his fingers through the fishpond. "You better watch out, Sonny. Maaag-EEE! If you get your fingers stuck on one of those catfish whiskers, you're gonna be sorry. Maaag-EEE!" The black and white bird cocked its hand and shuffled sideways to the left on the dowel Andrew had used for its perch. "Maag-EEE!"

Sonny peered into the murky water. "You aren't the boss of me. Besides, I don't see any catfish there. I bet they didn't make it through the winter. This pond was frozen solid."

"Maag-EEE!"

The magpie squawked, "KAAK-kaak-kaak-kaak"

"I think she's getting it. Maaag-EEE! Maaag-EEE! Maaag-EEE! You've seen some of the goldfish, haven't you? Maaag-EEE!"

"Hermy, I'm getting sick and tired of hearing that!"

"Why don't you throw a bug in the fishpond and see if anything comes to the top? Maaag-EEE!"

Max came out toward the goldfish pond with a cigarette in his mouth and a fishing pole under this arm.

"You guys back already?"

"What's it look like, Sonny? Hey, there goes one, Sonny! A damn Zero!"

"Where? Where?"

"And you missed spottin it. You won't ever find them Japs in a fishpond, ya know."

"Where, Max? Where'd it go?"

"Sonny, he's just pullin your leg."

"Cut it out, Max. And get away from here with that fishin pole. The catfish aren't for catchin."

"Don't tell me what to do, squirt." Max poked the end of his fishing pole into the pond.

"Make him stop, Hermy."

"Aw, he couldn't make anybody stop. But I'm goin anyway. Got bigger fish to fry than you, you little squirt." Max walked back to the garage.

Sonny looked through the grass and then lifted one of the flat paving stones next to the pond. The rust from its surface stained his fingers, and he wiped them on his fatigue shirt. "I see a rollie bug. Do you think a catfish would eat one of those?"

"Try it. Maaag-EEE! Maaag-EEE!"

Sonny dropped the bug in. It floated on its back, its tiny legs wriggling randomly. Then it tipped to its side. It tried to curl its shell. Herman sat down by Sonny. "I wonder if these rollie bugs are related to armadillos? Matthew talked about seeing those down in the desert when he was on maneuvers. You ever see one?"

"Shh! Look, Sonny, look!" The water swirled slowly beneath the bug and slowly there gaped a huge mouth into which the green water evenly flowed bearing the still insect. The mouth closed. For a moment, its whiskers floated on the surface of the pond. Then the catfish rolled, exposed a charcoal side and sunk out of sight under the lily pads.

"Wow…"

"I guess you still got catfish. Your Dad caught them?"

"Yeah."

"Why don't you eat them? You eat deer and bear and rabbits."

"Nobody eats catfish. They eat all that crap from the sewers."

"My stepfather eats them. He's from the South. They all eat them there."

"Yuk."

"I don't eat suckers. They live on crap, too. Once I caught a big one in Lake Washington and brought it home—it was really big, you see—and he cooked it.!"

"He cooked a sucker?"

"Yeah. And he made me eat some."

"Stepfathers are worse than stepmothers. You're worse off than Cinderella, Hermy."

"Yeah." Herman picked up a small stick and splashed the pond with short, jagged strokes.

"Herman, tell me again what a dirty Jap fighter plane looks like. What shape is it against the sky? I can't remember and if I can't remember, I can't report it. Wouldn't it be somethin if we spotted the first Jap plane in Idaho?"

"No, dummy. They'd be trying to kill us."

"Come on, Hermy."

"Well, the wings look like this." Herman drew in the dirt while Sonny leaned close to his hand, breathing heavily through his mouth. Then they lay on their backs and stared into the clear blue Idaho sky, looking for planes. "I read in the Statesman the other day that another Jap balloon killed some people."

"Yeah?"

"Yeah. These two kids had found it tangled up in a fence and they dragged it home and had been playing with it for a couple of weeks and then it suddenly exploded."

"How could a balloon explode?"

"They think it had a fragmentation bomb hooked up in it."

"That makes about six, doesn't it?"

"Yeah." Herman stuck a blade of grass in his mouth. So did Sonny. They looked up into the sky.

Herman yawned and stretched. "I saw Dusty again."

"Dusty?"

"Didn't I tell you about Dusty?"

"Huh-uh."

"Dusty's my squirrel. He lives over in the trees around my Dad's. He's a black squirrel."

"Squirrels are red."

"Not Dusty. After Tank died, my Dad gave him to me. Then we had to leave the Schultz's and I slept on a sleeping bag in my Dad's basement room. Dusty slept with me—except I called him Rusty instead of Dusty then. One day, I wanted to give him some exercise so I locked him in the furnace room next door while I went out. When I came back and looked in, he was gone. I couldn't believe it. I looked all over. And then I heard a scratching inside the furnace, so I figured maybe he got in there. I looked along the pipes and saw this little trap door, so I propped it open and I left. When I came back after dinner, there was soot all over everything! Gosh, the landlady was mad. That's when Dad really started looking for some place else for me to live. And we let Rusty loose. Except the black never came out and I call him Dusty now."

"Gosh, Hermy, you don't have very much luck with your pets."

Herman sat up and looked at Sonny. "Oh, my God, Sonny..." Herman ran for the house, Sonny following. Deserted, Maggie called after them "KAAK-kak-kak-kak. Maaag-EEE! KAAK-kak-kak-kak!" They didn't notice.

When the boys got to the basement, they found Fred Astaire lying on his side, his eyes pressed shut, his teeth bared, his black and white pelt flat and colorless and a little ruffled over the roll of his ribs, his paws curled back as if he were still running. His water dish was empty. The rabbit food was gone. The grass in his box was yellow. He smelled. **Like garbage.**

"Charlie was wrong, wasn't he, Hermy?"

"About what?"

"About nutty not killing you."

Herman sat down beside the cage and looked at Fred. He breathed in his smell. He put his cheek on his palm. "What's getting into me these days? Why'd I forget?"

"Hermy, let's do somethin."

"Huh-uh."

"Why?" No answer. "You still sad about Fred?"

"Yeah, well, what I really am is mad. I'm mad at you, Sonny. It's your fault. If I wasn't always baby-sittin you, I'd have remembered to feed Fred. Can't you give a guy any peace?"

"Baby-sittin!"

"And now Fred's dead. Gypsy's dead. And Tom's dead."

"Who's Tom?"

"Forget it. Why don't you just leave me alone, Sonny? You bore me. Because you're a little kid. Did that ever occur to you? Just leave me alone. I know I'm supposed to play with you, but I don't want to. I don't want to do anything."

"Jeez, Hermy. You don't have to go gettin mad or nothin."

Six

"How come you got that on your arm, Hermy?"

"Hmmm." Herman rolled over. The sun was glaring in his eyes. **Sonny. Canaries.**

"How come? How come you got that on your arm? Your left arm?" **Polio. Snakes.** Herman pulled the pillow over his head. A quill pricked his cheek. *"This is what it feels like."* The needle pricks his arm. *"Now that ain't bad, is it? Hold it out straight. Here. Stick your fist under my armpit."*

"Hermy?" Sonny's voice is dim outside the goose down.

"Go away." He pulled the pillow against his ears. Farther away, louder and still clear: "Can I look at it?"

"Can I look at your arm, Sandy?"

"Sure, kid."

"That's the gypsy's tattoo!"

"Aw, come on, Hermy. Wake up."

"The snake and flowers."

73

"Tell me Hermy. How come?"

"What's his folks gonna think?"

"They'll prolly think they better take better care of him next time."

"You been drawin on your arm, Hermy?" No way was this pillow going to keep that voice out of his life.

"Sonny."

"Yeah, Hermy?"

"Bug off. Or I'll bust you one."

"I gotta pee. But when I come back, will you get up? Please, Hermy. I'll bring the Sunday funnies in. Come on. You can take the pillow off your head now." There was silence. "I'm goin." The door opened and closed. He flipped the pillow under his head and turned from the morning sun. The plastic key chain lay across his upper lip. The air was cool on his moist cheek.

Guitar music sings from the rust-mottled blue panel truck. Sandy shouts "Murphy!" The rear doors swing out revealing a man in an orange plaid flannel shirt, legs spread, arms open, holding in one hand a black guitar trimmed with glowing mother of pearl.

"How they hangin, Sandy?" Murphy is broad and big bellied, his freckled face capped by tightly curled red hair.

"They hangin."

"Playing ball?"

"Just back in Seattle. I'm showin my stuff tomorrow."

"He yours?"

"No. Hermy, Murphy. Hermy's got a problem. Nobody showed at the bus station to pick him up last night. His old lady's nowhere in the Seattle phone book. So we're waitin to get through to the goddamn aunt in the Cashmere area. Party line's just like radio to those hicks. How's things with you?"

"Been down at the Sandpoint parkin lot, drawin on the swabbies. Anchors, U.S., Mom, and all that good shit. Hey, by the way, if you need a room, I know some swabbies who have got one— one of the guys livin with them just went to the South Pacific. Housing's real short in Seattle."

"Thanks, Murph. So you're gettin tired of the tattoo business?"

"Haven't done a decent job since your arm. Music's better. Think I've got a gig at the Royal."

"Who's playin?"

"Just some guys. Only piano and drum and never played together before. Sort of a Kenton sound. They're pullin in crowds. Problem's there ain't nothin to see but us—no food, no booze. And it's a shitty lookin place. The bastards who had it last stripped it. So our boss uses apple crates for chairs and tables. But that's got its good side. So hard to sit on the crates, the crowd turns over every half hour, so the ones in line outside won't go away. They get free peanuts and a waiter comes around every once in a while and throws all your peanut shells on the floor. The dumb bastards dig it. Like workin in a dump yard but the music's somethin around the corner."

"Sounds like I'm gonna have to be there tonight. But you givin up the tattoo business?"

"I could make more dough drillin anchors but I'm tired of that shit. Let's see your arm." Sandy rolled up his sleeve. *"She's healin real good. Now that's a masterpiece. I'd like to hang that up in Old Lizzie."*

"Not my throwin arm, friend."

"I'll bet that gypsy got that in Europe. I ain't seen a design like that around the states. Not on the street and not in the carnies. Maybe somethin like the style down in New Orleans, the snake and flowers and stuff. Oh, maybe I seen somethin like it in New York once in one of them side streets."

"This is better than the gypsy's, Murph."

"Well, you spread the word. I'd like to do some more like that. Look." Murphy rolled up *his left shirtsleeve and bared his thick arm at the elbow. Under the gold hair and crawling across the freckles was the outline of a snake pointed toward a fully rendered ruby rose blooming from his forearm.* *"Just started it this mornin."*

"It's gonna be a real honey. Hey, I got a customer for you right here. Another snake in a rose patch."

"The kid?"

"Yeah."

"Never done a kid before. What's his folks gonna think?"

"They'll prolly think they better take better care of him next time. Waited hours at the bus station for his mother. Nobody showed up. And his aunt threw him out cause his uncle shot him."

"Shot him?"

"Just a graze. See? Right…here. Sorry, kid."

"Son-of-a-bitch."

"Yeah. Well, he's a glutton for punishment. Wants a tattoo now. Like mine."

"You want this, kid, or is Sandy up to one of his tricks?"

"I want a tattoo. Will it hurt?"

"Well, it don't hurt a man full of beer and dumber than shit. I don't know about a kid. They hurt easier."

"I don't know."

"Well, I guess you gotta weigh the hurt against the gain. And there ain't no way to do that until you feel the pain. Least that's what Gramps always said. I'll tell you what. We'll do some little somethin that can fit into the picture and if you wanna finish, well, fine. Or you can do the rest later. And if you don't like it, it's on the house."

"And it's on your goddamn arm, too."

"Can it, Sandy. Okay?"

"Okay."

"Well, let's see now. I'd give you a rose like me but the other kids'd think you were a faggot. I guess I better settle for the snake. Maybe a little snake for a start. We can make a whole nest of them later. Yeah. A whole goddamn nest. How'd you like that?"

"I'd like that. I like snakes."

"Well, sure you do. Lessee. You roll your sleeves up some of the time?"

"Uh-uh."

"No? How come?"

"Well, it's my left arm."

"What about your left arm?"

"Well, I got polio in it when I was a little kid. It works okay now but it's skinny because I keep forgetting to do my exercises. So I wear long sleeves all the time."

"Polio, huh? The arm numb anywhere?"

"No. It all works okay. Just skinny."

"Lessee. Roll up your sleeves. Up to where mine is. Okay. Now hold em out. Real straight. Hold em still. Here, make me a muscle. Both arms?" Herman bunched his arms. "You play any sports, kid?"

"Yeah, I started playing tennis. You can do that with one hand. But I don't like playing on a team or anything."

"Why?"

"I get nervous. And I drop the ball all the time. And nobody wants me on their side anyway. I'm always the last to get picked."

"You see what I'm seein, Sandy?"

"Yeah. Hey, Hermy, your left arm isn't skinny. It's the right one that's big." "Huh?"

"You got a hell of a right arm for a kid. I'll bet you gotta good throwin arm."

"No."

"Well, that's because nobody ever showed you how to use it."

"Dad did. He tried, that is. But he got mad."

"Like I said. Nobody ever tried to teach you. He play ball?"

"No, he wasn't big enough. But Uncle Frank played football…and they let Dad help around the team."

"Well, you're not gonna be any little squirt, Hermy. Here." Sandy tosses a small pine-cone at Herman's chest. "Herman, look at which hand." The pinecone was in Herman's left hand. "Shit, boy. They just got you buffaloed. You got no problems except people, Hermy. Other people. Hell, they need you as much as you need them. Think about that." Murphy clears his throat. "Bad cold, Murph."

"Yeah, well I got to get back to playin my guitar. You guys ready? I know what I want to do with that snake."

"You gotta agree to one thing, Hermy."

"What?"

"Snake goes on your left arm. We gonna dress that arm up. Make it proud. Give it a goddamn snake. What do you say, Sandy?"

"Right flipper tosses, left fields. Gotta get em both to work. If a snake don't do it, I'll be damned if I know what will."

"Okay, Hermy. Let's go. We're gonna see about the pain and the gain now." Guitar in hand, Murphy climbs back into the panel truck, hands out three chains, disappears, rattles metal and then jumps down. "Here's my gear, Hermy. Problem is the only power I got out here is the truck. Lot smoother with electricity. But it ain't gonna make much difference. Sandy, start up Old Liz will you?" While Sandy gets the truck running, Murphy prepares Herman's arm.

"Hold it out straight. Here stick your fist under my armpit." Herman does so and Murphy clamps his own arm tightly, holding the boy's fist firmly against his side. "Now they ain't so much problem about you jumpin around and gettin yourself a dot on your nose or somewhere even more embarrassing. Look, if this hurts and you yell out, I'll stop right away."

Herman feels his heart beat still and hot in his chest, feels his heart tripping. He is dizzy and the pine trees and Murphy and Sandy and the motorcycle and Old Liz move away into a softer place. **I'm not going to cry. I'm not going to jump.** *"I'm gonna give you your first dot, Hermy." Herman closes his eyes.* **Ouch.** *He opens his eyes and sees a small blue dot on the crease between his forearm and biceps, close to the vein there. He smiles. "Okay, Hermy. We're in business." Murphy bends his head and Herman looks at red curls. Time moves.*

Herman closes his eyes again. The pain becomes broad burn, becomes heat. Murphy stops. "Let's give it a rest. Look." Herman looks. The blue outline of a small snake. Its body coils twice, its head pointing up his arm. "Now, I'm gonna fill it in." Murphy's head bends again and Herman closes his eyes. **It's hurt worse. Like the exercise from the Seattle Orthopedic. Mom forcing the arm up over my head. That hurt. That hurt a lot more. This is just sort of hot.** *Murphy stops again. "Almost done. Just the eyes now. Don't look. It's bad luck." Silence. Click of metal. A prick of pain. "Ta-daaa!"*

Herman looks down. There, coiling upon itself, moving through an oval patch of grass, under a red rose was a tiny snake, its back ornamented by intricate patterns, its ruby eyes looking up at him. He grins at Murphy. "Okay. Wow. Hey, this is great! Wait'll everybody sees this! It won't wash off or anything, will it?" Murphy laughs. "No, kid, you got this for the rest of your life. And even after that. And I put some extra stuff in it so when you grow and the skin stretches, it'll show. You'll like it when it comes out."

"What extra stuff?"

"Some details. You'll see…"

Herman bends closely over the tattoo trying to see the detail in the snake. **I can't wait. I wonder what he's put in there for me to see? I'll bet it's neat.** *"Can I touch it?"*

"Better leave it alone for a while. Just like a scratch. I'll put a little bandage on it before you leave. But right now, let's let it breathe." Sandy stands and stretches. "Nice work, Murph."

"Thanks."

80

When the men begin to talk, Herman sits at the foot of an evergreen, his legs crossed. **Like an Indian. Some of them had tattoos, too.** *He looks down at the snake. He closes his eyes and feels the heat in his arm spread up and up. Each moment, he feels bigger as if his body is something large and light, spreading out.* **Like a cloud.** *He looks down.* **It's really clear now. There's Mom. She's standing in front of a little yellow house. On a hill. Evergreens. She looks fat. Look at Sandy! And he's catching. Out. Double play. And over there. Over there's the gypsy in the front seat of a truck, her arm leaning out the window. What a great tattoo! Just sitting there smoking. She's looking at me! She sees me!** *Herman's eyes open. He looks back down at the snake.* **"What's happening?"**

"Take her muzzle off! I wanta kiss her." Murphy and Sandy laugh. Sandy looks over at Herman. "You okay, Hermy?"

"Yeah."

Murph stands. "Here, let me fix the arm." With a roll of gauze, he binds Herman's arm. "You're a good kid, Hermy. When Sandy here gets your phone number, I'll give you a call to see if you wanta take over where we left off." The motorcycle roars as Sandy guns it. "Looks like he's hot to trot. See ya, Hermy." Murphy waves as the boy climbs behind Sandy. Both wave back. Then the motorcycle begins climbing up out of Murphy's camp.

"I'm back!" Herman heard sniffling by his left ear. "Kelly wants to say hello. And here's the Sunday funnies. You can read em to me." Herman leaned back to rummage through the jacket hanging on the headboard. He pulled out a Lucky Strike and a wooden match, caught the match head with the nail of his thumb, and as it flared, lit the cigarette. He inhaled deeply. **Dizzy. Wow. Good. Right behind the baby blues. Mmmm-hmm. Yeah.** "Okay, Sonny, what do you want?"

"You smoke?"

"What's it look like?" Herman coughed.

"It looks like you're just beginning." Herman took another drag on his cigarette and, this time, let it dangle on his lower lip. "Can I have one?" Herman shook his head. "Better not let Mom catch you, Herman." Herman flicked some ash into one of his shoes. "So what's that?" Sonny pointed at Herman's left arm.

"What?" Herman scooped his faded blue flannel shirt off the floor and slipped it over his shoulders. **Like that guy in Casablanca. The one that took Bogart's girl.** He withdrew the cigarette with thumb and forefinger. **European style.** He exhaled smoke from the corner of his mouth. "What are you talking about, Sonny?"

"Come on, Hermy! That mark on your left arm."

"Oh God, Sonny, Don't you ever give up?"

"No." Sonny sat upright. "Never."

"Okay, but don't tell anybody. You promise?"

"I promise."

"Cross your heart and hope to die?"

"Okay." Herman lowered his voice. "It's a tattoo."

"A real tattoo?"

"Yeah."

"Will you give me one?"

"Can't."

"Couldn't you just draw one on me?"

"Listen, Sonny. It'd wash right off. A real tattoo artist has to do it. Like my friend Murphy. Besides, your mother'd never let you. She'd get rid of me first and then she'd kill you. My Dad almost killed me when he saw this."

Sonny leaned over Herman's arm. "Where's its eyes?" Herman licked a grain of tobacco from his lips. "Where'd you get it?"

"In Seattle."

"How much did it cost?"

"A sawbuck."

"Jeez."

"Who's Murphy?"

"Murphy tattoos sailors, plays a guitar, and works over at Boeing's as a riveter. He was a friend of Sandy." Sonny looked up at Herman. "You know, the baseball player. Catcher. The guy who gave me the cap?"

Still looking back down at Herman's arm, Sonny nodded. "I wanna know somethin."

"What?"

"What does a tattoo feel like?"

"It feels like normal, Sonny."

"Ya know, Hermy. You oughta roll up your sleeve and show those boys at school the snake on our arm. Bet they'd want one, too. Bet they'd stop hitting you."

"I don't like people looking at this arm."

"Because of the tattoo?"

"Because it's gimpy. Like Charlie's. It's bad enough being called Four Eyes."

"It doesn't look gimpy."

"I had polio in it."

"It looks O.K. to me. Does it hurt?"

"No. Hey, Sonny, you want me to read you the funnies?"

"Yeah! Read me Blondie and Mandrake and Terry and the Pirates and Popeye..." Down the hall came knocking. "Sonny, what's all that banging on the front door?"

"Dunno."

"Well, go see. Nobody's up. You said so yourself."

"But, Hermy, you said you'd read the funnies."

"Don't whine, Sonny. Listen to that racket. First the door and then the funnies." Sonny left and came back moments later, his face sobered.

"Who was it?"

"Max and a guy in a uniform. They knocked like Max don't live here. The man had hold of Max's arm. Said to go find my parents. They were already awake enough to send me back here like they always do before somethin happens."

"Well, leave the door open, then, bean brain, so we can hear."

They sat quietly on Sonny's bed with the funnies spread out in front of them. Gladys' voice came dim and small from the living room. "My daughter Helen's a WAC and my other daughter's husband's in France. And my oldest boy, Matthew, well, he was lost. In Africa. God knows if the others will come back." Her voice quavered.

Andrew cleared his throat. "It isn't that we don't want to do our part for Mr. Roosevelt. Sick as he's been and all. We couldn't be more grateful to him. It was the government gave me a job when there wasn't one. Hadn't worked for a year and a half. I don't know how Gladys managed to feed all of those mouths. We ate lots of potatoes. So we all appreciate what Roosevelt's done. But Max has a year of school left."

Gladys continued, "He isn't eighteen, if he told you different."

"But Ma. This war's been goin on for four goddamn years. The war's over in Europe. I wanna go to the Pacific. If I don't get in now, I'm gonna miss all the action. Maybe never get another chance my whole lifetime. Sign it, Ma. Dad all you gotta do is sign and I'm in uniform. Come on, Ma. You sign." Silence. Wood hit wood. "Goddamn!"

"Pick up that chair! And don't wheedle and don't you goddamn me, mister. You should be so lucky not to see another war in your lifetime."

"Max, I already told you. It isn't like the first war. Boys fourteen and younger running away to join the troops. Now, without your parents' permission, Uncle Sam doesn't want you."

"Ya mean they can pick me up off the street to fight fires but I can't be a soldier?"

"How'd you find out he'd lied, sergeant?"

"We've got our ways of tracking these things down, ma'am. But this one was easier than usual. Woman, a friend of yours, Mabel...Mabel."

"Jesus Christ! Ya mean it was Mabel talking outta both sides of her mouth. Again. Bart musta told her. Stick ya for anything she can get, Mabel. That bitch ruined my life. My only chance for combat in this century. Wait'll I get my hands on her."

"Now settle down, son. I'm gonna ignore what you just said, you been hot under the collar and wantin a uniform so bad. But you better not do it again."

"Well, goddamn it, Mabel!" Max shouted as his hand slammed down on wood.

"There goes the end table Dad just fixed," Sonny smirked.

"I'll just go to Seattle or California and enlist. None of you can stop me."

"Now, son, I don't think you see the writing on the wall. I notified all the recruitment agencies in all branches of the service for about a thousand miles around. Hell, boy, even the Japanese probably know about you by now. Best thing you can do is finish school, and then help the war effort. Now I gotta get back to duty."

"Let me show you to the door, sergeant. Thank you for everything."

"Thanks, Mr. Andrews, and..." The voices became soft, wordless.

"Jesus Christ, Hermy!" Sonny shook his head. "Hermy, we all better stay outta Max's way for awhile. He gets mean when he gets mad. He threw a bottle at me once. I wouldn't wanna be Mabel." Sonny scratched Kelly's ears. Then he looked up at Herman. "Well, you gonna read me the funnies?"

Seven

Gray tendrils stretched from sagebrush desert to city, charcoal clouds glimmered lightning, smeared the rosy late afternoon light in the west. Herman and Sonny lay on their cots beneath the marigold canary flock. Fingers locked behind his head, legs extended and crossed at the ankle, plastic key chain in his mouth, Herman listened to the thunder and counted the steps of the storm toward them. Curled into a pillow on his own cot, Sonny turned the pages of an Andy Panda comic book. Thunder rumbled. Canaries fluttered. Sonny looked up.

"Hermy?"

"What?"

"We're going to have rain."

"I know."

"Mom let some of these damn canaries loose this morning."

"Don't say 'damn'. She'll blame it on me."

"She did."

"Did what?"

"Let some canaries loose."

"I know."

"How do you know?"

"Look out there." Herman pointed toward Maggie's maple tree. The branches above Maggie's cage bloomed canaries.

"They're gonna get wet."

"How many did she let loose?"

"Those three cages that were at the foot of your cot."

"I liked those. They had bars on their wings."

"Well, a lot of people don't like those and anyway none of them sang."

"They made a hell of a lot of noise..."

Suddenly, Max sprung sideways into the sun porch with the clatter and crack of wood on doorsill and floor. Canaries exploded onto cage bars. Wood planks slid from his arms, bouncing slowly in separate rhythms, knocking one another, radiating from his body in odd and many angles.

"Hey, Max, playin pick-up sticks? We got some little ones here under the cot."

"Goddamn it, Sonny...God DAMN, Charlie!" He lunged into the room, a plank from the dark hall stabbing at him. He let his armload crash to the floor and back-pedaled until he fell onto Herman's cot. Herman pressed against the wall. Charlie edged neatly into the room with another load of wood under his good arm.

Sonny jumped up. "What's goin on, Charlie?"

"We're gonna let you boys in on the opportunity of a lifetime." Charlie leaned his planks upright against the doorsill. Scowling, Max bent to gather his lost load, as Charlie thrust a sheet of paper at Sonny. "Here are the plans."

Herman joined the pair. On the paper was a sketch. "Is this a boat?"

"A canoe, Auerbach, a canoe! Here. Look at these plans. It will cost us next to nothin. We're gonna make it ourselves."

"What do you know about canoes?"

"Hell, what don't I know about canoes? Down in California…"

"Hey, stop that!" Sonny jumped off the cot. "That's my corner, Max! Hey, Max, those are my things! How am I gonna find my marble collection under all those planks?"

"Look at this, Sonny." Max grabbed the paper from Herman. "It's a real boat. Doesn't need gas or nothin that's rationed. Just get in it and go. Down the river. This is our freedom, squirt. Can't you see what we can do?"

"Don't call me squirt! Me and Herman will never get to go in that canoe. The only reason you're givin us this opportunity of a lifetime is cause Ma won't let you put this junk anywhere else in the house. Go away, Max."

"Ya got me all wrong, Sonny. You like boats. Remember the one we took you on when you were little, the flat-bottomed one through the caves and they turned off all the lights. Ya liked that, didn't ya?"

"Yeah, Max. Hey Hermy, it was about a hundred degrees outside, but it was cold in the cave. This boat went way back into the cave. You could touch the walls with your hands. They were wet. They said it was a wet cave, not a dry one, so that cave was still dripping those long rocks from the top and the bottom. Ya should've see it, Hermy."

"He's tricking you, Sonny. Watch out. When's the last time these guys even talked to us?" Herman pushed his glasses back up onto the bridge of his nose.

Max laughed and began to tickle Sonny. Then he grabbed his ankles and held the squealing, laughing boy upside down. "We're gonna paddle down the river, Sonny! Hey, Charlie, wanna see some magic? I'm gonna make Sonny into a snake!" He began to bend Sonny's heels one way, his head the other. The boy struggled loose, slipped upside down toward the floor, Max reaching, falling sideways, Sonny squealing louder, Max barking his sharp laugh.

Charlie and Herman watched from the cot. The wrestling brothers rolled against Herman's legs, and he lifted his feet onto the mattress.

"Hey, Auerbach." Charlie lit a Chesterfield.

"Yeah?"

"Go along with this one, will ya? First time Max has stopped being a son-of-a-bitch for days now. Wanna butt?' He tapped out a cigarette.

Herman took it. "I'll save it for later. I'm cuttin back."

"Got somethin else for you." Charlie rose and pulled a bent envelope out of his hip pocket. "Oops. Sorry. Forgot it was back there before I sat down."

Herman squinted at the return address. **Uncle Frank!** He went over to his cot, stooped to reach under it for his shoes. As he laced them up, Charlie watched. "You need new shoes, bud." Then he knelt down beside the planks with the canoe plans. Herman stepped over Max and Sonny and walked outside. He sat against the maple tree. Canaries twittered.

"Mag—eee?"

"Shut up, Maggie." He began to read.

> Hermy, old boy.
>
> How's the pitching arm? I think a lot about that day with you, Sandy and Maxine. That was the last decent day that I had.
>
> I'm back at sea again. Sorry, no details. Censors think you might tell a Jap. But I think it's going to get hot and heavy before you see me again.
>
> Your dad told me that you guys lived in a baseball park after you left Seattle. Hey, that sounds great to me! I bet Sandy would love that. He'd bunk on the pitcher's mound. I haven't heard from him—from anybody really. I know from my last tour that sometimes it's pretty hard for the Navy to find the sailor. I got twelve letters all at once during the campaign in North Africa.
>
> Well, kid, hang in there. It's a tough world we're living in now and it's probably not going to get a lot easier. I just hope that all this is over before you get out of school.
>
> Think of me. And take care of your Dad. Remember what I said?
>
> Write, will you?
>
> Love, Frank

Splash! Herman looked over at the fish. Concentric circles widened. *Herman leans out of the window of the prefabricated home and looks at the western sky. Sunset breaks into blacks and oranges, tinting his bare chest rust. He leans farther out the window.* **It's like Halloween up there. Boy, those black clouds make it hard to see Zeros. Now if I spotted a Zero, I'd be a hero. Hey, I'm a poet and I don't know it but my feet show it.** *He picks up his airplane spotter's manual and looks again at the silhouettes of the Japanese Zero.* **If I had been at Pearl Harbor two years ago, we would have won the war by now.** *A child's cry comes from the next room.* **Little Jacky. Jeez, he cries a lot. I can't even sleep sometimes.** *And then he scowls.* **And he really looks stupid under all that curly blond hair. Just like Gorgeous George. When's she going to give him a haircut?**

Herman watches two men in civilian clothes walking from a taxicab slowly up to the door. **Is that...?** *He stands and removes his glasses to polish them. He looks again.* **Dad! And Uncle Frank.** *They bang on the door.* **They look mad.** *He hears the door open and the soft voices of his stepfather and his mother and then the voice of his father.* "I don't give a damn what you want, Hope! You can't take Herman to Georgia. I won't allow it. And I have custody."

"Hermy!"

"Dad." *Herman cracks open the door and looks into the living room. Uncle Frank, large, bald, in Navy blues stands before Jack and his mother, his fists bunched, his white cap cocked on his bald head. Behind him, smaller, stands Jake. His mother calls. He opens the door and walks into the room. His father walks over to him and puts his hand on the boy's shoulder, suddenly leans down and examines his neck. Herman smells beer.* "What's this scar on his neck? What the hell have you been doing to him?" *He turns to Jack.* "Have you laid a hand on my boy because if you have, I'll..." *Herman hears his stepfather shout, but the world moves away from him and he stands beside himself. He watches everyone. He watches himself. He is comfortable, relaxed. His father grabs his arm and pulls it up. The pain brings him into himself again.* "...tattoo!" *The world moves away again. People slide slowly and silently, like ballet dancers. Jack sweeps toward his father. Jake steps behind Frank. Frank moves toward Jack.* "Hurry up and pack up your suitcase, Herman." *Herman smiles at his mother. Her mouth is open.* **Like a fish.** *Darkness slowly moves down like a window shade. And there are two words:* **custody** *and* **tattoo.**

"Maggie?"

"Shut up, bird." Herman shifted his weight and stretched his cramped legs straight before him. He looked at the envelope.

Herman's father and uncle sweep outside through the door. Herman is between them. Frank carries his luggage. "What the hell you got in there—bricks?" A black and white checkered taxi door opens. His mother calls out to him. He can't hear the words. The three of them press together in the back seat for the ride back to Uncle Frank's, the cab smelling of beer and the driver's cigar smoke, his father and uncle laughing loudly and fiercely—"Sure caught that son-of-a-bitch by surprise—a goddamn blitzkrieg!" Singing Anchors Aweigh, My Boys, Anchors Aweigh and Coming in on a Wing and a Prayer. The world still stands a step to his right, mute and far in itself, outside him and there he is now, over there, in the hum between father and uncle, a small man and a big man, and yet somewhere, somehow the tattoo glows and curves, no longer hidden, no longer his, just another scar. But then it coils and warms, seeds something to begin growing here, in this long moment.

Uncle Frank laughs, curses, sings, talks so loudly that Herman can feel the big man's life thrum against his side, through his body into the ribs of his thin father and bouncing back into his own heart. He looks up at the large bald man with the villain's black moustache. He smiles. He turns to Jake. He, too, smiles up at the big man.

Herman smiled. He rose and slipped the letter back into its envelope, both into his rear pocket. He stooped to lace his shoes tighter. Thunder cracked. Maggie fluttered, rose, settled. Herman looked up. The canaries flew in a small cloud among the branches. Some settled. Others flew a distance out from the tree and then returned.

"Hey, Hermy! You better get in here before the storm hits!" Sonny stood in the doorway of the porch.

"I like storms." Herman saw lightning over the desert.

Sparks trickle down from the cable as the trolley clacks and clatters around the street corner, disappears behind a gray building, leaving the street open and empty fog. Frank looks around the crowd at the Seattle Lake Washington ferry dock. Herman shivers, pulls into his neck, into his jacket. "There they are!" Herman follows Frank's point. **Sandy!** *He smiles.* **Is that Frank's girl friend?** *"Hey Maxine!" Frank shouts, "You're going to lose your good name talking to bums like that! Ball players are all ex-cons."*

A woman in a green and white print dress turns, grins, shouts back. "Honey, I lost it years ago. That's why you're my date." But as Frank and he move closer, Hermy can see that Maxine is blushing. The ferry horn drones. "Come on, honey. We got the tickets." They enter at dock level, weave among the few automobiles parked there, climb the stairs, open a door. Herman sees lined-up seats facing the bow. **Like school.** *Near the windows of the structure are tables toward which Frank moves. All seated, Frank and Sandy gone for drinks, Maxine smiles at Herman. He smiles back.* **She's got freckles. Like Mom.**

"So you're Jake's boy?"

"You know my dad?"

"Well, sort of. Not really well. How you doing?"

"Okay."

"Sort of rough on you, isn't it? I mean, your folks splittin up and all."

"I don't know."

At that moment, the men return and pass around coffee, and, for Herman, a Royal Crown. Frank looks around, arches up one eyebrow, and gives a villain's mad chuckle. "Little rum'll juice it up some. Make the ride go faster. Let's have a toast. Here's to a short war and a long life. Come on, Hermy. Toast with us." Outside the window gulls scream and dip to the water for garbage.

"Herman!" Mrs. Williams stood at the side of the house beside the kitchen door. "Get out from under that tree and get in here! Lightning's gonna blow you right off the face of the earth!" **That damn Sonny, always tattling.** He rose and brushed the seat of his pants with both hands and walked to the porch entrance. Charlie and Max sat on his cot. Charlie's back was to him. Max was scowling.

"And I say we make the Peterborough! It says here," Max picked up a book, "that it's the 'first white man's canoe'."

"Yeah, but it also says it's only good for light trips. Your best canoe on the fast water is the Chestnut Prospector and it carries a hell of a lot more. Look at how deep it is in the middle and it's about nine inches wider."

"What?"

"Max, you don't know how to read the plans. Look, this is measured from the centerline, not all the way across. It's twice what you think it is."

"Yeah, well..." Max bent over the plans. "Okay, I guess so."

"You see what I mean? We wanta get some distance out of this baby. Stay out for a long time. Get through the fast water. The Chestnut Prospector's just what the name says. The prospectors in Canada used em. If we wanta get out of this hole...What?" Max had put his hand on Charlie's knee and was nodding toward Herman. Charlie turned and grinned at Herman. "He's okay."

"You sure?"

"Yeah, want another butt, Auerbach?"

"Sure." Herman took a Chesterfield from the extended pack.

"See, Max? We all got something on each other. Light up, kid."

As Herman lit the cigarette, Max and Charlie returned to the plans. "Now this here's the baseline, Max..." Herman looked out the window. The sky had grown black. Rain was spattering between the rose cane, splashing on the window. **I like the rain. I really like it.**

They plunge into the water, splash each other, shout and shriek. Herman doesn't swim. **They think that I can dog paddle. I wish I knew how to swim.** *"Hey, look at this, guys!" He puts his hands on the sandy bottom of the lake and kicks till his feet break the surface.* **They think I can swim.** *The minnows that swarm close to the shore move toward him, nibble, tickle his toes and fingers.* **This is so good. I will always remember this. I want it to go on.** *But the morning becomes noon. All tire of swimming. Clean, drying in the sun, they sit on bright towels spread on the grass, sit close together under the maple trees, leaning against gray park benches or great smooth rocks, silently watching each other.* **This is a kind of family. I love them.**

Herman looked at the baseball cap and mitt hung over the bedpost. He put the cap on and unhooked the mitt.

Max looked up. "You play ball, Hermy?"

"Never tried out for a team. Not much on batting. But I can throw and catch."

"Football's my game."

"I know."

"Ever see me play?"

"No."

"Hey, Max, your attention's wandering. Now look at this. We don't have all the materials yet. And some of them are gonna be hard to get. Look, Max. Max!"

"The kid's in with us, isn't he?"

"Yeah, yeah."

"Well, I'm just talkin to him."

"Talk to me, Max, talk to me. Please?"

"Let's play catch!" Frank seizes the ball as it rolls out of his bag.

"Frank, where's my glove?"

"Maxine, honey, this isn't a softball. Didn't want you to get hurt."

"Damn you, Frank. You're the one that's gonna get hurt."

"Honey, now honey. Hey. Hey! Not there, not..." Frank and Maxine collapse onto the grass.

Herman stands by Sandy. "But I'm no good." Sandy stoops, seizes Herman's shoulders, draws him close, gazes at him steadily. "Don't say that. Everybody's good. Good enough."

"Hey, kid."

"Max." Charlie sighed.

"Kid. Hey, kid. Wake up, kid."

"Yeah. Yeah, Max."

"Sonny tells me you got problems on the playground."

"What?"

"Some junior high school kids pushin you around."

"Yeah."

"Some guy named Karl Schultz."

"Uh-huh."

"Look, Max. We got to make us a miter box. You think your Dad can help?"

"What's a miter box?" As Max turned away, Herman looked down at his mitt. **Karl.** *"Well, if it isn't little Herman the German again. Look, boys. Hey Hey! Get the little son-of-a-bitch. Howie. How…"* **I'm a coward. I'm no good.** *"Everybody's good. Good enough."*

Smack. *"Damn! Not so goddamn hard, Sandy. Sorry, honey. Excuse my French."*

"Sea water softened the old gob's hand, Hermy."

"I'm gonna poke you right in the jaw, draft-dodger."

"Save your arm, Frank. Back at me." **Smack.** *"Now over to Frank. No, no. Here."* *He walks over to Herman.* *"Now hold it this way. Now when you bring your arm back, do this. And follow through. Like this. Here. Okay, try it. Yeah, yeah. Hey, you got it. Here it comes, Frank!"* **Smack.**

"Damn!" Herman laughs as his uncle blows on his hand. "That's it. When a kid burns me out, that's goddamn well gonna be it. Come on over here, honey. Let's sit under that tree over there. I need some consolation. When you guys get through, let's hit the carnival and see how the kid does on the wooden bottles."

"So tell me more about this kid. He still in junior high?"

"He just finished the ninth grade. He'll be in high school next year."

"He play football?"

"He doesn't play any sports."

"How'd you get him pissed off at you?"

"After my folks got divorced, my dad and I lived with his family. We didn't get along."

"Your folks got a divorce?"

"Yeah."

"This kid, this Karl…" Charlie returned to the room. "What'sup Charlie?"

Herman looked out the window again. **No more thunder. Just raining. Just a little rain.** *North, west, south, east, the four of them lean against the trunk of the maple tree. Herman looked southeast, at a point between him and Maxine.* **Mom's going that way.** *At his back he heard Frank: "Let's hit that carnival!"*

"Dinner! Boys? Hear me? Get washed."

"The only canoe I can get hold of is one that guy Jeff swiped from the Scout camp up at Payette Lakes. And it paddles like a rowboat. We just got be careful and figure out what we want."

"Mom said for you guys to come to dinner."

"Beat it, Sonny."

"Mom!"

"Okay, okay. Hey, Hymie."

"Hymie?"

"Yeah. Hymie. Your buddy over there."

"Why Hymie? He's Hermy. Hermy Auerbach."

"Why not Hymie? I like it. Come on, Hymie, let's chow down."

Hymie. Huh. Hymie. Yeah. "Okay, Max."

"Try yer luck. Hit da bottles. Win a duck!" Sandy stops. He looks down at Herman. "Ready, Hermy?" Herman looks at Sandy. He walks to the booth. Sandy lays some change on the counter. Frank and Maxine stand together, watching. Sandy quietly explains the layout, the weight of the bottles, their special positioning, where to hit the pyramid.

"Hey, kid?" Sandy and Herman looked up. "It's a slow day. So I'm gonna make ya a deal. For the cash yer friend just laid down there, I'm gonna give you some practice balls. When yer ready to shoot, if ya can knock down three of them bottles in three tosses, ya can have Donald the Duck up there."

"Thanks, mister."

"Don' thank me. I just need a shill to get things started here."

"A what?"

"Here's the balls, kid."

Herman throws half a dozen balls. He feels the weight of the ball and the distance in his arm. He hears Sandy. **Good enough.** *He finds a still place inside.* **Right off the side. Here.** *A breeze takes the maple branches above them into a dance. He calmly watches himself* *find position, take motion, throw. Some balls strike bottles, some miss. None brings down the pyramid. A seagull cries. Herman smiles. "I'm ready." He throws. "You win, kid."*

"Hey, Hymie?"

"Yeah, Max?"

"Don't worry about that Karl guy no more."

Eight

Herman listened to the rain rattle against the window. **Isn't this ever going to stop?** Lightning flashed, the topple of thunder. The birds rattled against their cages. He felt something, **something in this space, near.** He jumped. Charlie stood there, grinning. "Auntie Glad said to give you this, but it's gonna cost ya." Charlie had a letter in his hand. **Mom. A bus ticket?**

"Hand it over, Charlie." Herman reached and reached again, but the letter was always just out of reach. "Come on, Charlie. This is important. It's from my mom."

"Mama's boy. Mama's boy. Sissy mama's boy."

"How much, you bastard?"

"Bastard yourself, shorty. Just one thin dime," Herman sighed and searched his jeans for his last dime. He held it out. Charlie gave him the letter. **Uncle Frank again. But Mom should have written...**

"Blackjack?"

The room was warm and close. "You got my last dime."

"Get some chips. Your credit's good with me." Herman went down the hall for the poker chip box in the buffet. **I'll get more cash off Dad's dresser.** When he returned, he tossed the box on the cot.

"Got a butt, Charlie?"

Charlie began to shuffle the deck. "Lock the door first, so Auntie Glad don't come in unexpectedly, huh?" As Herman turned to lock the door, Sonny burst into the room followed by Max. The birds battered themselves against their cages.

"Hermy!"

"Look, kid, can't you see me and Charlie are busy?"

Max snapped, "Not busy enough, goddammit!" He brushed past Sonny and held out sandpaper and a saw to Charlie. "Don't ya wanna be ready when the river's high and the weather's right?"

"Gotta win Hymie's money first, buster. The white chips are a penny apiece. I bet two Camels. That's four cents to you."

"Two cents for a fag! You're a goddamn robber, Charlie," Max muttered, looking around for a place to put the saw and sandpaper.

"Yeah, yeah. Well, nobody's gonna sell this kid butts except me, so if I'm gonna get my ass in a sling, he might as well pay for it."

"Yeah, but two cents…"

By this time, Sonny was dancing. "Hermy! Hey, Hermy! Listen! Jack Armstrong's off. It's the President."

"So what, Sonny? So what? Is it another Fireside Chat or is the whole damn war over?"

"Mom better not catch you cussin, Hermy." Sonny stopped talking and thought silently for a moment. "Oh, yeah. The show's off because the President died!" He stopped and looked around the room. For once, he had everyone's attention.

"Well, come on, kid, you're usually clatterin away a mile a minute. What happened?"

"Jack Armstrong isn't on."

"Probably just the lightning, kid."

"No, Max. He...died."

"Jack Armstrong?"

"No. The President. He died. It's all they're talkin about on the radio."

Herman stood. "Yeah, Sonny, we heard you the first time. So what happened?"

"He died in Georgia." **Where Mom is.** "He was sittin for his picture and he fell over. He should've listened to the Nez Perce." Everyone stared at him. "You remember the Nez Perce? They don't let nobody take their pictures. Somethin about their souls. They say if somebody takes their picture, they'll die. Well, he did. The radio said he had a stroke. What's a stroke, Hermy?"

"My dad's father had a stroke. He died. He had a car accident and banged his head. He was all right everyone said, but six months later, he had a stroke. He was sitting at the breakfast table with my grandma and, she said, he was eating this piece of toast with apple butter on it, and suddenly stood up and fell over and he was dead. Right away. Dad said he had too much blood in his veins and it came gushing out his nose and everything, and then he died. My grandmother didn't know how to do nothing by herself. So Frank and Dad had to take care of things and not go to college or anything. Dad was as old as you are, Max, when it happened. So when he had a stroke and he died, then nobody knew what to do."

Max sat on Sonny's bed. "Just what I wanted, Hymie. Your family history." Herman threw his cards down. "Got a problem there, kid?" Herman rearranged the cards. Max looked around at the group, "Hell, I could take care of things around here. First, I would knock you kids into line and get you to do some of the work around the house for a change."

"You couldn't find your butt with both hands, Max," Charlie retorted. Herman and Sonny snickered.

Max gave him the finger. "Spin on this, buddy." The boys laughed outright and Max turned around, pleased. The front door slammed. "So who's gonna run the war now, Sonny?"

But Sonny was running down the hall toward the living room. "Ma, Mabel. Did ya hear? The President died."

"Mabel. What's Mabel doin here?" Max scowled. He left the room. Charlie and Herman looked at one another. Charlie blew a smoke ring. Max's voice echoed in the hall.

"Ya hear that, Mabel? I missed the Big Show, Mabel. Now Roosevelt's dead. Just because you're runnin your goddamn big mouth."

"Max!" Gladys shouted. "Gettin too big for your britches, mister. Mabel, I'm really sorry."

"Goddamn it, Mabel. Why're you always buttin in other people's business where ya don't belong? Suckin around the recruiting officer and anybody else in a uniform."

"Out, Max! That's it! Get your mouth out of here."

"I'd be outta here, mouth and everything, if it wasn't for that old biddy."

"Get out, I said. You just wait for your father to get home. And you leave Mabel alone."

"If she leaves me alone."

"Mom. Mom! The President died."

"Sonny, stop that. Don't talk about the President that way. It's not funny."

"But he did!"

Charlie cleared his throat. Herman looked back from the hall. "You standin, buddy?"

"What?"

"You got a pat hand, Hymie?"

"I guess so. Yeah."

"Twenty beats nineteen. Too bad, kiddo."

* * *

Later that week, Sonny and Herman sat on the carpet in front of the radio. They played Old Maid. The curtain cast dappled shadows on the cards, dancing over sun glare on the white surface. Herman pushed his card back into the shadow. "Hermy, you looked."

"I told you. I don't want to play this stupid game."

Shamrock on her shoulder, Gladys stood in the kitchen doorway, looking down on the boys. "Seems like you boys haven't moved from that rug in two days."

"Well, there's nothin on the radio and I'm sick and tired of it. It makes me mad. What good is it bein out of school if you can't do nothin? I haven't heard Jack Armstrong or Jack Benny or anything good all week."

Gladys answered him, "The President's dead, Sonny. He's been president for all you boys' lives. Look at all he's done for us. Won't be anybody able to fill his shoes."

"But Ma, that goddamn..." Gladys stooped and swung at Sonny. Shamrock flew onto the side of the lamp, right claw clutching a tiny fringe ball. Sonny dodged, but she backhanded him across the tip of the nose. "Ma! That hurt! You almost put my eye out!"

"You're listenin to Charlie and Max and now you, too, Herman. Smoke isn't the only thing coming out of that room while that canoe's being built. What goes in your ears doesn't have to leak right out of your mouth."

"But Ma," Sonny gingerly touched his nose. "It just popped out."

"Quit whining, Sonny, or I'll give you something to whine about. Nothin worse than kids whining. It's been a sad enough day. That reporter broke down and cried while he was tellin about the funeral. And you, Sonny Williams, ought to be willin to take time out to honor a great man. And a brave man. You know he had polio, just like Herman. Just thank your lucky stars, Sonny Williams, that you haven't been a polio victim, too." Gladys went back to the kitchen and began clattering pans.

Herman looked down at his cards. **Brave. Because of polio.** He looked at the king of spades. **I wonder why Dad doesn't like Roosevelt.** He looked over at Sonny. **He's right about the radio programs. Roosevelt was just an old sick man.** Sonny rubbed his nose some more. "Hermy, you had a lot happen to you." He dropped his voice to a whisper. "Hell of a lot. Polio and coming here. Don't it hurt to have polio?"

"No, squirt. It feels good." He flipped another card over. "But it doesn't hurt as much as getting shot."

"Somebody tried to shoot you?"

"Didn't your Mom tell you?"

"No! What happened?"

"Oh, my uncle Cory got mad at me because I brought my pet rat Gypsy into the barn. I don't know why. He's pretty crazy, I guess. From being shot up at Corregidor—that's where he got his nickname. Cory. Short for Corregidor. He was at the carnival with me when I got Gypsy and didn't say anything then. I guess he got upset because it was so close to the chickens. I guess rats eat eggs or something. So actually, he shot at it, not me. I think." Herman picked up the three of spades. He pulled its edge across his left thumb. "And then he shot at…" **Tom. Yes, he shot, he shot…** "He shot at something else." **He fell over. At least I got to show Tom how to catch snakes. Uncle Cory. The blood. Blood on the straw. Uncle Cory…**He carefully placed the card on the pack, squared up the cards and shuffled them. He looked up at Sonny.

"Do we have any juice in the icebox?"

"No, Charlie drank it all. That's too bad about your rat. Gee, you have pretty bum luck with your pets. Look at Fred."

"Yeah. And I had another mouse besides Fred. I almost forgot about that one."

"What was its name?"

"Lionel. You know, after Lionel Barrymore?" Sonny shook his head. "You know, Dr. Gillespie." Sonny looked blank. "In the Dr. Kildare movies. God, Sonny, you're dumb."

"I don't like the Dr. Kildare movies. Mom does. But I don't."

"Well, I like Dr. Gillespie."

"So what happened to Lionel."

"Remember when I said I had polio?" Sonny nodded. "Well, the March of Dimes people sent a lady, some other kids, and me from Walla Walla, to a place in Seattle called the Orthopedic to get some exercises. It was really a funny kind of place. There were kids in it with big heads and little bodies—just like Dr. Silvana."

"In Whiz?" Herman nodded. "I figured out why you like that comic book so much."

"Why?"

"Cause Billy Batson's a cripple, too."

"I'm not a cripple. Anyway, my Uncle Frank took me around Seattle after I finished at the Orthopedic. And we went into this huge pet store with all these animals in it—parrots and monkeys, snakes, chipmunks, and some animals I didn't even know."

"Gee. Did they have an elephant?"

"No, Sonny. Use your bean. They're too big for anybody to keep as a pet. But they had alligators. Little ones. Anyway, Uncle Frank brought me a little white mouse. That was Lionel. They put him in a cottage cheese box, you know, with the little wire handle on it."

"I hate cottage cheese."

"Who doesn't? Are you gonna shut up so I can tell this story?" Sonny picked up the cards and began to shuffle them. The deck fell apart. "When it was time to take the train home that night, I brought Lionel into the Pullman with me. But the March of Dimes lady took him away when I was showing him to this kid who couldn't walk and had those braces on his legs. Like President Roosevelt. Well, she took Lionel into her berth across the aisle. The next morning I was asleep and I heard her screaming and looked out and she was jerking. Like this." Herman started laughing and Sonny smiled. "And hitting at her blanket. Lionel had chewed a hole in the box and crawled out into her berth and got away." Sonny laughed. "Anyway, when Mom called up the railroad to see if anybody had found Lionel, they told her they hoped their porters never found out about him or they would never come back there to work."

"Why's that?"

"I don't know. Maybe they are afraid of mice. I don't know."

Herman took the cards from Sonny's hands and stood up.

Sonny rose. "Do you know any other funny stories?"

"I scared a Sunday school teacher once. Like the March of Dimes lady."

"Tell me." The boys sat at the dining room table. Herman grinned.

"Well, where I was staying in Auntie Ide's apple orchard around Cashmere there were a lot of snakes, mostly little snakes like garter snakes, but there were some dangerous ones, too. Rattle snakes. Auntie Ide told me how she and Mom got caught up an apple tree one day when they had been thinning all morning and found out that the sun woke up the rattle snakes in the dew and grass below them and they started buzzing."

"Jeez. How'd they get out of that?"

"They yelled till somebody came. Well, I was like my Mom. I used to be afraid of snakes. A lot. But I was really interested in them, too. When I had polio, Dad gave me this book about snakes, by a guy named Raymond Ditmars. I think I read it three or four times."

"You read too much, Hermy. It's bad for your eyes. That's why you gotta wear specs."

"Anyway, I decided one day when I was watching a garter snake lying out in the sun that I would get over that. So I picked it up by the tail."

"You picked up a snake."

"It wasn't scary. Well, it was a little scary at first. It kept reaching up, trying to bite me, but it could bend its head only a little way as long as I held it out from me. Then somehow it started getting itself going around and around in circles. Big slow circles. I wondered what was happening and then I realized. It was going to break off its tail! I read about lizards doing that in the Ditmars book. So I had to do something."

"What?"

"Well, I got a stick and held it out and let it rest its head on the stick. But that wasn't right, so I…"

"Get to the teacher part."

"Okay. To make a long story short, I learned how to tame them so that they would nestle down in my shirt pocket. They like it in there because it's dark and warm. They just stay down and every once in a while their heads will come up and they'll start sticking their tongues out. They're looking around. Ditmars says they can't see and they use their tongues to smell with."

"Smell with their tongues? That's nutty."

"That's snakes. Well, Auntie Ide took us all into Cashmere one day to go to the Baptist Church. Except Iris and I went to the Sunday school."

"Who's Iris?"

"She's my cousin. She's my age. We're friends."

"Friends with a girl?"

"She isn't just any girl. Iris likes snakes. She's sort of a tomboy. She does chores, milks cows and everything. She goes into the orchard during the rattlesnake season and she's never scared. She just wears tall boots and kicks the hell out of one if it comes close." Herman looked at Sonny. "Where was I? Oh, yeah. This teacher was standing right in front of me tellin us about Genesis and the tempting of Eve and she looked down and this little snake head was looking up at her. She sort of grunted—like a pig—and she jumped way back. Her eyes were as big as saucers!" He widened his eyes, dropped his jaw, and gaped at Sonny. "Holy Jesus!" Sonny bounced up and down on his chair, laughing. "And then she jerked. Like the March of Dimes lady. And then she let a scream out..." By this time, Sonny was laughing so hard that he tipped his chair over and lay on his side on the rug. Herman began to laugh, too.

Finally, Sonny sat up, wiping his eyes. "That was a good story. Hermy? Teach me how to catch snakes."

"Well. Okay. There's nothing else to do today. I know where there are a lot of them. Down by Pioneer Park."

The sound of boys' voices came from outside. "The iceman! The iceman!" Herman looked out the window to see two blond boys running down the alley toward the Williams' garage. "It's the iceman!" Sonny and Herman jumped to their feet and ran down the backyard sidewalk past the garage and into the alley. A mule hitched to a cart stood beside the garage. At the cart's rear, a broad, burly man in a thick leather vest glanced up. Wielding tongs, he resumed wrestling a huge block of ice onto his back, and bent, began to trudge up the backyard sidewalk toward the Williams house. "Look at the size of that block. Gosh, he's big." When the man entered the house, the four boys ran to the cart and began fishing for ice. Soon each was sucking at a fist-sized chunk.

Herman reached into the cart for a second chunk and began rubbing it on his forehead. Sonny did the same. "Do you remember how hot it got last summer? It was way up in the hundreds? The tar in Walla Walla was melting so much that I got some of it off the street and made a big black marble out of it."

One of the other boys said, "Yeah we were doing that here, too." The boys were so blond that their hair was nearly white. They were identical twins.

Sonny said, "That was the summer Max got pulled off the street to fight that fire. Boy, was he mad!"

"You mean they just took him?"

"Yeah, he was walking home from a movie and this truck pulls up and it has a couple soldiers in it, and they made him get into the truck and took him off. We were worried because nobody was home when he tried to call and we didn't know where he was." There was a squeal. One of the twins had stuffed a chunk of ice down the other's neck and ran down the alley. The other fished out the ice and chased him with it.

"That's Sammy and Lenny."

"Lenny?"

"Yeah." Sonny made his voice low and hollow. "What's up, George? Huh, George, huh? Can I have a rabbit, George? Huh?"

Herman laughed. "I like that movie. It was sad."

"So who are those kids anyway?"

"Just kids I know. Their dad's the warden at the State Penitentiary. They get to eat anything they want. Sammy and Lenny, not the jailbirds. Those guys don't get to eat good stuff like the warden and the guards and Sammy and Lenny."

"Do they live there?"

"They live here in that brick house." Sonny pointed south. "Their mom is nervous about the prisoners. But the warden stays out there except for the weekends. You ever been inside a real prison, Hermy?"

"Naw. Why would I want to?"

"Well, I wanna see a real prisoner. Somebody who's killed somebody."

"Don't have to go to a prison to see that."

"Wadda ya mean, Hermy?"

"Nothin, kid."

"You see somebody kill somebody?"

"Forget it. Tell me some more about those kids."

"Sometimes I go to play with Lenny and Sammy and they say I can come to have lunch at the prison with their father, but it never happens. About the time it's supposed to happen, they decide somebody else is their best friend. I wish I could go there. It's out in the sagebrush."

The iceman returned, tossed his tongs in the back of the cart and pulled away. "Can we catch snakes today, Hermy?"

"Go and ask your Mom. Tell her it stopped raining. But don't tell her about the snakes. Just tell her we want to go to the park."

"Okay!" As Sonny ran toward the house, Herman went back to the lawn and sat by the fishpond. A catfish slowly rose and descended. He looked up from the water at the thick stand of bushes against the garage.

It is after school. The rain mists down to the streets. He unzips his jacket, slips a hand into his shirt pocket, and scoops out a small snake that easily coils and uncoils in the palm of his hand. The creature is warm and dry. Its tongue flickers. "It's okay. You're going to like it in the Zoo." He places it on the ground and carefully parts the thorny branches of the large wild rose bush. **That makes eighteen...What in the world...?** *He starts and then leans forward.* **A two-headed snake! I can't believe it.** *As he leans forward, the heads slowly twist up, tongues flickering.* **At me. Only one body. Or are they coiled together?** *He reaches for them. His sleeve catches on the bush.* "Hermy!" *Aunt Ide calls. When he looks back, the snakes are gone.*

Herman looked down at his tattoo. "Hermy. Hermy. Hermy!" A shadow fell across his arm. Herman looked up to see Sonny standing over him. "She says I can go."

"Okay." Herman rose. "Hey, I got an idea. Let's make a snake zoo."

"Huh?"

"Sonny, you look dumb with your mouth hanging open that way." Sonny closed his mouth. "A snake zoo. I had one going when I was over on Auntie Ide's farm. We'll catch a lot of snakes and bring them home and put them right over there." He pointed to the bushes beside the garage.

"Keen! Let's go."

"Okay, where'd I leave my bike?"

"It's over by the kitchen door."

Herman mounted the bike, waited for Sonny to jump up onto the cross bar, and then with a grunt pushed off, the bike wobbling down the narrow path parallel to the house until he reached the lawn and bogged down.

"You got to get off, Sonny, until I get out on the street." Sonny slipped off, Herman walked the bike down to the curb, bounced it off onto the street tar, and soon they were off again, slowly weaving under the green awning of maples and elms, Herman panting at first with the effort and then falling into the rhythm and glide of the bicycle until Sonny suddenly shifted his weight and rocked them.

"You got to stay put, Sonny! You're going to tip us."

"This cross bar hurts. How come you don't get a thing I can ride on in back?"

"I don't carry passengers. Now hold still!" They soon were out of the residential district.

He rides the Schwinn on the sunny path outside the park, then under the trees, feeling Dad behind pushing and running, hearing his breath rasping. **Faster, Dad, faster. Boy this is great!** *The air is cold on his face, drying its sweat.* **It's so quiet. I can't even hear him!**

He looks around. **Where is he?** *He twists further.* **Way back there!** *Dad shouts and waves his hands. "Keep going, Hermy!" Herman crashes into a small bush.*

Now the boys were back again in the shade under the trees of the public park. "Can we visit the park zoo, Hermy?"

"Sure." The boys walked down the path to the zoo. It was a collection of small, rusty cages shaded by a grove of maple trees. The cages contained animals native to Idaho: a deer, a black bear, some squirrels, a collection of birds. No one else was there. "This isn't much of a zoo, Sonny. You ought to see the zoo in Seattle. Uncle Frank took me to that, too. It's got monkeys, tigers, bigger bears."

"Your Uncle Frank sounds like a neat guy."

"He is. I sure...Look! There's a rattlesnake!" The boys paused before a cage, stared through the diamond-shaped screen at a hard clay floor, coated with light dust where a large snake lay, its body partially concealed by a tangle of branches.

"Why doesn't he move?"

"I don't know. Maybe he's hot. The ones in the Seattle zoo don't move, either."

"Let's go catch snakes." The boys walked out of the zoo into the sunlight. Soon they came to a sluggish stream, its bank on the park side a lawn, on the other side marsh grass.

"Okay. Keep your eyes peeled. There are lots of them in here. Keep quiet and move slowly." Herman began to edge along the stream, taking a step, searching, taking another step.

Herman walks down by the little trout pond in the middle of the meadow to see if he can find a garter snake for his Cashmere snake zoo. He has just caught one—a nice ten-incher—and has about tamed it when he hears a familiar pop with a soft punch to it and a half-second later a crack. **A BB gun. There's another kid out here.** *He searches the clump of birch trees by the river. Letting the snake crawl into a coil in his shirt pocket, he begins to walk cautiously that way, coming from behind the other person, a boy, a boy shooting at one of the squirrels that rule that side of the meadow.* **An Oriental boy. Tom.**

"Look, there's one!" Herman looked over at the still water of the stream. A small snake swam there, its body an S, S-curves flowing behind it. "Quiet, Sonny. Wait." The snake made the bank and lay for a moment, half in, half out of the water. Then it began to move onto the grass. "Let me get this one. Watch me, "Herman whispered. "Don't let your shadow fall on it. Come slowly from behind. Wait for it to stop. And catch it by the tail!" He seized the snake. He held it out to Sonny, who shrank back. "It won't hurt you. See? I'll tame it."

Herman draws the snake across the stick until it stops twisting and begins to pull itself ahead. Then he lets it touch the ground, again, and again, lifting it lightly whenever it turns on him.

"See, it's getting calmer now. Finally, he lets it crawl on his palm, then slowly from palm to palm. "It's starting to like me." Tom sits on the ground cross-legged to let it crawl on his thigh. "Come here. Just put your hand under him when he crawls off my leg. Now let him crawl to the other hand. That's the way, Tom."

"That's the way, Sonny."

Tom lays down the BB gun and sits cross-legged in front of Herman. They both watch the snake slowly crawl from palm to palm.

"Okay, Sonny. Now let him go into your pocket. He'll like it there. Just tip your hand up so his head points down. There. No, press his head down a little— he doesn't know about pockets. Okay?"

They look at each other for a moment. Then the boy picks up his BB gun and starts toward the river. Herman follows, watching his red flannel shirt light up and dim as he steps in and out of slanting orange sunlight filtering through the birch leaves.

"Hermy? Hermy?"

"What?"

"Let's catch another."

Nine

"Bye, Dad. Yes. I'm sorry, too. Yes. Next week. I'll get my allowance off the dresser." Herman held the telephone receiver tightly to his ear. He heard the click. He could feel his breath coming back from the mouthpiece, warming the skin of his upper lip, moistening it. He sighed. The moisture condensed.

"Number, please." He hung up the phone and looked across the living room at Sonny. Sonny was juggling two blue balls above his head. Suddenly he tossed up a third ball. All three fell, bounced at three different angles. Herman sighed again. The weather had warmed. He expected to hear from his mother any day, just like the turtle came with the Christmas package, unexpectedly. **The bus ticket.** Maybe she would send for him. Or maybe she would just walk through the door with her old hat on, but when he heard "Number, please?" as he hung up the telephone, he felt his stomach sink. **Telephone calls are always bad news, Mom says, that's all they're good for. Another weekend without Dad.**

Gladys came into the living room from the kitchen, flour ghosting her arms, Shamrock dancing for balance by her ear. "When's your Dad picking you up, Hermy?" Silence. "Herman?" He scowled and parted the chintz curtains to the left of the radio to stare out the window, into the sunshine. "When are you going over to his place?" He let the curtains drop. "Are you going over to his place?" He shook his head. His neck muscles pulled. **Left. Right.** Her thick brows knit, Gladys pressed her lips together. She walked into the dark hall. Herman could hear her rough voice in the bathroom. **Talking with Mr. Williams. About me.**

He looked over again at Sonny. Sonny smiled. Kelly jumped off the davenport and walked into the kitchen, his thick claws tapping the wood floor, clicking the linoleum, his pump handle tail a pendulum. **Left. Right. I'm shaking my head.** He stopped. Sonny cleared his throat and shifted on the davenport but said nothing. Herman heard Gladys' high-heeled shoes, heavier and louder on the hall floor. **She's coming back.** Outside, Maggie screeched. "**Mag—eee!**" He looked at the hallway entrance. Gladys stood by the dinner table, wiping her arms on her apron, powdering white the golden petals and russet centers of its great sunflowers. "Do you boys want to go to a baseball game today?"

"Sure, Mom!" Sonny jumped from the davenport. Herman leaned forward. "I didn't know they had started yet."

"They're having an exhibition game this afternoon. They have brought together most of the men from the old team and we're playing a team made up from the League. It was in this morning's paper." Herman smiled. **Sandy.**

"That's sort of why I'm here, ma'am. I'm a baseball player. Team's folded and my head's too banged up for the Army. So read me them cards you got there." The gypsy shuffled the deck. "Here's some questions. When's this war gonna be over? When am I gonna to play again?" Herman looked at the man's heavy flannel shirt. **A black C. Number 33. Wears my luckiest number. Baseball player! Look at him. He couldn't play the outfield. No pitcher. A catcher! That guy's a catcher. Boy, that's what I'd like to be. I wish Dad could see him. He sure would be proud of me if I grew up to be a catcher.**

"Come on, Hermy." Sonny was outside already.

"Thanks, Mrs. Williams." Herman went through the kitchen, down the steps—one-two-three-lucky—and out the screen door.

"Hermy, don't slam that door."

"Okay, Mrs. Williams!"

"Hurry up! Mom says the game's gonna start soon." Down on the sidewalk were his Schwinn and Sonny, pulling on his fatigue cap. Herman mounted the bike, waited for Sonny to join him, and then heaved his weight onto the right pedal. "This is going to make a man of me." Fifteen minutes later, they were at the ballpark. Sonny slid off the crossbar. "The baseball park!" Sonny shouts. Herman pulled up to the park wall and leaned the bike against it. *The baseball park," Jake says to the taxi driver after their suitcases were loaded in the trunk.*

"The baseball park, Dad? Is there a game?"

"We're going to live there."

"At the baseball park?"

"Yes, the baseball park. I was keeping it a surprise. Walker closed it to get ready to do something with circuses. And he needed somebody to watch the grounds. It's just for a little while. And it's next to the Boise Park and Zoo. You can get down to the Natatorium in five minutes—and take some swimming lessons. We'll get something else in a few weeks. Before school starts. Housing is tight now with all the Air Force families in town."

"We're going to live there? You mean right in the ballpark? In the bleachers and all?"

"Well, almost." Jake smiled.

"Where? Where do we live?"

"Wait and see." At the park, Jake lets them in through a door next to the ticket seller's window, and they walk up the wooden stairs into the bleachers behind home plate. Herman paid their admissions and they walked up the wooden stairs into the bleachers behind home plate. "Remember I told you I used to live here? Last summer, and look at this." Herman signaled to a boy selling food and bought a bag of popcorn. "See that boy on the front of the bag?"

"Yeah."

"Look familiar?" Sonny silently stared at the bag. "That's me."

"That's you?"

"Uh-huh."

"On this popcorn bag?"

"One of my father's jobs was making this popcorn bag for the owner of the ballpark. They're friends."

"And you lived here?"

"Yeah. Now watch the players warm up. Here. Have some popcorn." Herman looked around for Sandy. **Where's the team?** He stuffed popcorn in his mouth and looked out at the diamond. **The grass is green. Base paths straight and neat. Paint peeling over there on that billboard. But it looks okay.**

"Let's go downstairs, Hermy." Jake leads the boy back down wooden stairs one flight to the main floor, through a hall to the left, and then down concrete stairs. "There are the locker rooms over there. The showers are still running, so we can clean up after we get settled. Here. Here's the caretaker's room." He opens a wooden door onto a small room with two cots, a dresser and mirror and a closet. "This is where you sleep." Jake points to a bunk. "Leave your stuff here. Let's go out onto the field."

Outside, Herman crouches down behind the plate as if he is ready to catch a ball. "Gee, this is where Sandy played." He glances up at his father and sees him frowning. "Is something the matter, Dad?" Jake shakes his head, turns away and begins to take off his shirt. "What are you doing?"

His father steps out of his pants and then his underwear. "I'm going to get in some sunbathing. Come on. Join me." **What's wrong with him? What's he doing? I've never seen him naked before. Look at the hair on his butt.** *Herman turns his back. "I've got to go to the bathroom."*

"Well, I'm going to stay out for a while. Wake me up in an hour, will you? I don't want to get sunburned. You can play anywhere you want to. If you'd like to go to the Nat this afternoon, I have an extra set of keys for you. I put them on a plastic neckband so you don't lose them. Here." Jake fumbles in his pants and tosses two keys on a ring to Herman. "Good catch. Have fun."

Herman dropped the neckband back into his shirt. "Sonny?"

"Huh?"

"This sure is a great place to live. It's like having the biggest house in the world, bigger than a castle, with the biggest yard in the world, and all these walls, everything green and quiet, except for maybe a plane flying overhead. Hey, can I have one of those?" A boy sold him a program for a nickel.

"What's that for?"

"You keep score in them. And you can find out the players' batting averages and everything."

"What do you wanta know that stuff for?"

"Well, look at the visiting team's lineup here. Maxwell—he's number five out there—he's going to bat first—that's because he was good at stealing bases, so he's fast. See? No, look at 'SB'—that's stolen bases. You have to be fast to steal so many. So's the next guy. But even though the next guy—Simpson here-- can't run, he has a really good batting average—see the 'BA' column. So's the next guy. Now the fifth batter doesn't, but look at all the home runs he's got. He's cleanup."

"Cleanup?"

"He'll knock in anybody on base. Look, here comes the other team. Hey! Sandy! Look, see thirty-three out there? That's my friend. You know, the one that got me a tattoo?"

"Yay, Sandy!" shouted Sonny. He stood. Boise began warming up. The boys watched, growing still and silent in the summer sun.

Just outside the men's room, Herman stops. Looking steadily at him is a man in a short-sleeved gray shirt and black slacks. "Hey, kid. You got a familiar face." The man clasps his bare arm, looks down at it, suddenly smiles and looks back up. "Gypsy." Herman looks at the man again. **It's the catcher.** *When the man removes his hand from his arm, Herman sees a tattoo.* **Snakes and roses. Like the gypsy.**

"What are you doing in Seattle, kid? Where are your folks?"

"I'm waiting for my mother. She's supposed to pick me up."

"How long ago?"

"About five hours."

"Five hours!" The man looks at Herman a moment longer. "Tough luck, kid." He turns away.

"Mister." The man turns back. "Aren't you a baseball player? A catcher?"

The man smiles. "Yessir."

"Would you give me an autograph?"

"Sure, kid. Got some paper?"

"I don't have any with me but I have a diary over in my suitcase."

"Okay, but let's make it snappy."

They walk to the boy's seat and Hermy pulls the suitcase from under the bench, opens it and rummages through it. He pulls out a red book and ruffles through it to find a blank page. The man writes "Yours, Sandy Pritchett" and hands it back to him. Hermy smiles. "Thanks, Mr. Pritchett. I'd like to be like you some day—a catcher, faking out the batters, calling the pitches, running the infield. You really run the show when you play."

"Well, thanks...uh...what's your name?"

"Hermy Auerbach."

"Thanks, Hermy. Well, so long." Sandy reaches down to shake Herman's hand and then walks away. Herman watches him go to the luggage counter and get a suitcase. Then he puts the diary back in his own suitcase and latches it. He looks down at it, his stomach tightening again. **Cory. Tom.** *The wound on his neck stings. He feels his eyes fill with tears and clears his throat. He swallows.*

"Did you phone her?" He looks up to see Sandy standing before him. Herman wipes his eyes.

"I can't find her in the phone book. She just moved here."

"Well, she probably got side-tracked. It'll work out." Sandy looks at the boy a moment longer. Herman looks down at his suitcase.

"Did you ask the operator for a new number?"

"The operator?"

"What's your mother's name?"

"Hope."

"Come on." They go to the phone booth where Sandy makes a call. "I want a new phone number." He covers the mouthpiece and looks at Herman. "Is it A-u-e-r?" Herman nods. "For Auerbach. Yes. A-u-e-r. Hope." Sandy stands listening, his eyes on the boy. "Okay. Thanks." He hangs up. "No luck, kid."

"Wait a minute. I just thought of something. She got married."

"Shit, kid. What's her name now?" Herman swallows. **I can't remember. Arboroo. Berooto.** *"I don't know."*

"You don't know your stepfather's name?"

"No."

"Well. Jesus. Jesus, kid." Sandy reaches into his hip pocket and pulls out a package of chewing tobacco. He takes a bite. "Who were you staying with in Cashmere?"

"I was living outside Cashmere. With my Auntie Ide."

"Now don't tell me you forgot her last name."

"Pillton."

"Got a number?" Herman shakes his head. "Shit, kid." Sandy turns back to the phone, shifts the tobacco into his cheek, and drops a coin in. "I want to make a collect call to Ide Pillton." He looks up at Herman. "T-O-N?" Herman nods. "Yes. Cashmere, Washington, from Herman Auerbach." He listens and then sighs. "Thanks." He hangs up and turns back to Herman. "It's busy."

"They've got a party line. Somebody's always talking."

"Well, we'll wait till they go to sleep. Then we'll wake the bastards up. You eaten?"

"No."

"Come on. Let's get a bite."

"Shouldn't I wait here?"

"I don't think she's got the news yet, kid. But I'll leave a message with the agent over there. Take our suitcases over to Luggage there and check them. They will give you a ticket. I got to call a friend."

When Herman rejoins Sandy, they walk out into the Seattle night. "We got a ways to go. The place I'm headed is where I used to wash dishes one winter. They opened it up Christmas of 1922 and threw away the key. Never been closed since. Not for a minute. Cafeteria. You can get almost anything. I know some guys there that'll give us some free grub."

As the Star Spangled Banner played, everyone saluted the flag. Someone shouted, "Play ball!" And the game was on.

"Boise's got a really good pitcher," Herman said as he pushed the program back in front of Sonny. "See?"

"But his numbers are lower than the other guys' pitcher."

"That means he's good. It's his ERA, his earned run average. Batters get less runs off him than the other guy. Look…that's two outs now." The third batter stepped to the plate, swung, connected and hit a high foul behind the plate. Pushing back his facemask, Sandy weaved back and forth under it, fixed his spot, and palmed the ball. "Yaay, Sandy!" the boys shouted as Boise headed for the dugout.

"What are you writing on the scorecard?"

"I'm keeping track of the game. This K means the pitcher struck out Maxwell, and a 5-3 after Green's name means the third baseman got a grounder and threw it to the first baseman to put him out. And 0 above 2 with a little line coming down means that Sandy caught a pop fly. You get the numbers by starting with the pitcher, 1, Sandy's 2, the first baseman, 3, and around the bases, then 7 with left field and around the outfielders. You watch. You'll catch on. Here, you take the pencil and I'll tell you what to write until you can do it. It's really neat. We'll be able to look at this scorecard when we're old guys and know exactly what happened today."

Boise was at bat. After a strike, the first batter hit far out to left field. Herman rose and shouted. The left fielder moved slightly toward center and caught the ball. The second batter made it to first on a hit between second and third. Both boys were standing and cheering as the third batter whacked a long fly out to left field again. "Pitcher's rattled, Sonny. They're knocking him around, hitting balls into the outfield. They're really laying wood on everything he's got." Sandy Pritchett stepped up to bat. The men just in front of them stood. The boys stepped up onto their benches to see over them. Sandy bunted to the third baseman, who threw him out. The runners advanced to second and third. Sonny looked at Herman. "It's the way the game goes, Sonny. Sandy's got a lot of control over the bat and the manager told him to move the man along. He'll get some glory the next time." Just then the crack of leather on wood yanked them both back to the game to see the ball soaring over the right field fence. They looked at each other and grinned.

Later as the smiling, excited crowed left the park, Herman turned to Sonny. "What'd you think?"

"Wow! Gee, that was really somethin, Hermy!"

"Sure was. Look, Sonny, would you wait here for me? I want to go down to the lockers and see if I can talk to Sandy."

"Can I come?"

"No, you wait. It's going to be hard enough for me to get in there by myself. I got to work up some kind of a story."

Sonny frowned, but he nodded and sat down. Herman walked down to the iron fence surrounding the playing field and slipped beneath it. He entered the dark tunnel that led to the player's lockers.

Herman stands in the stadium's dusty shower room. He holds a little frog in his hand, examines the small round balls on its toes, the brightness and richness of its glittering eyes, deep in their brown and, under the bright glare of the naked light bulb, bright enough to be jewels, like the ones in the purple box on his mother's dressing table.

Herman saw a guard standing in front of the Boise locker room. He stopped in the shadow of the tunnel and waited. He could hear the sound of the showers and men laughing. *Alone in the evening in the ballpark, Herman reads on into the night until a persistent sound, like that of crickets chirping, begins to break his attention. It is louder and clearer than any cricket. He walks into the hallway.* **It's coming from the locker room.** *He turns on the light, and the noise quiets. Then the sound that broke his attention begins again.* **It's the frogs.** *There are hundreds of them on the dusty concrete floors of the showers, dark and singing, their chirp echoing.*

Where's Sandy? Where's Dad? Where's Mom? Sometimes I can hardly remember her face. She's never here when I need her. Not since polio. *He turns off the light and quietly leaves the room. Minutes later, undressed and in bed, he goes to sleep to their song.*

Herman finally moved into the light and approached the door. The guard blocked his way. He had a gun in his belt. "Hold it, son. Where do you think you're going?"

"I came to see Sandy Pritchett."

"I don't think he's here. Left before I got here."

"Can I check?"

"No, you can't go in there, son."

Herman felt the tattoo burn, the soar of courage, the current a blue stream sweeping him on. "He's my father!" he blurted.

"Oh, you don't say. Look, kid, I knew Pritchett way back when. He don't have no kids, and he ain't never likely to---leastways to any that he'd fess up to—he likes the gals too much." The guard chuckled.

"Look. I can prove it to you. If you know Sandy Pritchett, you'll know he's got a tattoo, one with a snake like this in a patch of roses." He rolled up his sleeve to show the guard his tattoo.

"Well, I'll be goddamned." The guard looked back up at Herman. "Okay, kid, go on in." Herman pushed open the door of the locker room, now misted with steam and bright with clothing blue and cream, dusted with dirt and grass. He looked down the silent aisle of lockers before him. Six men were there. One looked up. Sandy was gone.

"But Dad, I like the baseball park. I don't want to move to a house."

"Herman, the house is beautiful. It's made out of stone. It looks like cottages in England. Has apple trees and everything. And Mrs. Schultz will cook for us and be there when you come home. Besides, she has two boys for you to play with. That's a lot better than hanging around here all the time." They are in the bleachers. Sunset fills the western sky with purple and peach. A cool breeze ruffles Herman's fine hair. A cigarette dangling from his mouth, Jake sits with his shoulders hunched forward.

"No. I don't want to move again. People are always telling me to move. I like this place. Nobody's ever lived like this before. It's big and it's quiet and it has all those little frogs singing and looking through their beautiful eyes at you. Please don't make me leave. I want to be alone with you. Just you and me. Please." Herman's voice is loud, breaking, liquid with tears. "I don't need anybody to take care of me. I have you." Jake puts his arm around Herman's shoulder. They sit together silently, Jake looking at the sunset, Herman looking at home plate.

"Can I help you, kid?" It was the second baseman.

"No sir." Outside the guard was gone. Herman leaned against the wall listening for frogs. The frogs were gone, too. Only Sonny, waiting on the bench and swinging his feet.

Ten

S*loping street. No traffic. Concrete walls on both sides. Bicycling.* **Marzidotes and dozidotes and lil lamsbsidivy.** *Policeman at rest on his motorcycle on the edge of the intersection.* **A kiddledidivy too.** *The policeman's eyes follow the bicycle.* **I guess he can hear me.** *The houses begin to go by faster.* **These Seattle hills.** *Suddenly there is space.* **Ohmygod!** *The curve breaks into fall, into the railroad yard so far below. She'll be sorry. She'll finally be sorry. Oh God, the ground.*

Herman's eyes opened. Shadows of tangled gold outside dusty windows. Canes heavy with roses in a gray dawn. A canary peeped. He sighed and relaxed. **It's a dream. Just a dream.** His eyes closed.

Depot Vista fills with women and babies. **The baby will die.** *Pulling out of the station, the train slowly passes a policeman standing alongside the track, then a photographer bending over a tripod.* **I forgot he was a policeman. Not just a policeman. The Chief of Police. In the old photograph of Grampa on Gramma's dresser, his badge is pinned on his uniform.**

Herman woke a second time. This time, Sonny was sitting on his bed and pulling on his socks. "Late for school?" Herman asked, his tongue thick with sleep. Sonny's eyelids drooped over large brown eyes. "Naw, school's over. Way over. Remember?"

"So if there's no school and nobody's hollering for me to get up, what's up?"

"Ma and Max. They're at it again. Max's saying 'Look what happened Easter Sunday in Okinawa. I wanna go after those dirty Japs!' Then she's sayin 'Okinawa Schnokinawa. All those Jap names we never heard of before.' Then she starts in about Kamikaze pilots. And then he says he's gonna miss the whole goddamn war." Sonny's voice modulated between an imitation of Max's growl and his mother's raised voice. "One of them slammed a hand on the table, hard. I think it was Ma this time. She was madder than heck. Hollerin about life and death and how Max didn't know nothin. That's prolly what woke you up."

"Where do you get all this stuff, Sonny?"

"Listenin. What else is there to do? Come on, Hermy. Get up. Let's go play catch." Now Herman noticed the baseball glove in Sonny's left hand and the ball in his right. "You wanna get some breakfast first?"

Herman coughed. **Damn cigarettes.** "No." He coughed again. "I don't wanna get around all that. Hell, she doesn't know a damn thing about people leaving. People leave all the time. They gotta leave."

"Hermy, my other brother's dead somewhere."

"Yeah, okay."

In the small side yard near their bedroom windows where the rose bushes drooped with summer blooms as heavy as weeping willows, the boys played catch. Herman threw the ball. Sonny's arms were spread wide as he ran toward it. The ball went over his head. He ran to retrieve it and then threw it back as hard as he could.

"That hurt! Why'd you throw it so hard?"

"I guess cause I had a nightmare."

Sonny looked up with interest. "About what? About Frankenstein?"

"No, I drove my bicycle off a cliff. The highway just ended in a cliff and out I went."

"Gee." Sonny waited. "Did you get killed?"

"I guess so." **She'll be sorry she didn't come to get me.** "Forget all that. Bygones be bygones? I'll show you how to hold the ball."

"Walk back and think a little before you throw. Grip the seams like this. Feel it in your body. Focus." Something moves inside him. Like a double exposure. **Settle.** *"There's the pyramid. Aim for the center bottle. Now throw. Hard."*

"Now grip the ball by the seams like this. Walk back and think a little before you throw. You have to feel it in your body. And grip the ball by the seams. See how good the ball feels in your hand?" Sonny threw the ball into Herman's mitt for the first time that morning. "You're almost good enough to win a duck, kid."

"Whatta ya mean?"

The ball strikes the pyramid of bottles. "Step right up! Winners all the time!"

"Softer."

"That's it, kid. Take your duck and leave. Only one to a customer."

"Once I won a stuffed duck pitching balls at a carnival."

"Where is it?"

"In Cashmere."

"You think I'm good enough to do that?"

"Sometime you'll be. But you gotta let it happen. Same thing with juggling. To get all three of those balls up, let it happen. So you don't bring home the duck first time out, what the hell?"

"Yeah. What the hell?" Then he frowned. "How come?"

"Stop how-comin me."

"Okay." Sonny sat on the ground to tie his left shoelace. Herman knelt beside him. "That was some mouse, old Fred."

"Yeah, I miss him."

"Do you think it really did have a nervous breakdown, Hermy?"

"Who knows?"

"The Shadow knows." Sonny dodged as Hermy swung at him.

"It's too early in the morning for that, Sonny."

Sonny pushed his fatigue cap back further on his head. "Want to play some more catch?"

"Sure." Thwack. The ball made a solid sound in Sonny's glove. They threw back and forth for a while, closer to one another and much more gently, falling into the rhythm of the exchange.

"Do you think you'll ever see Sandy again?"

"Don't know. I almost got to see him at the game. I told the guard he was my father. At first the guard said Sandy had no kids, but when I showed him my tattoo, he believed me." They threw in silence again, backing up a few yards, picking up the pace, the silence punctured only by the smack of leather. "My father doesn't care about me any more. I think he's mad at me." Smack. "How long has it been since he spent a weekend with me?"

Smack. "Gosh." Sonny grunted when he threw. "I don't know, Hermy."

"I wish I could go to Mom's. Or that Sandy would come and get me."

"Hi, Ma."

Herman turned. Orange hair wild, Gladys stood on the sidewalk, her heavy eyebrows knit downward, her full-lipped mouth tight. Herman's stomach clenched.

"Herman Auerbach, you don't know what you're talkin about. No, don't you talk back to me now. You said enough. You know what a fine man your father is? You know how hard he works? Why, there isn't a person in Boise who doesn't know him. He's always doin things for people. He's raised thousands of dollars in Idaho for the war effort. And he'd give you the shirt off his back."

"How many other boys can point to their Pa's ads in the newspaper? Florsheim shoes, Wurlitzer pianos and that beautiful ad for the war bond drive? Your father did those. You just don't appreciate that man." As Gladys moved toward him, Herman backed away. "For the past few weekends, your father has been workin on startin his own business while he's still holdin down his job as advertising manager. Some day you'll come into that business. And the sign will read 'Jacob Auerbach and Son'."

"And as for your mother. Your mother and her sister Ide. One man right after another. Those two have married more men than we have on this block. Look at Ide. Three husbands and the last one that low-life Cory. Do you know he killed a man? Before Corregidor. He grabbed up a rattlesnake out in the orchard and just jammed it in this apple thinner's face. If the thinner hadn't been a Mexican, he'd gone to jail." Herman felt the scar on his neck prickle. **Tom.** "And as for your mother, she's nothin but a whore." Gladys brushed Herman on her way back to the house. The side door slammed.

Sharp heat fanned across Herman's forehead and down the back of his neck. He looked at Sonny. Sonny just looked back. Herman walked past the house, past the side door, toward the alley. "Aren't you going to teach me any more baseball?" Sonny called. "You goin back to look at rabbits? Will you feed that big buck for me?" Herman spun and threw the ball. It went over Sonny's head. He ran to chase it while Herman stalked on. **Whore? It's bad alright. But what exactly is a whore?** *He sits in Shelton's Restaurant with his father and some ad men drinking beer. Al laughs. "Walla Walla's got four whorehouses—two for whites, one for the spicks, and the Union Bulletin."* But Mom never worked for a newspaper. Just for Sears.

Herman walked under the open kitchen window. He could hear cans rattling, doors slamming, Gladys' mumbling to herself. He walked on into the back yard, under Maggie's tree. "Maggie!" **Damn bird. I was crazy to teach it anything.** He walked out by the garage and looked in at the rabbits. Startled, a doe jumped and rattled her cage. **Damn rabbits. They oughta eat that buck. What's Mrs. Williams mean anyway?** He sat down in the dust and leaned his head back against the warm wood of the garage. He closed his eyes against the sun. **Johnny. Dis. And dat. And Joisy. Can't he speak like an American? Damn New Yorker.** *"Dat punk kid of yers can't talk to me like dis, honey. I'm gonna teach him a lesson."* Door to the attic stairs creaks. Johnny's voice. **"It's for his own good."** *Black hair parted in the center, the shoulders of the blue wool uniform. Herman unhooks the punching bag from its swivel.* "Get away, Johnny." *He throws the punching bag from its swivel, then down the stairs.* "Get away!" He opened his eyes.

He was breathing hard. He threw a pebble against the garbage can. **Clank.** *Throwing books at her.* **She's crying. The big Uncle Wiggly.** *"I'm so sorry, Hermy. I'm so sorry."*

Faster, faster. Her arms are before her face. *"Get out of here! Get out of here!"* *The door creaks.* **I'm going to fall apart. I can't stop this. This is just going to break me up. I can't stop. My books.** *A Hardy Boys cover lay at one angle, the pages at another.* **Like that little kitten with a broken leg. It walked in a circle around its broken leg.**

Herman dried his eyes and looked around him. **What a dump.** He looked at the rose-colored hollyhocks on the other side of the alley and stood up. He walked over to them. He kicked the ground. Dust rose. **Everything's dusty out here.** He fingered a broad, soft leaf. **And I thought it was Johnny she married while I was at Auntie Ide's. But it was Jack. And I never heard of him. "More men than we have on this block."** His lips stuck to his teeth. The roof of his mouth was dry. **I sure would like a soft drink. One of those new drinks Mr. Johnson is selling. Dr. Pepper. Cherry taste. But Max says they're made out of horse hooves. Max is nuts.**

"Maggie!" **Damn bird.** He looked at the Victory Garden. **What does she want sunflowers for? They're gonna be big as trees. There's that damn Sonny. What's he doing? He's looking at the yellow flowers on the tomato plants. That's crazy. Who wants to look at a flower before it's a tomato? Uh oh. He sees me. He's smiling. He's gonna come over here.** Herman took his jack knife out of his pocket and began scraping away the dust until he came to hard clay. Then he began to dig a hole with the point of the knife.

"Wanta play some mumblety-peg?"

"No."

"What about marbles? I got a couple a new steelies. Max brought a couple a ball bearings from work. You wanta see em?"

"I guess so."

Sonny fished around in his pocket and drew out two silver balls. Herman picked one out. He could see his reflection, small and distant, warped by the curve. "I saw a guy break another guy's marble with one of these. But you got to shoot harder than I can."

"Let's see." Herman reached in his pocket. He drew out three marbles. He and Sonny cleared away a flat hard area on the clay, scratched a circle about a foot in diameter, and putting Herman's marble in its center, got down on their knees and began taking turns shooting at it with the steely. "I guess I'm not good enough to break any marble but this steely whams the heck out of that marble. Look at it go!" He knocked the marble a couple of feet out of the circle. "Look. The steely stays right there and I didn't put hardly any English on it...Want to play keepsies?"

"No. I just got these in my pocket. Most of my marbles are all in the house somewhere. I lost them. You can have one of these steelies."

Herman looked at the boy. Then he took the steel marble. "Thanks, Sonny. Look." He dug into his pocket. "I got these marbles here. You can have three of them." Herman held back a clear glass marble. "Except this one. This is my lucky one." **Christmas stocking. Not last Christmas.**

"Thanks, Hermy." Sonny rummaged through the marbles and chose three while Herman started shooting much closer at the green marble with the steely. "Hey, look." Sonny looked over. "I knocked a chip out of it." They both examined the marble closely, feeling the chip with their fingers.

"Hermy."

"How come you got mad at me?"

"I didn't get mad at you. I just got mad. When your mom jumped on me out there about my dad, and when she said those things about my mom."

"What was she talkin about? That stuff about your ma and your aunt?"

"I'm not sure."

"How come your dad doesn't see you? My dad is busy and he sees me all the time. How come you don't live with your dad?"

"We used to live together. Last place I lived. But we got kicked out."

"How come?"

"Because of some stuff I did."

"To that guy Karl?"

"Yeah. The one who beat me up at school. I hit him. I told you about that. The turtle. Remember? We didn't get along. I didn't get along with his little brother either."

"Is your dad mad at you?"

"I think so."

"Why doesn't he just spank you?"

"I think it was bigger than that."

"Why didn't the kid like you?"

"Well, we were working on these airplane models together. It was Karl's hobby. He had planes hanging from the ceiling down in the little basement room off the furnace. A Messerschmitt. A Piper Cub. I was building my first one and he was showing me how. It was a glider, a troop carrier that had a little Jeep in it. I put together the Jeep and I painted it olive drab. But I never finished the glider. I think that's when Karl lost respect for me. Because I wouldn't stick to it."

"I never ever stick to things. Except jugglin."

"I know."

"So what happened then?"

"Then he got a chemistry set for Christmas, and we burned sulphur that smelled like farts."

Sonny giggled. "Farts." He relished the word. "Farts."

"We did some test with litmus paper that turned water blue in a test tube. But I got bored. And then we stopped playing together. He started teasing me a lot and I got mad and hit him. Well, not really. I got mad at him before. When I stopped making the plane with him."

"How come?"

"I think it was because of Christmas. Last Christmas was awful. It was the first Christmas I ever spent without my Mom. She had been gone for two months and I thought she was going to marry this sailor from New York City named Johnny. Ended up she married this guy named Jack instead. Anyway, Karl's little brother was sick with something. Really sick. Everybody was gloomy. Well, the Christmas tree was up and all the presents for the Schultzes and Dad and me were packed around it and Karl's little brother was always lying in the living room on the davenport looking at all those presents. And he decided he wanted to open one. He nagged his mom and she said, yes, he could open one present. Well, he chose mine. My mother had sent me this funny-shaped present—like one of those air tubes they send back and forth at Sears—and it had us all curious. And he chose it."

"Your present?"

"Yes."

"From your mom?"

"Yes. Well, I said, 'No, that's mine.' And his mom said, 'Don't be selfish. Can't you see he's sick? Really sick? Who knows what might happen to him?' Dad was on her side. Karl didn't say anything but he started giving me dirty looks. After that, whenever I would say something, he'd always sigh and look like he was bored."

"What'd you get?"

"Huh?"

"For Christmas. What did ya get?"

"Lincoln Logs. A big set. I had never had a set before. We all got down on the rug and played with them and had a pretty good time. But that kid got to open the present and touch them first, and it was like they weren't mine. It's like nothing's ever been mine since the divorce."

"Divorce? What's divorce?"

"It's when your mom and dad stops being married and one of them leaves."

"What's bad about that?"

"In less than a minute, I lost everything that I had all my life. That's what's bad about it. It was like I had been working for weeks with those Lincoln Logs building me a cabin with all these rooms and these little side roofs and some-body kicks it and---Bang! Just like that. It's all wiped out. Anything like that ever happened to you?"

"I never worked on anything for weeks."

"Well. I don't know how to explain it. It's like…You remember that nice new blue flannel shirt of yours that Kelly chewed up, the one with the black checks?"

"I sure do!"

"It's like you were that shirt, just washed and dried a little and only worn for a month. And rip-p-p-p. Kelly tears you up. Rips right up the back. And there goes a pocket. Not the whole pocket, though—it's not all off. Like this pocket. See? The corner, how heavy it's stitched at the top? Well, that little corner stays with threads all sticking out like porcupine quills. But the rest goes. And an arm from the cuff up." Herman sighed.

"Hermy?" Herman was looking down at his pocket. He looked up. "What are you talking about?"

"Divorce."

"Divorce?" Sonny waited.

Herman looked over at the bushes. "And where are all the buttons?" He looked down at the ground. "You ask, how am I going to be a shirt now? Who will want to wear me? How in the hell am I supposed to act?" He paused. His throat was closing up. He tried to hold back tears. "Like rags. That's how. Like rags." He sobbed once and his voice became choked. "Just some damn rags used for wiping up spilled stuff, for polishing cars and windows." He paused. "Well, it's like that. I still think of myself as a shirt. But I'm not. I'm even worse than an old shirt."

"I don't know what you're talkin about."

"No." Herman looked up. "You have a family."

Eleven

The screaming in the back yard wouldn't stop. It fell and came again and rose and fell and rose and fell like an air raid siren. "Ohmygod. My god!" shouted Herman.

"Oh, get him," shouted Sonny. "Get him! There—there he goes. There he goes. He's runnin around the tree."

Maggie began to screech. "Maggie, Maggie, Maggie, Maggie, Maggie."

And Kelly screamed. **"Yulp/yulp/yulp. Kiyiyiyi. Yip/yip/yip."**

"I got him I got him, no he's slipped away. Here he is. Here he is. Okay. We got him in a corner now. You little devil. Oh God. He's going right into the Snake Zoo! Ohmygod, get him outta there! He's going to step on somebody. Maybe he'll get Billy. Billy's just a baby, Sonny. Get him, get him now. Okay, okay there he is. And there he goes again. Sonny…"

"He bit me! Hermy. Look."

"There he goes."

Herman and Sonny chased Kelly over the back yard around Maggie's tree, into the freshly spaded earth of Gladys' Victory Garden, back around the tree, along the north fence, and across the yard again before they finally captured him in the corner of the house made with the south fence. They sat there, cross-legged, panting, looking at one another, scowling. "It was your fault, Hermy."

"Well, when I want to get the ticks out of myself, the thing that I do is use alcohol and turpentine. It seemed like it would be just as good on a dog. They're both good for removin stuff from wood and that sort of thing."

"You almost killed Kelly."

"What are you boys doin out there?" shouted Gladys. She was leaning out the kitchen door, looking down the walk at them. "What's that dog screamin for? You killin it? Calm down that darned magpie. I can't hear myself think in here. You got all the canaries going and everything." She disappeared. Her voice echoed from the recesses of the house. "Charlie? Charlie! You go out and take a look at what those kids are doin. And then stop em from doin it."

With his stiff arm, Charlie shoved the screen door. It slammed against the outside wall. He strode into the back yard. "Okay, okay, you little shrimpos, what the hell have you been doin to that pooch?"

"Kelly had a tick in him. I found it. I was afraid he was gonna get Rocky Mountain Spotted Fever like those kids in the paper. And I asked Hermy to help me get that tick and Hermy put turpentine on him. He got some from the garage, the turpentine Dad had been usin to paint with. And he put it on him and then Kelly just took right off." Sonny sobbed. Herman scowled down at the grass. **Crybaby. Is he afraid for the dog? Or for him? The little brat.**

Charlie turned to Herman. "Hermy. Hey Hermy. Look at me when I'm talkin to you, buster." Herman slowly looked up. The pimples bordering Charlie's widow's peak had turned maroon. "What the hell were you thinking of? Putting turpentine on a dog. Jesus."

"Well, I didn't know. I thought dog skin was like people skin."

"Hey, son, dogs are sensitive to things that people aren't. Don't you know that? Jesus, Hermy." Charlie intently squinted down at the boys and then surveyed the yard. "Why are you kids in your bathing suits? Why's the sprinkler goin? For Pete's sake, would somebody mind tellin me just what the heck you were doin out here anyway?"

"We were runnin through the sprinkler. That's when I found out about Kelly."

Kelly began to squirm in Charlie's arms. He handed the dog to Herman. "You and Sonny go back over to that sprinkler and wash this mutt off. That'll take care of it."

"Okay." Charlie looked back at the house and lit a cigarette. "Can I have one of your butts, Charlie?"

"Go to hell, Hermy." Charlie ambled down the walk toward the alley. As the boys walked toward the sprinkler, Sonny reached over Herman's arm and petted his dog. "I believed you when you told me that stuff would help Kelly."

"Sonny, I didn't do it on purpose. I wasn't trying to hurt the dog." They were silent as they knelt in the grass and began splashing water over the squirming dog's hindquarters. Kelly yelped and arched back to snap at Herman. "Now hold him, Sonny."

"The tick's still in there Hermy."

"Well now, isn't that just too bad. Why don't you get Charlie to take it out— he's so smart." Herman gave the dog back to Sonny. "Here. You take care of your own damn dog."

"Mom doesn't like people saying 'damn,' Hermy."

"I don't care. This isn't my house. She isn't the boss of me." Herman plucked a blade of grass and put it in his mouth. "Who gives a damn?"

"Well, the grass sure is getting wet here."

"Good observation, Sonny. You got pretty sharp eyes. Or a pretty cold butt."

"I guess I can put Kelly down."

"Uh-huh.

"Well, Hermy." Sonny stood and rubbed his hands over his rear. "Hey, I got an idea. There's gonna be nightcrawlers out tonight. Ever hunt nightcrawlers?"

"Yeah." Herman paused. He spit out the grass. Then he squinted up at Sonny. "Yeah. Yeah, Sonny. Yeah, I hunted nightcrawlers. So what?"

"Weekend's comin up. Maybe we can get some nightcrawlers and Dad will take us up fishin on the river. He'll take us if we get a lot of nightcrawlers."

"Maybe."

Sonny grinned.

"Maybe not."

The boys looked away from one another. Herman stood up.

"Where did you catch nightcrawlers, Hermy?"

"We used to catch them in Walla Walla. My gang and me."

"You had a gang, Hermy?"

"Well, sorta. Sorta my gang. For a long while we were just a bunch of kids hangin around the neighborhood. Nobody was in anybody's gang or anything, but one time I got in a big fight with a lot of the guys."

"You got a pretty bad temper, Hermy."

"Yeah, well, so one time I got in a fight with these guys…"

"Did you actually have a fight? Did the fists go and everything? Was there any blood?"

"Oh, it wasn't a real fight. We were just yelling at each other. I told everybody to get off my yard. That's where we were yelling. And then a little later on I climbed this big tree that hung over the crick behind my house. Got some planks up there and sorta rigged up a little platform. And pretty soon the guys came down the sidewalk and stood under the tree lookin up at me. Clarence—he was the oldest one of us—said, 'What you doin, Hermy?' and I said 'Well, I'm startin a clubhouse up here.' I was sittin up there and I was readin comic books. 'What kind of a clubhouse?' Clarence shouts up. 'Well, I'm gonna have a club where I'm gonna read comic books.' And so we started talkin back and forth. And everybody said, 'Let's get this club on the road', so we got it together. Pretty soon we started meetin up in my attic and my mom would fix peanut butter and jelly sandwiches and we'd read comic books. It was a lot of fun."

"So how did you and your gang hunt for nightcrawlers over in Walla Walla?"

"Well, we just decided we'd go out and hunt for them."

"Are there good places to fish over in Walla Walla?"

"No, we were just huntin for the nightcrawlers for themselves. We didn't go fishin."

"Didn't go fishin? Just caught worms?"

"Well, what's the matter with that? It's as hard to catch a nightcrawler as it is to catch an old fish. And it's more fun too."

"Isn't there any good fishin out in Walla Walla?"

"I don't know."

"Didn't you guys' fathers take you out fishin?"

"They weren't around."

"How come?"

"Billy's dad was killed in the war. Norman's folks died somehow—he never told me how—and he lived with his grandparents. And I never heard anything about Clarence's dad."

"What about your dad?"

"He was over here. He had left my mom. Besides, who wants to fish? I stood by Lake Washington for hours and hours watchin these old suckers swim back and forth along the shore. They didn't even come up to get pieces of bread I threw out for them. The one bite that I got—you know the one that my step-father made me eat—I think the thing got hooked on my hook by accident." Herman moved over to the sidewalk and sat on the warm concrete. Sonny sat beside him. "Now fishin on the ocean's fun. But there's no ocean around here."

"How come it's fun on the ocean?"

"Well, my Uncle Frank took me from Seattle down south to Coos Bay in Oregon. We were down there seein a girlfriend of his and we went fishin off this dock. They got this place where they do a lot of crab fishin and they catch crab and shell em and everything in this plant and they have a lot of crab guts and stuff around that they call 'crab-ack.' And there are always a lot of fish around that dock waitin for the crab-ack to fall in. Uncle Frank gave me a stick with this thick green line wrapped around it. There was a big hook on the end of the line and a weight on it about the size of a golf ball. So you put some crab-ack on the end of the hook. And you throw it off the side of the dock. Then you just wait."

"You just wait? That isn't any fun. We hike all over the country, squeeze through the trees, jump rocks and everything."

"Let me tell this story, Sonny. You see the exciting thing is you don't know what you're gonna catch. You don't know what's gonna come up. You might even get a shark. That's what Uncle Frank said."

"A shark?"

"Yeah, you ever see that picture about all those people who were sunk by a submarine and they went in this rowboat. It's called 'Lifeboat' or something like that and this guy falls over and a shark gets him."

"Mom wouldn't let me see that. She said it was too scary and I'd get nightmares."

"Well, that's what I'm talkin about—sharks. And they eat people. Frank told me about some sailors that went swimming and one of them lost a leg."

"Sharks. You really got sharks at this place, this whose bay?"

"Yeah. Sharks. That's one thing Frank said you can catch. Anyway, there I was with my line over the side of the dock and this fish hit and the line went out and I thought I had a shark on the end of it and I pulled and pulled and when it came out it was just a little tiny fish except all of it seemed to be head. This big head and this big mouth and this tiny tail. I forget what Uncle Frank called it. Dog fish or something like that. It was strange. But the best thing I caught that day was a flounder."

"A flounder?"

"A flounder. My line went straight down and somethin was on the end of it and it just went and went and went and I just hauled and hauled. I finally got it in. It was really hard to get out of the water. And when I got it out of the water I could see why. It was flat. It was harder pullin a flat fish straight out of the water than it was one of those regular little trout."

"Trout are hard to get out of the water."

"Well, let me tell you about this flounder. It had eyes comin up the side of its head."

"Eyes on the side of its head?"

"No. Comin up the side. The eyes had been movin. Frank said that once when it was young it would swim upright like a trout and its eyes were on either side of its head. But when it got older, its eyes were movin up to the top of its head so it could see better. This one was still sort of young he said because its eyes hadn't made it all the way to the top. It was real funny when his girlfriend tried to cook it. She didn't know where the belly and stuff was so she just cut it all to pieces while we laughed. But it sure was good. For fish. That's what they use for fish and chips out there."

"What are fish and chips?"

"An English way of makin fish. Frying it. Chips are french fries. So that kind of fishin is fun. But we didn't have it in Walla Walla either. That's a lot like Boise except we got wheat fields and pea fields around the town instead of sagebrush."

Sonny sat silently. He looked around for Kelly. Then he rose and went over to Maggie's cage. He looked back at Herman. "What about catchin nightcrawlers? In Walla Walla?"

"Well, me and my gang would all go out with flashlights into this park on a night after they finished watering it. They had sprinklers out there. And the park would be really wet. There'd be about an inch of water on top of the ground and even some places where the ground was lower. We'd be really quiet and then—all of a sudden—flash our lights there on these nightcrawlers. Some of them were huge, Sonny. There was one that was about—I think—about a foot long. They'd just lie out there like big pink snakes. Now, you'd have to come up on them from behind and you'd get down on your knees and jump for it. What you had to do is go right for the spot where the nightcrawler's body went into the hole because they're so fast that if you went any higher you'd miss him. So you'd generally catch him right at the hole and—here—you'd hold your hand like this." Herman made a V out of the doubled-up knuckle of his forefinger and his thumb. "You'd catch them like this, sort of pin them to the ground with that little V there because if you didn't, if you tried to pinch him, you'd pinch him right off! Boy, those things are fast."

"Well, it don't seem to me that there's much difference between your nightcrawlers over in Walla Wall and our nightcrawlers over here in Boise. That's how we catch em out here in the back yard. Except we use em for fishin. And you're wrong about fishin, Hermy. You ever fish for trout?"

"Well, no. I really haven't. Dad never took me fishin for trout."

"Well, fishin's a lot different than you think it is. Wait'll you go out with my dad. Ma says he picks those fish out of the river just like he was shopping down at the meat market. It sure is fun watchin him."

155

"Well, what about you? Have you caught any fish?"

"You can't catch much after he's been ahead, and he doesn't want you up there scarin the fish. But when he's got his limit, he'll wait for you for a while and show you some tips and stuff. I'm just learnin right now."

"But have you ever caught a fish?"

"Well, not yet. But I'm goin to. Maybe this year. So. So, let's get some night-crawlers tonight. Okay?"

"Well, it's okay with me." Herman stood up. "Okay. Okay let's do that. I'm willin to try out trout fishin, go out after your father. See what he catches."

"Well it's a lot more interestin out on the streams than it is on your lake. I never really fished for anything in a lake before. I don't know if I'd even call that fishin. Maybe it's somethin like fishin on a river. Fishin on a river is different, a big, deep river. But, anyway, okay. Let's try that out, Hermy. Hey, look at my fingers! They're like Mom's washboard. Let's dry off and get into the house, huh?"

"Okay."

The boys went over to Maggie's cage where they had hung their towels, and they began to dry off. "Get real dry before you go into the house or Ma's gonna get mad."

"I will, Sonny. Don't you think I know that? Jeez."

Standing in the stairwell, Herman and Sonny looked up into the kitchen. Shamrock nesting in her frizzy orange hair, Gladys was pouring sliced and chopped carrots, tomatoes, celery, and onions from a green stirring bowl into a Dutch oven, its cast iron sides streaked lightly with rust. To her left sat a small, plump woman, dressed in white except for rows of gaudy necklaces shimmering like rainbows, ordinary except for her hair, a splintered gold glow. Sonny whispered, "Rose." Herman started.

Out of the midway, in a quiet and dim clay patch, before a tent striped red and white and blue, a small, fat woman, shoulder-length gold hair curling to her gaudy blouse sits at an oval table across from a stocky man with a baseball shirt stuffed into his jeans. **Something white's on her shoulder. It's a rat. A white rat!**

Her elbows on the flour-powdered dishtowel before her, Rose sat at the kitchen table, rhythmically gathering and fingering rows of necklaces studded with a rainbow of ruby, sapphire, and emerald beads mixed with silver Indian pendants studded with turquoise. She listened intently to Gladys. Sonny looked up at Herman and smiled. Herman shook his head and then pulled on his shirt.

Rose glanced at Gladys. "Now...Charlie?" Gladys didn't look up from the pot, but she nodded, her lips thin. Rose sighed and closed her eyes. She inhaled and slightly lifted her chin, the folds of fat tightening into a gentle curve. She was still. Then she exhaled and spoke, her eyes still closed. "Twenty years from now. I see him. He wears a brown suit with a vest. He gives a speech. He speaks to a hall full of hundreds of men in blue shirts, workin men. Now some of them stand and cheer. A man stands behind him. He has a gun inside his jacket. But he won't hurt Charlie. He will help." Rose opened her eyes and stood. She stretched her thick arms above her head, the wide sleeves of her white blouse slipping down around her dimpled elbows. Dropping them heavily, she moved to the stove and with a wooden spoon tasted the vegetable soup, first catlike, then twice, faster. "Basil. More basil, Gladys."

Herman leaned against the wall framing the stairwell. His eyes never left Rose. **The gypsy with the rose tattoo. Who told Sandy's fortune. Who gave me her rat. But her clothes are different. And where's her tattoo?** As she tasted the soup again, he stepped up into the kitchen and spoke, "My father wants me to get rid of my tattoo. How did you get rid of yours?"

Rose turned and stared at him. Then she laughed. "Carnival?" Herman nodded. "Happens all the time. Don't it, Gladys?"

Gladys smiled. "Herman, Rose has a twin sister who follows the carnivals. She's the one with the tattoo." Shamrock fluttered to the rim of the flour canister and began preening.

"In fact, the rose in the tattoo is me." She looked at Herman. "Rose. Get it?" He nodded. She smiled. "Let's see your tattoo."

Herman flushed. "Okay." He rolled up his sleeve.

She bent over his arm and touched the tattoo. "Beautiful. There's more to the snake than you can see." Her fingers slid down his arm to his wrist's pulse. "Now." She closed her eyes. Everyone in the kitchen fell silent. "You have a brother but he is a long ways from here. Along water. An ocean." Herman nodded. "And your mother's pregnant again. But all is not well. There isn't enough money for another child."

Herman sighed. **Gypsies seem to know more about Mom then I do. Another baby?** "It is dark. Shadows. Water. A river. You…Be careful." She opened her eyes and looked into his face. Herman's stomach churned. He carefully removed his wrist from Rose's fingers. Turning away, she joined Gladys.

"What happened, Hermy?" Sonny asked.

"I don't know."

The woman moved out of the hot kitchen to the front porch to shell peas and trim snap beans for the soup. Sonny and Herman poured glasses of lemonade from the pitcher they had left behind and then followed them, hanging back a little, watching, listening. The women's fingers worked quickly as they talked.

Herman watched Rose's soft, full lips. They moved in gentle rhythms, delicately, continually. **I like it when she laughs.** A bee entered the porch and flew around her head. She paid no attention to it. Then five more. Then more and more. They seemed to form a pattern above her. **Like Zeros.** And she was smiling. Gladys looked up from the peas. "Rose, what kind of perfume you got on? Look at those bees. Look out, boys! There's bees on the porch."

"Not the perfume. They just do this sometimes. Circle round my head. They don't hurt me."

"Don't do that, honey," Rose ordered Herman just as he swatted at a stray bee searching his lemonade. But Herman cried out sharply. He had been stung in the meat of his left forearm.

"Sonny, go get some mud!"

"What do you mean, Ma?"

"Mud. Out back, Sonny. By the pond. Hurry up! Go put some in this dish and bring it back for Herman's sting." Before Sonny got back, Herman's hand and arm, then his face, began to redden and swell. **I'm cold.** Gladys looked sharply into his face. "Boy, this ever happened to you before? Answer me. You ever been stung before?" Herman nodded "Did you swell up like this?" Herman nodded. "Dammit!"

Sonny's lower jaw dropped. "Mom!"

"Well, his father never told me. He should have told me. Rose, you go call Doc Murphy. His number is on the wall right next to the phone." Herman started to protest, but he could feel his throat swelling. **Air.** He looked out at the sidewalk that suddenly tipped. *Blue water. Whales.*

"Don't take the little boats. Whales can swallow the little boats." Merle Oberon *showed him the ignition keys.*

"But I don't know how to drive, Miss Oberon."

"It's just water, honey. You can't hit anything in the water. Except whales. And they'll get out of the way. Now pay attention. The big brass key turns the ignition on the right, the little silver key is the one on the left. Use the silver key. Then the motor will hum. And the whales will stay away."

Way, away. Way. Way. Weigh. Lift the baby up. It is bloody and naked. Big head. Like the kids in the Orthopaedic. Like Doctor Silvana. Nemesis. Marvel. Where is its face? Where are its eyes? Someone threw this baby away. Its mother. Its mother threw it away. What a shame.

"Hello, little guy. Upsy, daisy. Whoops! Hello. Beetle-de-weedle-dee, bump-de-bump. Round and around. Spin the baby-bee! Dad used to spin me. This is what you do with babies. Isn't it, little guy? Let's dance with the snakes on the floor. Blue snakes on linoleum floor. De boomp, de boomp, de boomp. Beetle-de-weedle-dee. Snakes around the claws of the bathtub's jigging legs. <u>The Runaway Bathtub.</u> *Anthony Burgess. You'll like that one, keed."*

"Look at us in the silver moon mirror. Beetle-de-weedle-de, beetle-de-weedle-dee…" Slower *and slower, deeper and deeper. Like the victrola winding on down.* "Boomp!" *the baby grins. Grins right at Rose.*

Rose? Damn it. Damn you, Rose. "Why didn't you tell me this was going to happen to me?"

"Do you know where you are, Herman?" **That's not Rose.** "You're in the hospital. We're going to take very good care of you."

"Seeing is believing."

"Herman, can you see this?" White light danced in his eyes. He frowned, clenched his lids. A peach danced in the room. **Don't do that.** He opened his eyes. The peach darted about on the woman's forehead. He squinted. **She's clear. I can see better. It's like I can see without my glasses now. Hey.**

"Herman, do you have any pain?"

Do I? Yes. Yes I do. Yes, indeed. Damn it. Anger rose, heavy, insistently heavy behind his eyebrows. "Nobody ever stopped it."

"Where does it hurt, Herman? I'll give you a shot."

"In my head. I don't want a shot in my head."

"A shot will make the pain go away, and you'll feel better."

"I want my mom. She took care of me when I had polio." Herman waited. The woman smiled. "I bet she's not here, is she?"

"Your father's here. And a little boy who's worried about you." She gave him the shot.

"Ow. That makes it worse."

"Relax. This shot will lessen the pain and it will probably put you to sleep for a while. Sweet dreams."

"Wait a minute. Where is everybody, huh? Where is Dad. And Sonny? I wanna talk to Sonny. He knows what happened to me. He was juggling those damn balls."

Herman feels warm sun rising from the desert. A river in the desert. **There's old Sonny.** *Sonny stands on the shore of the river. He juggles balls. They catch the sunlight. Then Sonny catches them.* **Three balls. Three's my lucky number.** *Sonny tosses them in perfect arcs,* *in gentle rhythms, over and over again. Herman stands in the river and watches. He squats and then stretches back.* **I'm gonna float this time.** *He slowly rolls over, face down in the water.* **The dead man's float. Only thing I can do.** *He looks at the bottom of the river, at the sand, at a rusting can half-buried in the sand.* **Gotta save that for the war effort.** *A minnow swims out of the can.* **Look at that.**

Someone stood beside him. Arms, bare and slippery, lifted under his chest and stomach, slowly turned him over onto his back, held him up. **It's the woman in the picture. Helen.** *Helen Williams stands beside him in a white bathing suit, a strap slipping down over her left shoulder. She brushes against him. Her bare arm is soft, warm.* **I'm floating.** *He stares into the blue and cloudless desert sky.* **I love her.**

A pinhole of night punctured the sky and filled the room, the black hollow room. Herman smelled medicine sharp and tart. Voices echoed. The voices of a boy and a man sitting on chairs to the side of his bed.

"I know who you are."

"Who are you, kid?" Jake dug into his pocket to pull out a thin, long pen-knife. Delicately, he lifted out a narrow blade and began to clean ink from his fingernails. Printers' ink. He spread his fingers and examined the back of his hands.

Sonny began again, "I know who you are. You're Hermy's father."

Jake inspected his other hand. "So if you know who I am, it's only fair I should know who you are. So who are you, kid?"

"Sonny. Sonny Williams. You smell like my grandfather when he's been drinking whiskey in his coffee."

"Oh, you're the little Williams kid. What are you doing here?"

"My dad said I could stay until dinner. He said he'd come if you didn't show up. I got to ride in the front of the ambulance with the driver. How come you're so mean to Hermy, anyway?"

"Who says I'm mean to Herman?"

"Herman says you yell at him." Sonny pulled out of his pocket three blue balls and began to toss two of them gently into the air.

"All fathers yell at kids sometimes. It just happens. Don't your parents yell at you?"

Sonny dropped one ball. He stooped to pick it up. When he had both balls in the air, he started juggling again, forming his words slowly in between each catch and toss. "Yeah. Well. They yell at me but they do other stuff like hug me too and take me fishin. I see my parents every day. How come you don't come and see Hermy anymore? Huh?"

"None of your business, kid." Jake tapped a slim and shiny shoe on the black and white squares of the hospital tile. "I'm busy." He closed the penknife and slipped it into his suit pocket. "I want to start my own ad agency when the war ends. I got an idea. A good one. I'll write ads for politicians." Sonny now juggled the two balls quickly in short, tight arcs. "The agency will be Herman's one day. Auerbach and Son. Fathers need to provide for their kids."

"But Herman don't have nobody now."

"Herman's got a whole house full of people. And a woman to cook for him. That's what he needs."

"Ya know what Herman's lucky number is?" The arc grew longer, the balls rose and fell more slowly, began to float.

"What kind of question is that?"

"It's a magic question. Like the magician who says how many balls do I have? Well, I have two up here right now. But I wanna juggle three. Because that's Hermy's lucky number. Three for the three people in his family. Hermy. His mother. And you." Sonny slipped a third ball into the arc about his head, dancing white and high. The ball caught the sun coming through the window of the hospital hallway. And when it came down, he caught it.

Twelve

G lowing red globes with dark green stars. Herman laid the tomato on the kitchen table and looked at the other vegetables. **Bell peppers. Squash. Cantaloupe. Something sticky. Damn sticky wax lid. Crumbs in the oleo. All of this mess. And that old oilcloth. With that Mexican on it. Why does Mom have to have babies? She's somebody else's mother. Wiping up somebody else's kitchen table. Mom used to like gardens.**

"Ma's got those goddamn vegetables all over the table again. Vegetables and canaries. Won't it ever stop?" Max swung his leg over a chair and started shoveling in oatmeal with a large spoon. "Bet the chow in the Pacific ain't oatmeal, Hermy. Sure wish I was bombin the hell outta those Japs. Dirty rotten bastards. Instead of goin to school for Christsakes."

Sonny entered, juggling. "Aw, Max, I like lookin at vegetables. Look at those tomatoes," Sonny said.

"Only you, Sonny. We'll probably be callin you Sonny when you're fifty years old and you'll still be dreamin about tomatoes."

"Hey, it's getting late. We don't wanta miss the cartoons. And they're startin a new serial!

"Give me that paper, will ya?"

Cool dark interior of the newspaper office. Gold-lettered glass. Garbled voices. Jangled phones. Typewriter clatter and bells. Sharp odor of rubber glue. Flat and shining thick ink. Big beat of the press. "Who're you looking for, honey?" Telephone cradled against her shoulder, she gestures down the hall. Jake is on the phone. He frowns up at Herman when he enters.

Yellow pencils in a coffee cup. Square tan eraser. Pulp paper. Paperclips hooked together in a chain. Herman picks up the chain and unhooks a clip. Jake frowns. "Sit down, Herman. I'm busy." Jake leans back in the old cracked leather chair. "Look, Bill, you know the printers. Those bastards march to a different drummer, friend. The whole campaign will have to be moved back to the morning issue. Goddamn unions. Time we got rid of Roosevelt." Herman crosses his legs. "Can't leave, son. Here's four bits. King Kong's about to start at the Pinney."

"Look! It's my dad. He won second prize in the Trout Derby. Look at him! His picture's in the paper."

Shamrock bobbing its head on her shoulder, Gladys turned from her conversation at the dining room table with Mabel. "Now don't you boys play with those vegetables. I'm preserving them today. Just as soon as you kids leave for the movies."

"Ma, where you gonna put the jars? On the roof?"

"Shut up, Max."

Max turned in his chair to stare into the living room. "Hey, Ma, where's Charlie? That lazy bast...son-of-a-gun. The river's open and old hot-to-trot's flat on his back, dreamin those California dreams. And I'm lookin at a canoe without any sides."

He looked at the paper Sonny was waving in front of him. "Too bad it was a female with all them eggs. Shoulda weighed in first. He sure was proud of that fish. Look at him grin. Looks a little fishy himself."

"Hey, look at Shamrock!"

Shamrock was peering into the corner of Gladys' mouth while she talked. The boys began to giggle. Max shouted, "Hey, Shamrock, watch out or you're gonna fall in!."

"You stop that. Just like a bunch of girls. Here. Let me have a look at that newspaper." Gladys entered the kitchen, Mabel following with the coffee pot in one hand and a cup from the buffet in the other.

"Good morning, boys," Mabel patted her tight black curls.

"Not if you're here, Mabel. Even school's better than all that yakkin. Ain't that right, Shamrock?"

"Mabel, don't you pay any attention to him. In spite of his blathering, he's alive. And I for one am mighty grateful you kept him from enlisting. Don't know what this war's going to come to, but I'm glad he's not in it."

Mabel lowered her coffee cup to the saucer. "Letter I had from Alexander, my nephew—he's in France now—said shells just keep exploding around him. And you know what he did? He said he just went to sleep! Nothin else to do, he said." The boys laughed.

Gas pierces the air in small needles. Utterly black air hangs in the nasty aroma of aging moist clothes. The gentle percussion of a laundry wringer's gears poses black rubber riddles. The wringer taps its code. **Get out, Hermy. Get out while you are alive.** *He falls to the concrete and crawls the low crawl, a soldier in shrapnel rain, always going forward to victory. More glass blows and shatters, clatters on the basement floor. He inhales sharp old stone.* "Herman, come back here. You're going to get cut!"

"*I can't find it, Mom. Was it your blue purse?*" *He crawls ahead. Another root beer bottle explodes. He slithers his flat course across the bottle battlefield, bottles of homemade root beer* *creating more new explosions as he enters a special room, a black room within a blacker room where all sound ceases. Here he is. Safe. **At last.***

Herman picked up the cup of cooling black coffee Max had left on the table and poured sugar into it. *Shells exploding.* **Jesus, Mabel sounds like Mamie. Mamie in the All Night Battle Cafeteria.** *"I'm not supposed to drink coffee. Stunts your growth."*

"Hell it does. Puts hair on your chest. Here. Let me put some sugar in it. One swallow. That's all." Herman sips from the cup. **It's good. Not as good as it smells. But it's good.** *He took another sip. "Hungry, kid?" Herman shakes his head.*

Herman watches elderly men and women in booths. "Skid Row, huh, Hermy? Home of winos, drunks. Actually, Skid Row started here in Seattle, south of here. We're in the fourth shift now. These guys come in here after the all-night movies let out, around three, three-thirty. Looks like you slept through the third shift. The faggots. They come after the swabbies that the whores can't pick up." **He left me?** *"I left you here a couple of hours. But I told the busboy to keep an eye out when I left. Had to get an itch scratched. Okay? Ain't gonna screw around with a kid. Not with Cap lookin on. He carries a bar of Ivory wrapped up in his mop-up towel. Better'n a sap."*

"Sap?"

"Blackjack. I tried a to get through to your aunt twice, but no luck. Damn phone was still busy. Prolly someone left it off the hook. Is the whole goddamn town of Cashmere usin that line?" Sandy rises. "Well, I'm gonna get some flapjacks. I'll bring you some in case you change your mind."

Herman watches him walk to the steam tray. He looks over at the swinging doors to the kitchen. An elderly lady stands beside the left door, next to the water fountain. She smiles at Herman. **Why's that old lady lookin at me? She's coming over here...**

"Hello, boy. My name's Mamie." She leans toward Herman. He can smell her breath, the sweet rot. "I used to have a boy like you." She sits beside him on the bench. "Scoot over, honey.

Had blue eyes like you. Fine brown hair. But no glasses. I wish something had been wrong with him, but no." Her voice breaks. "He was a pilot." She shivers, breathes deeply. "They shot him down over the English Channel..."

"Well, what's this? Mamie?" Sandy was back. "Now don't bother my friend, here. You been cryin again, honey. Yeah, I know. Come on. Let's go over to the water fountain and get you somethin cold. Come on, now, Mamie. You know that it's about time for the offices to open up. Carl isn't gonna want you here gummin up the works when all those cute little secretaries come in for their toast and orange juice. Now, upsidaisy." Sandy takes the woman off to the water fountain where they pause, talking.

Glass shatters. **Mamie.** *Her face a witch mask of rage, she pulls another glass out of the rack beside the faucet. "Get AWAY from me, Pritchett! You son-of-a-bitch!" Mamie's gaze locks on Herman. Her twisted mouth relaxes and the glass poised by her head, drops from her fingers. Sandy deftly catches it before it hits the floor. "Please. Please, ma'am." Herman walks to the fountain. He reaches out his hand. Mamie gently takes it. They walk down the aisle to the door, which he opens with his left hand, still holding hers with his right.*

Herman calls after her, "Goodbye," but she doesn't turn. He goes back to his booth in the cafeteria.

Sandy rises, his mouth full of flapjacks. "Good job, Hermy! Jesus what a handful that old bag can be." Herman silently sits down. "What's up, Hermy?" The boy looks down at the scarred table. "Say, don't take it so serious. Just a lonely old drunk. And you did one hell of a job. Why, I bet Carl makes you an offer as a bouncer today. Did she tell you about her son?" Herman nods. "Thought so. Tough way to go—being shot to bits while parachuting out of a dogfight. The Nazi bastards."

"Come on, Hermy. Snap out of it. Eat some flapjacks." Sandy's flat voice brings him down to his plate and a stack of flapjacks.

Herman picks up his knife and begins to slip butter between the flapjacks and then pours syrup carefully over the top, watching it trickle in short streams down the sides. **Like** *lava. Lava coming down on the Romans, slowly but surely.* "Okay. Now eat. Hermy?"

"Yes, Sandy."

"I like you." Herman smiles. **Sandy likes me. I wonder if I was sick and dying, if he'd hit a home run for me and bring me out of it? Like Babe Ruth? Just stand there and step up to the plate and...** "But eat your goddamn flapjacks."

"Hey, Hermy? Hermy! Answer me!" Herman focused on Sonny. "Did your mother ever have a Victory Garden?"

"Not now, squirt. We're late. The movie. Remember?" Herman rose from the table.

Sonny continued as they left the kitchen for the living room. "Ya know, Ma's picture was in the paper last year. She was holdin onto a tomato as big as your fist. That's how they said it. As big as your fist. I wonder if that means my fist or Max's fist?" Herman sighed. "Ya know what her secret was?"

"Sonny, have you ever heard the word blabbermouth? If it's a secret, keep it!"

"Jeez, Hermy. All I wanted to do was tell you how she got tomatoes so big they wouldn't fit in a Mason jar. You know how she did it? Do ya?"

"Listen, kid. If I listen to you, you have to leave me alone after that. All the way to the Pinney Theater."

"Deal. It's my grandma. Little chunks of her bones. And ashes. Max knocked the vase with her in it off the mantle. An ugly old vase. Kinda purple red. Made outta that kinda glass you get at the carnival. It was one day when Max was mad. When he first tried to enlist. Anyway, when the vase broke, Ma said that's it. It shouldna been there in the first place she said. So she swept up all those pieces of bone and ashes into a dustpan and took them out to the garden. Then everything grew like crazy. Ya know you can still find some pieces of glass out there. Kinda purple red."

Mabel's voice came from the kitchen. "...Hope." **Mom? Why's Mabel talking about Mom?** "Pregnant, pregnant, pregnant. Big as a barn, I hear. And no time for her firstborn. Rose says there's trouble."

"Not enough money for another child is what I hear."

"Well you know Gladys, it all started with Jake hitchhiking all over Idaho trying to get politicians to go to bat for him, even the governor so he could get into the O.S.S. For the war. Everything was for the war. And when they wouldn't take him, man of his age and family and all, he was embarrassed. He just took off. Left her and the boy in Walla Walla, and took a job at the Statesman here where nobody knew him. He took to drinking and whoring. Didn't send any money home either. That's when Hope went to work at Sears in Walla Walla. She and those girlfriends from Sears. They started going out to meet soldiers and sailors. I think she just wanted to get even with Jake. He thought it was fine for him, but not for her. 'An unfit mother,' he said. I know you think highly of Jake, but he isn't the pretty boy in this story."

"Even so, Hope didn't have to be whorin around with a nineteen year old sailor. Lordy, she was more than thirty and had a boy to raise."

"Hermy?"

"Shut up, Sonny. Go out to the porch and get your shoes. And snap it up, for Pete's sake!" Herman couldn't hear Mabel's reply. He flushed, the heat spreading across his forehead and down his throat. He put his jacket down and stared at the huge blue and white morning glories on the cover of the davenport.

"I'll bet she tricked that sailor again. Remember how she got him to marry her when she was pregnant?"

"Now, Mabel, I remember how your own daughter got pregnant and married pretty fast."

"That's not the same and you know it. Hope had one husband right after the other and a couple a men in between. One husband was enough for me. I nursed him along for years till he died. Buried him." She sighed. "Good riddance. No more husbands."

Herman heard clinking. **Mabel's scooping cream out of the bottle's bulb! What's the matter with her? And why doesn't Mrs. Williams like Mom? I'll bet if she knew her better… Talking about me and Mom like that. Who does she think she is?**

"Mabel, I just don't know what to do with Charlie. He knows all the tricks. He's got those little kids following him around. Up to all kinds of shenanigans. I know he's teaching them to smoke. I'm sure of it. I smelled it the other day."

"Well, Gladys, all the boys smoke around here."

"But Herman's just turned twelve and Sonny—why, Sonny's just a baby. Beside Herman's father's paying me to keep his kid out of trouble. The police picked the boy up once for something. That's why he's here."

"Step over to the car, son."

"But, officer…"

"Why are you out this time of night? It's forty-five minutes after curfew."

*"I just got out of **King Kong**. Right behind me there—at the Pinney. My Dad said that I could go and then I should come to his office at the <u>Statesman</u> across this street—right over there. He's working late. I'll see him in a minute or two."*

"Step over here, son."

Herman rose. The room swayed, steadied, swayed further. **Damn cigarettes. Must be those butts, all this stuff goin around in my head. Like a movie that won't shut off. I gotta get out of here. Where's that kid?** He picked up his jacket, but the women's conversation stopped him again. "And Charlie's out there teaching them to gamble. For money. And you know how I feel about gambling. And Andrew feels the same way. I don't know how they're doing it, but I heard Sonny say Herman lost all the allowance his father gave him. To Charlie. Hermy didn't have money for comic books this week and Sonny didn't like that. But I couldn't worm out of him how Charlie done it." **What's wrong with playing blackjack?**

"Now, Gladys, you know how Charlie never had a man around. Whatever he learned, he learned on his own. And besides he's just here for three more months. How much can happen?"

"What I really want to know is what do you think she's going to do while Charlie's gone? Why does she want to be alone with that woman? You know something about her? Is something funny going on in Los Angeles?"

"Something funny's always going on in Los Angeles. How do you know any particular thing's going to happen?"

"Rose said, 'Death under mysterious circumstances.'"

"Sometimes Rose don't know that much. Aren't you going to be late for work, Mabel?" Porcelain rang sharply on the table.

"You wait and see if Rose and I aren't right." Footsteps. A door slammed.

Herman bumped into Sonny as the boy barged in through the door.

"Hey, Hermy, where've you been? I been outside here waitin for ya for an hour! Come on! We're real late!"

As the boys went down the steps, Herman asked, "Did you hear them talk about Charlie?"

"Naw, I missed that. Was it good?"

"What about Charlie's father?"

"Charlie's sort of like you. I mean he don't have a father so they call him a bastard. You don't have a mother. What do they call you?"

"Where do you get that stuff, Sonny? I got a mother. She just isn't here right now. You know that. I told you that. Jeez! Don't you know anything? Don't you ever listen? You keep talkin, and you keep changing the subject. No wonder you never know what's going on. Charlie's father. We were talkin about Charlie's father."

"Pop would say you're as bad as Mabel. Wantin to know the story. Pop says Mabel should write it all down somewhere."

Herman grabbed Sonny's shoulder. "Sonny. I don't want to hear about Mabel. I don't care if I never hear about Mabel again. Tell me about Charlie. C-H-A-R-L-I-E. Charlie."

"Charlie's just Charlie. He's tough. Some people don't like him. The way he talks. But he's just being tough. Cause of his arm and all. Tough like the Dead End Kids last Saturday."

"Charlie's father, Sonny. What about his father?"

"Nothin much. Only enough to get Mabel excited."

"Why?"

"He's a married man. And he's not married to Charlie's mother. He doesn't want anyone to know about Charlie."

"Is that it? Is that all you know?"

"Yes."

"Poor bastard." **Charlie's a lot like me. Screwed-up arm, screwed up family.**

"You know, Rose was the one who found out who Charlie's father was. It was sort of like a detective story. Not spooky like grandma dyin. Just somethin Ma and Mabel never knew. Like one of those Hardy Boys books you been readin to me."

"So?"

"Well, Charlie's mother's a nurse. She was stationed here at the Air Force base before she got transferred. And her next door neighbor in Los Angeles is a woman who is real, real sick."

"What kind of sick?"

"They say nerves. She shakes a lot. Somethin funny about her blood. So Charlie's mother takes care of her some of the time. And Charlie's father is that woman's husband. He's in the Army."

"Lives next door, huh?"

"Yeah. Mabel says Rose thinks Charlie's mother is goin to give that woman something to do her in, so she can run away with her husband when he comes back from the war. A mercy killin, Mabel calls it. What's that mean, Hermy?"

"I dunno."

"Mabel talks and talks, like Rose. Ma says she's catty. I don't think she looks like a cat."

"Sonny, she doesn't mean she looks like a cat. She means that she acts sorta like a cat. So how did Rose know who Charlie's father was when your ma and Mabel didn't?"

"Well, I don't think she had special powers for this one. She was just lucky. One day, Rose was stayin a few days with Charlie's mother, and she saw that man out in the garden and there was somethin about his hair, somethin about his nose. Anyway she says she began to see a resemblance."

"So maybe she's not a gypsy."

"Yeah, she's a gypsy but sometimes she's also just lucky with seein and hearin. She says it pays to be in the right place in the right time... Look! Nobody's out on the playground! They're all at the movie, Hermy. We're late and it's your fault."

When he returned from the movie that afternoon, Herman found a letter on his bed. **Mom! This one's from Mom!** He tore it open:

June 30, 1945

Dear Hermy,

How I have missed you. I am sorry that I haven't written you for some time, but the baby is keeping me so busy. They keep saying that the war is nearly over but it goes on and on. Jack is still in the South Pacific. I am so worried about him. They say that the Japanese will fight to the last man and the battles over there are hard to win. So many of our boys are dying.

I got a letter from your cousin Phil. He just finished flying 28 missions as a bombardier. Can you imagine that big lanky guy all squeezed into one of those little belly guns? He said he's going to get married to an English girl!

I'll bet you're so big now. I wish I could see you! But there isn't any room here. Jack's folks are poor and I think they're not very happy that their boy married a divorced woman, especially a Yankee. You wouldn't be very happy here. I'm not. I don't know where we will go. We may stay here in Georgia. Maybe Columbus will be easier to be in after the war. There are so many bad feelings here between the southerners and the soldiers at Ft. Benning—they said that General Patton trained artillery on Phoenix City across the river in Alabama (a place where there's a lot of gambling and fighting—death every weekend). He told them that if they killed one more of his men, he'd blow it off the map! The government sent him to Europe after that.

I'm joining the Episcopal Church. The whole family goes to church every Sunday to pray for our boys. I hope you're still going to church, too.

I know your father is taking good care of you. He was right. This is a time for a boy your age to have a man around. Your mother would just make a little sissy out of you.

Think of me once in a while, Hermy honey, and remember I love you.

Love, Mom

Herman carefully folded the letter and pulled out from under his bed his cardboard suitcase. He placed the letter inside, closed and locked the lid. Then he went into the bathroom. He locked the door behind him and looked at his face in the cabinet mirror. He brushed the long floating hair from his face and pressed back the two wings of hair that jutted out of each side of his head. **Like Dagwood Bumstead.** He opened the cabinet and reached in for Max's razor. **Double-edge Gillette. Save it for the war effort. We still need metal.** Setting the razor down on the sink, he rolled up his left sleeve. **Damned arm isn't worth anything anyway.** He looked at the tattoo, bending close to the snake. **I think he's getting more scales. Just like they said.** He sighed. He picked up the razor, unscrewed the top, and pulled out the blade, holding it between his right forefinger and his thumb. He twisted his left arm until the tattoo was out of sight. Biting his lip, he pressed the corner of the blade into his forearm. **It just dented me.** He pressed harder and pulled the blade to his right into the pinched flesh. A drop of blood spread into a circle around the blade. Black ruby, a tiny round light glowing in its center. He pulled the blade further down the arm for three-quarters of an inch. **It doesn't hurt. Whatta you know about that? It feels...keen. Like someone singing a high note.** He pulled out the blade. The wound opened up, a small, smiling mouth quickly filling with blood. He smiled back. **Nothing can hurt me now.**

Thirteen

"Hey Ma, how come Mabel gave you her ration coupons? She hardly ever gives anybody anything. Max says she hoards stuff in her mattress."

"Max says, Max says. Sonny, of all the kids I had, you are the how comin'ist kid I have ever seen. Don't you dare say bad things about Mabel. She's a widow lady. She's just had a hard life, makin it on her own and then the war on top of that." Gladys brushed back an orange wisp of hair and returned to the coupon books spread on the kitchen before her open brown leather purse with the large gold clasp. Shamrock clung to the strap of an apron hung over the back of Gladys' chair.

"Aw, Ma, I just wanted to know how come she gave em to you." As he talked, Sonny juggled. Suddenly, one ball skidded across the kitchen counter and knocked over a green tumbler.

"Sonny, I told you to use those bean bags! It's the only way Max ever learned to juggle. You're not ready for balls yet."

"Ma, you haven't been watchin me. I can get all three up now. If I just keep sayin to myself it doesn't matter, so what the hell if they fall."

"Sonny!"

"Sorry, Ma. Anyway, beanbags are for little kids. I won't hit anything again, I promise." Gladys returned to her coupon books. "So what about Mabel?"

"Enough about Mabel! She didn't give me the coupons. I traded her. You know I want this dinner to be special for Helen. It's been two years since she's been home. Lord, I've missed that girl!"

Sonny had retrieved his balls and began juggling again. "What'd you trade her, Ma? What'd you have that Mabel wanted?" Another ball skittered across the floor.

"None of your business, mister. You're makin me nuts with those balls. Out of here. Right now!"

"Aw Ma, the only reason I'm droppin em is cause you're making me nervous."

Charlie and Herman appeared in the doorway. "When's Helen's bus due?" Max asked.

"Bus gets in at 6:20. And the next thing you better be askin is what you can do to help. What are all you boys up to anyway?"

Steam was rising from three pots on the stove, and in dented rectangular pans along the edge something white was rising from yeast, smelling sweet and covered with red and white checkered towels.

"Where'd you get sugar, Ma?"

"From Mabel. Ma traded her for her coupons, but she won't tell what she traded."

"Come on, Auntie Glad, nobody can get sugar. In her letter Helen said she'd been tryin to get us Milky Ways at the commissary but she said not to count on it. What'd you give Mabel?"

"None of your business either, mister. Important thing was I traded her fair and square. I certainly didn't steal them." There was a moment of silence as she looked at Charlie through heavily lidded eyes. Charlie looked away. "Now you and Hermy start on those pots and pans. I want this kitchen all cleaned up when I get back." Heaving herself out of her chair, she left the kitchen, Sonny following.

"Charlie, you think she knows?"

"Naw, the old bat just made a lucky guess. Uh-uh-uh-uh-uh." Charlie machine-gunned Herman with his finger. "Dirty Jap rat. Now if you tell Sonny, then she'll know plenty and ship my ass out to LA fast as a rat's ass. But I'm not goin back to waitin for sick people to die. Not me. I'll just keep on runnin. Damn war be over pretty soon they keep sayin. Course they been sayin that for years now." He aimed again at Herman. "Uh-uh-uh-uh. War over, we can steal us a car and take off for good. Darn tootin. Neither of us got anything to look back on. Uh-uh-uh. How come you never run, Hermy? Always doin' just like they tell you to. Uh-uh-uh-uh. Run, run, Hermy."

"My mother's cousin ran away to join the Navy a long time ago in World War I. He got killed."

"Runnin don't mean dead, jackass."

"You kids get movin! Get those bushel baskets of apples from the basement right now!" Gladys shouted down the hall.

Charlie took Gladys' chair, rocked back, and swung his feet on the table. "You get the apples, Herman."

"No. She told both of us."

"Listen, kid. You're forgettin who works for who. You work for me, remember? I got the moolah, you step n' fetch. That's the way the game goes. And even if you had scored real good off old Daddy's dresser and told me to piss off, you know what would happen? I'd have me a little chat with Max and Karl and his boys'll be right back on your butt."

"That's Max's business, not yours."

"Son, I got a way with Max."

"Yeah, yeah," Herman muttered and left to get the apples.

That evening, there was a knock at the front door. When Herman opened it, he saw before him a young woman standing straight in a military uniform smiling, smiling at him, then looking behind him, grinning and calling out "Mom!" She brushed past him. She smelled like roses, fragrant swelling roses. **Like Mom's on the back porch at Walla Walla. She's a Williams?** She wasn't like Gladys with her wild orange hair floating about her or lean and quiet Andrew, or Sonny with his chipmunk teeth and sleepy eyes or Max with his blond crewcut. Like Saturday matinee credits, the Williams cast flickered behind Herman's eyes, but Helen's dark beauty wasn't there. The mass of dark curly hair framed an oval face, lightly tanned and highlighted with the softest pink. All were hugging her, even Charlie, crushing her olive uniform. **I don't belong here. This isn't my family.** As he turned to close the front door, he saw Rose. **Hey.** She smiled at him and then walked in as casually as if she had only left that morning to go to the market. **There's two of us now. Rose and me. She's like a guardian angel.**

He sits in Ide's church, looking at the angel above the altar. It has a rosy face. Now he sinks in the immersion tank, still watching the angel's face on the ceiling of the church. Words flow out of her mouth but he can't understand them. She reaches for his hand. He pulls back. **Angels scare me.** *"Will I grow wings?" he tries to say but his words only bubble. She reaches again for his hand. This time he gives it to her.*

Herman smiled back at Rose. They joined the family. Gladys put her hand on her daughter's shoulder. "You put on some weight, honey."

"Army food. Lots of potatoes."

"Look at your cheeks. It's like they're bloomin right out of your face."

"That's cause I'm home again. Back in Boise. Did I ever write that nobody I know in the service has ever been to Boise? They talk about places in the Philippines like it's their backyard, but they always say 'Boise? Where's Boise.' Well, this is Boise and I'm here, and that's what makes my cheeks rosy." She hugged Gladys again. Herman blushed. He turned away. Rose moved into the kitchen where she stood quietly watching the sunset outside the kitchen door.

Herman said to her, "I've got some money, Rose. I want you to read my palm or read the cards. Mom's got another family and I think Dad's just tired of me. I wanta know what's gonna happen to me. Am I gonna stay here forever?"

"Poor kid. The war's made orphans of us all. Well, son, I'll tell you what. Gladys says there's a teakettle about to whistle out here. I was just comin to get me a cup. Now she says it's all hocus pocus and she don't believe it but she always makes sure there's tea leaves where I can get at them. These days, everybody thinks they can read leaves. Even Mabel, and you know how much Mabel don't know. Just lookin in that cup for a uniform, Mabel is." Rose laughed.

Sonny appeared. "Rose, how come Tokyo Rose's got the same name? You workin for the Axis?"

"Sonny, why do you keep askin how come? No, me and Tokyo aren't kin." Rose looked at Herman and shook her head. He smiled. "Now listen, Herman, I'll read the tea leaves for you for nothin since I owe you for that bee sting."

"No, I don't want tea leaves. I want you to read my palm or the cards. Like your sister. I got money."

Rose looked at him softly. "Now where'd you get that money, Herman?" **She knows. What am I gonna do now?**

"Workin a little. I don't have much. My dad doesn't come around much now. Tea leaves are okay, Rose."

Rose's deep laugh echoed in the kitchen. "I like you, Herman." She looked around for tea. "So you thought I was Mae. Couldn't believe there's be two of us."

Gladys and Max came through the kitchen door. Gladys began moving around pots. Max stood beside Herman, watching Rose. "What's up, Hymie?"

"Sit down, Max, and take a load off. You too, Herman," Rose said as she began to make herself a cup of tea. "It's been a long time since I read the leaves. Gladys, I was just tellin Herman that people are always readin their own leaves nowadays. When they come to me, they want palms or cards. Mostly palms. Some people are putting signs up with big palms on them, red as Helen's nail polish. I saw them when I was visitin my brother down South. Maybe one day I'll get me a little house and put a sign outside with a big red palm that says 'Sister Rose, Advisor'." Her laugh throbbed in the steamy kitchen. As she drank her tea, Herman's stomach tightened. **I want to know. Don't I? Why does she always talk in circles that way?**

Gladys cleared her throat. "Now don't get settled there, Rose. Pretty soon you're gonna have to move. Time to get this show on the road. Helen has been eating Army food for more than a year." She opened the oven. "I was real surprised they gave her a pass to come home, what with the war and all."

"The Army works in strange and mysterious ways," Rose replied and sipped more tea.

"Now don't you go making fun of Helen. Or the Army. She's doing more for the war effort than the rest of us."

"I'd be there right now if it wasn't...."

"Now, Max, honey..."

"Would I make fun of Helen's war effort, Gladys?" Rose rolled her eyes in dismay. Before Gladys could retort, she turned to Herman. "Now, Herman, what question are you gonna ask the leaves?"

Herman's face flushed. **I didn't know I would have to ask a question. I didn't last time. Everybody's looking at me.** He blurted out, "Everything! I want to know everything that's going to happen to me."

Rose looked into the cup. She paused and closed her eyes. Her brows knit in a slight frown. After a moment, she opened her eyes and focused on Herman. "Now I will tip the cup." She tipped the teacup towards him. The brown sediment had fallen into a circle separated into equal halves by an S-shaped line. "Herman, there is water in your future. See the way the leaves have fallen with a river through the center?" She looked up at him. "It's the river within. In and between." She touched the right half. "You think you're here, but..."

"Mae told me about that. It sounds sort of crazy." He looked from the cup to Rose. "I guess what I want to know about is my mother. When's she comin home after the war?"

"Herman," Rose's voice was sharp. "You can't change the question. We tipped the cup. Forget about her. This is more important. Do you know how to swim, Herman?"

Swim? Who told her about that? Herman looked over at Max. "Yeah. Sort of. Who doesn't?" Herman flushed.

Rose touched the back of his hand. "Herman. Listen. The dam is breaking. Listen to me. Be very careful around water. Especially the river."

"What river?"

Gladys suddenly took the cup. "Rose! You're scaring the boy. Stop that. He's got enough problems. Don't you know by now people only come to you because they want to hear somethin good? Because they want somethin to hold on to? Now move out. I told you not to get settled there because I need that table. You boys carry these plates and glasses into the dining room. This isn't a wake. It's Helen's celebration."

That night, Herman suddenly awoke, half in, half out of his dream. *He sees himself arrested and handcuffed to a seat in the back of a police car. Around him is everything that he and Charlie have ever stolen. He looks out the window as the car is driving away and sees Charlie on the sidewalk. A policeman is sawing off the rest of his right arm. The blood trickles slowly down from his arm.*

Rose and Helen open the door of a bright white room. Helen bent over, holding her stomach. All he can see is her hair, dark and curling. Following her is a man with a large camera. He tries to take her photograph. "Here, hold the face powder in your hand. In your hand!" he shouts.

Herman closed his eyes and lay back on the pillow. *He is at the police station. They take off his handcuffs, and he looks at an aquarium, one that had been in the doctor's office when he had had polio. The fish have flown out of the water and are circling above his head like Rose's bees. Herman tries to catch one to put it back into the water where the blood is dripping.*

"Blood!" The shout fully woke Herman. Someone was shouting "She's bleeding all over the place!" He looked over at Sonny. The boy didn't move.

"How could you do that here? I always knew you were no good. Nothin but a whore. But I didn't know you killed babies."

"Gladys, stop that!" Andrew said. "She's helping. You know how things will be for Helen if anybody knows. With Donald in Germany for the duration. If she hadn't done it here, she could be bleeding God knows where."

"That's a mixed blessing, Andrew. It's your daughter that Rose stuck the knitting needle into."

Helen's door closed. Herman now heard a low moan. **Stop it. Don't hurt her. Not her.**

The next morning Herman and Sonny sat silently on their beds and looked at the cracked and dirty wall. The day was gray, the porch shadowed, the canaries silent. Herman finally turned to Sonny and forced a smile. "Hey, kid, let's see some of that jugglin."

"Naw, Hermy, I'm not any good. I've lost my touch. I keep knockin over Ma's stuff and she don't like it."

"Well, she's not here right now, so go ahead. There isn't any of her stuff out here. Just canaries and they could use a thump or two."

"Naw, I don't feel like it."

"What's the matter?"

"Ma told me to take soup to Helen. Her face is white. She just lies there not movin, lookin at the wall. I even said I'd juggle for her but she said 'Not today.' She looks awful, Hermy."

"Yeah, but your Ma says she's gonna be all right. Doc Murphy looked at her. Don't you think he'd send her to the hospital or somethin?"

"Yeah. Did you hear her moanin? I never heard nothin like it."

"Yeah."

"But I took her soup."

"I bet she liked that."

"Doc Murphy says she needs nourishment. He says milk. Maybe Ma will let me take that to her. I like to think about Elsie and Elmer when I pour it. Ya know, Hermy, I never believed any of that stuff about advertising, but Elsie and Elmer make me want to drink milk. Maybe I'll show Helen the ads. They make me laugh."

"Let's go out to the living room, Sonny, and play Old Maid."

"You always beat me."

"I won't this time. You can win."

"Okay."

As Herman shuffled the cards at the dining room table, he could hear Mabel in the kitchen talking to Gladys. "Do you remember my telling you about Esther? You remember, she was working at Sears while her husband was in France. She went out and got drunk with a soldier one night and ended up pregnant. I told you about how she got rid of the baby herself. She didn't have to have any help."

"Help! You're beginning to sound like Andrew. Fat lot of help Rose was, makin Helen bleed all over the place."

"Well, Esther did it herself, but then she got what was comin to her. She found out she couldn't ever have children. Big price to pay for one night with a soldier. Let alone the shame she brought her husband and family," Mabel concluded. The boys were drawing cards from each other silently. Mabel spoke again. "Did you see it in the paper?" Gladys' response was an unintelligible murmur. Sonny looked at Herman. "Well, I only wanted to know if you'd seen it. I'd forgot all about him." Herman blushed. But he didn't know why.

Sonny whispered to Herman, "What do ya think it is? Last time Ma didn't want somebody to know somethin, she just cut it out of the paper. Somethin about bein drafted or enlistin, and she didn't want Max to get any ideas. So she just cut it out, pretendin it was something about bonus points or somethin. Big hole in the front page. It got Dad's goat."

"Well, if we look in today's paper and there's a hole in it, we'll know she didn't want me to get drafted. You're goofy, Sonny."

"Well, maybe I am. But I don't like Mabel. She talks to Ma a lot but she isn't good like Ma. She's selfish. Selfish shellfish. Can you see Mabel lookin like a clam? Clam up Mabel? No siree."

"Be quiet, stupid. They're still talkin. Let's see if we can hear."

But Sonny wanted to play. He rabbit punched Herman. "You can't see with your ears, dummy."

"Come on, Sonny. Deal the cards. Here. I'll shuffle for you. I want to hear. It might be something important. About my mother."

"You don't think he'd take out after the boy, do you?" Mabel continued.

"Probably don't even remember him."

"But Cory's in Idaho now. They know that much. And killin that little boy."

"Mabel, what a horrible thing to say!"

"Well, they don't call him Corregidor for nothing. He has been a real son-of-a-B. Even more since he came back from the war."

"Now, Mabel. I seem to remember when you were real young, you bein interested in him."

"Those were the days when he was young and everybody thought he'd out-grow bein wild. Those snakeskin boots and rattles hanging from his belt. Out shootin up a storm just to be shootin. 'Headstrong,' they said. You know how men are sometimes. Well, not your Andrew, I guess. Anyway, those days are long gone. The man's loose and he's shot a little boy. It's a dirty shame. Even if the kid was a Jap."

"He's crazy all right. Maybe we should worry about whether he'll look you up after all these years."

Mabel giggled. "We didn't leave on the best of terms." Herman picked up the cards. Tom? The women began to talk about canning what was ripe in the Victory Garden.

"Vegetables." Sonny rolled his eyes. "Notice how they never talk about the good stuff like pickled peaches and bread and butter pickles. Frills they call them. Don't you miss em, Hermy?"

"Yeah."

"Is your Uncle Cory the one who shot your rat, Hermy?"

"Yeah."

"Your uncle?"

"Yeah. He's married to my Auntie Ide. Her third or fourth husband. For a change, Mabel's right about somethin. He is a mean son of a bitch." Herman pointed to the scar on his neck. "You know the story."

"Tell me again, Hermy. Tell me. I don't remember so good. That where the bullet hit you? How come he shot at you, Hermy? Did you have a gun, too?"

"No, squirt. Now where would I get a gun? He didn't want me to have a rat. Mae, Rose's sister, felt sorry for me at the carnival and so she read my palm and gave me a rat."

"What about the rat?"

"I named her Gypsy and took her home and was gonna keep her in the barn, but I forgot about the chickens. Old Cory was drunk and totin a rifle around with him. I had the white rat on my shoulder and was playin the Guessing Game with this other kid. Cory shot at it and killed Gypsy and gave me this scar."

"Jesus, Hermy."

"Sonny, you know your mother'd beat you for sayin' that."

"Sorry. It just popped out. Good thing you didn't have Fred Astaire on your shoulder that day." Herman began to laugh, then stopped. **Dead.**

"What happened then?"

"Ide put me on the bus right away. Like Charlie would say, she threw my butt outta there."

"Where'd you go, Hermy?"

"She sent me to Seattle on the bus to my mother, but she couldn't get through to call her right away. My mother was at her job at Sears. So my mother wasn't there when I got to Seattle. That's when Sandy took care of me. I told you about that."

"Jesus, Hermy. I've never been lost anywhere by myself. Max was once, but not me."

"I told you about that Jesus stuff, Sonny. I don't wanna get thrown out of here. I don't know anybody who'd take me this time."

The kitchen door banged. The noise was as loud as a shot and startled the boys. "Aw, it's only Mabel goin to work. Hey, Hermy, where do ya suppose he is, that old Cory?"

"Hidin out if he knows what's good for him."

"And he shot a Jap kid." The hair on the back of Herman's neck prickled and he flushed, feeling the bullet grazing his skin again. Sonny continued, "Why would anybody kill a kid. Even a Jap kid? My dad never shot anybody. He ain't wild. Don't even yell very loud when he yells at me. Does yours, Hermy?"

"Sonny I don't know how you get so much out at one time. You go on and on."

"So does he, Hermy? Does he yell and shoot people, Hermy?"

"He yells plenty sometimes. He gets real mad. Like when he wanted to be an intelligence officer in the war and they wouldn't take him. I remember him doin a lot of shoutin then. But he wouldn't shoot anybody."

"So wadda ya think your Uncle Cory's gonna do, Hermy?"

"If he's in Idaho like they say, I dunno. Might follow the Snake River out into the wilderness. He's a tracker and a hunter. They even tried to get him to find Rainbow, Dad said. He's as smart as a mountain lion. Won't leave a trail for anybody to find."

"Maybe we should try to find him, Hermy. You know what he looks like. Maybe we could track him. We could be heroes."

"Look, pea brain. He's a mean old bastard. He'd shoot us on sight and me sooner than that. He'd remember Gypsy."

"Gee, Hermy, don't git mad. It was just an idea."

Have they found Tom?

Fourteen

"**H**erman, your father's here."

Herman ran down the steps. **Dad?** Jake sat stiffly on the edge of the large brown wing chair in the darkest corner of the room. He had a yellow telegram envelope in his hand. It was torn. His face was bleached, black lines carving white. Closer now, Herman saw that his eyes were sunk in shadow and the flesh around them dark. "It's Frank," Herman said.

Jake nodded, covered his face with his left hand. **What happened to the wedding ring? I never thought about that. Where is it? What's he doing? Maybe I should touch him.** In his tears his father shimmered, a ghost. *Frank stands with his arm around Jake's shoulder, laughing, singing, smelling of beer. Jack shouts. Mom is crying.* Herman sat on the edge of the wing chair's arm and buried his head against his father. Sobs jerked his body violently. **What's happening? What's happening to me?** He stopped sobbing. A long silence passed. He could smell the tobacco on his father's clothing. He looked at the tan blinds pulled against the sun. "I don't know anything, Hermy. Only that he's gone."

Herman stood but, not wanting to let go, touched Jake's shoulder. **Gone. Frank! That bald head and that moustache. The songs. Lake Washington. Swimming like a family. Darts. Frank laughing, teasing. Gone. Where did somebody like Frank go?** "He just never made it back from the Pacific." *Frank. In the water. Under the water. Salt water. Whiter than Jake. Strange fish swim slowly by. He floats on his back and then slowly, slowly turns until he is face down staring* *with white eyes into the blackest black ever. A shape corkscrews up towards him. Its mouth opens. Teeth.* "Hermy. Hermy! Were you listening?" Herman shook his head. "I said 'Get dressed.' Put on your good clothes. Your suit and tie. We're going out." Herman looked at his father but Jake said no more. The boy turned and went back to his room.

Herman returned dressed in his brown suit. **The arms and legs are too short.** He had his blue and red striped tie in his hands. "Dad, will you tie this again for me? It got undone." Jake took the tie and looped it around the back of Herman's neck. "Where are we going?"

"To Frank's wake." **What's a wake?** He started to speak but his father roughly jerked the tie. He closed his mouth. The flatness of his father's voice told him the closeness between them was gone.

When they walked into Murphy's Bar and Grill, a blonde woman met them with a large bottle in her hand. She waved it at Herman. "What's a boy going to do at a wake? Kids aren't even supposed to be in here."

Herman felt the hair on his neck prickle. He looked at the bottle. **Those are the black and white Scotties I got on my magnets.**

"But Jake, the boys got carried away already…." They walked into a dining room full of smoke and balloons and laughter and ad men from everywhere in Boise. Duck, his father's assistant, was the only woman present. She picked up a water glass from the table, filled it to the top from her bottle, and handed it to Jake. He took a deep swallow from it. On the wall at the end of the table, there was a huge photograph of Frank in a football uniform.

Jake laughed, "Where in the hell did you get that photo?"

"Over the wire. From the <u>Cashmere Daily World</u>. Didn't you used to work there, Jake?"

"Sure as hell did. They must have carried the shot when Cashmere won the conference. Frank scored three touchdowns that afternoon. Goddamn. That's beautiful. Now what in the hell is this?" Jake pulled down one of the balloons and looked at it more closely. "A rubber." Herman looked at the balloon more closely. **What's wrong?**

A fat, curly-haired man pushed through the crowd. "We thought that Frank would've appreciated the decorations. We got a stripper to come down from Kellogg. She'll be here around ten. Bill said she takes on mules, but we can't find any...except for that jackass Gallagher." The man and Jake laughed. The smoke was beginning to sting Herman's eyes.

Jake filled his glass again and looked over at Duck. "Why don't you take Herman over to the bar and get him a soft drink?" Duck nodded and took Herman's hand. They pushed their way through men and conversation.

"And then the cowboy said to the magic rattlesnake..."

"I sold five column inches to the son of a bitch and then he..."

"It was in one of the Walla Walla whorehouses. He cut her nipple off with a pair of sewing scissors. But it served the bitch right."

"I heard that the O.S.S. needs ad men."

Herman looked at Frank's picture behind the bar, looked at the grin, the knowing eyes, the strength and energy. His chest heaved and he looked away. In front of him, on the side of the bar was a poster the size of Frank's picture. **Coke, the little white-haired guy with a bottle cap. Cap. Get it? "My name's Coke."** Duck called over the bartender, a bald-headed man whose broad green suspenders curved over a great belly. "Ain't he a little young to be in here?"

"Take it up with Jake, Gino."

Gino looked into the crowd. "His kid?" Duck nodded. "Well what the hell? It's a private party. What do you want, son?"

"A Coke." Gino turned away and began filling a glass with ice.

Herman turned at the sound of laughter. Three men were standing around a sweating red-headed man who apparently had just told them a joke. He recognized him---Pat Casey, an agency artist. "So, old Peterson was always telling the artists that they didn't have the mouths right. He would say to Mike, 'Ah, Mr. Turnbull, at...'" The men around Casey erupted into laughter. "Ah, Mr. TURNbull."

"'Yes, Mr. Peterson!' Mike would always stand straight as a rod behind his drawing board as if he were getting ordered to take an enemy position. 'YesSIR!'" The men laughed again. Herman smiled and took a sip of his Coke. Duck had left.

"'Yes, Mr. Peterson. Ah, the mouth isn't quit right on this young lady.'"

"'And how would you have it, Sir? Please, Sir?'" Someone groaned. "No, really."

Peterson thought Mike was just being respectful. Anyway, he'd go on, 'Well, Mike, can't you make the mouth smile a little more?'"

"'What kind of a smile, Sir'"

"'Well, Turnbull, well. Let me see. Um.'" The men laughed again. So did Herman. "'A merry smile.'"

"'Merry, Sir?'"

"'Merry.' And then Peterson would peer into Mike's face." Pat moved closely towards one of the men and thrust his head into the man's face and then raised his eyebrows. "'Merry. As in Merry Christmas.' So Mike would knock off the shit and get back to the drawing board as they say. He had been on the staff for three years when he got this idea. He got the other artists together—Joe and Pancho—and a copywriter, a talented young Irish gentleman name of Casey, I believe, and he explained to us the Great Plan—Mr. Peterson's Birthday Gift. And later on, the copywriters got into it. So when Peterson's birthday rolled around—April Fool's Day, I think—" Herman alone laughed. One of the men looked down at him, then smiled and tipped him a wink. "And he came to work, there pinned up on the wall behind the secretaries were numbered pictures of mouths, bright red and thick lips being licked by a tongue 'as in lustful,' thin twisted lips underneath a pencil moustache 'sneering as in contemptuous' and of course one under a square moustache, 'maniacal as in Hitler,' one under a sheep's nose…"

"'As in sheepish,'" chorused men on each side of Pat.

"Thank you, gentlemen. I see that I need not develop the point any further. After all, I am among a group of failed English majors and writers of unfinished novels. Even a poet, if I am correct. All, as they say, poor little lambs who have lost their way."

"So. Mouths, mouths, mouths. Two hundred and sixty-three of them, each carefully numbered so that—as someone politely explained to a grateful Peterson later, the Boss could just call out numbers hereafter when the mouth question opened." A groan. "And dead center, numbered two hundred and sixty-three in Roman numerals, was Peterson's mouth—a stunning photographic representation with attention to the slightest detail, the loose and hanging nether lip, the hairy mole at the right corner of the mouth, the dentures stained yellow with Camel smoke and on the right, that little chip on the front incisor, the slightly wolfish canine and The Smile. You all know The Smile. When the big lumber account came in?" Pat beamed moronically down at Herman suddenly, his eyes slightly unfocused, his tongue protruding at the corner of his mouth. Herman looked around. The other three men smiled at him with the same idiotic and somewhat greedy smile. All burst into laughter. Pat suddenly regained his dignity. "Gentlemen! Allow me to conclude. And Mouth 263 was labeled 'Happy as in Happy Birthday!'"

Someone said, "Aww" and someone else asked "Where's the stripper?"

Then the group broke up and Herman was alone. Herman turned back to the bar. Sandy stood there in his baseball uniform. "Hey kid, I'm real sorry about Frank. He meant a lot to me too. We'd been friends a hell of a long time." He hugged Herman.

"Yeah," was all Herman could manage to say. He looked at Sandy, tall and tan in the pebbled gray uniform with dark blue trim.

"Draft dodger."

"Hey, Frank, Dodger's a compliment in my crowd."

Herman smiled. He hugged Sandy back. "Sit down here with me, buddy. I hear you tried to get in to see me at the ball park. Guard told me about it the next day. Been looking for you at the Sunday games."

Herman's face flushed. **What did the guard say?** "How's the team doing, Sandy?"

"We're winning." Sandy looked into his beer for a moment, then took a long swallow from it. He sighed. "Poor old Frank." He took another swallow. "I probably should be shootin at Japs somewhere but baseball's all I've ever known. It's the way I live."

"They say you're the magic of the team, Sandy, that you always pull the team through wherever you are."

"That's a lot of talk, Hermy. Old-timer talk. Besides, I'm getting too old for this. And the game has to change a lot when all those ball players get back from the war." Sandy looked around at the men gathered in small groups, talking, laughing. "They say the war's almost over now. Doesn't do Frank any good, does it, kid?" Sandy drank more beer. Herman looked around at the others. "I hear you were living right in the Pilots' ball park. Now that's something I've never done. Live in the ballpark."

"Yeah," Herman said. "I wish I was back there. I don't see my dad much anymore. Not like when we lived there."

"Your father's going through some hard times, Hermy." Herman watched some men popping rubber balloons with their cigarettes. "Hermy, listen to this. He's gonna be lost without Frank. Ever since your grandfather died, it's been Jake and Frank. Even before that, Jake followed Frank around. Water boy on Frank's team, whatever they'd let him be. Wasn't anything he wouldn't do for Frank. Jake always admired him. Now there's gonna be hard times." **God, omygod, when is it all gonna stop?** Sandy looked at him carefully. "Guess times been pretty hard on you already, kid." He took Herman by the arm. "Let's see how much the snake's grown on that muscle. Can you see more of the detail now?" Herman rolled up his sleeve and exposed the tattoo. "Yeah. Look at that. Look at the eye. That little arch of scales right over it. Tiny scales. God, he's good! Look." He rolled up his own sleeve. "He's done the same with mine, but it isn't the same snake. Look at the snout. And the eyes. Looks a little like a hog snake. Yours is a baby rattler."

Sandy turned Herman's arm, looked closely at the scab. "And what happened here?"

"I fell."

"On a knife?"

"Hey a coupla lumberjacks are gonna arm wrestle!" Pat grinned down at them. "My money's on the dwarf!" Two more men and then a third, and a fourth joined them. Each leaned over the tattoos. "Hey, look at that!"

"Did it hurt, kid?"

"You know, I always wanted one of those."

"Is that a snake?"

"Hey, Hermy here's the son of an ad man. We never feel pain. Can't afford to."

"Hey kid, where'd you get that cut?"

"Sandy's snake reminds me of my contact on the current account."

"Which one's that, Joe?"

"Your mother. Now why the hell would I tell you? You'd be over there so quick."

"Hey, beertendar, buy this man another Oly! Loosen him up."

Rose appeared suddenly, pushing through the men and threw her arms around Sandy.

"Rose. Where did you come from?"

"Hi, Sandy. Look guys, if you think that tattoo's something, you oughta see my sister's."

"I'd love to see your sister, honey, if she's anything like you. Who's the beauty, Sandy?"

"Rose. She tells fortunes. Her sister was tattooed by the same guy who did us."

"Well, tell my fortune, honey, and I'll buy you a drink."

"I prophesy for you great pain tomorrow upon awakening."

The men in the circle laughed. Sandy bent down and lifted Herman up to the bar counter. "Get up here in the bright light, buddy."

"Here you are. How's the bee sting doing?"

"You know him, Rose?"

"Sure do. He's living with Gladys Williams. You know her?"

"No, I guess not."

"Well, one of my bees stung him a while back."

"Bad sign, Hermy."

"No. We just got into a fight over who was going to get my lemonade."

"So, what's up Rose? You still got a warm spot in your heart for Frank?" They all looked up at Frank's picture.

"I do. Frank. I came to give him a kiss. Give me a hand, boys." Two men reached out to her and helped her step to a stool and from there to the bar, where she stood facing the photograph for a moment. "Goodbye, Frank." She leaned over to kiss the photograph.

"What's that woman think she's doing with Frank's picture?" Jake suddenly broke into the circle. "She's nothing but a two-bit whore."

"Like the rest of us, huh Jake?" Pat eagerly chimed in. Jake lunged toward him, but Sandy pulled him back.

"Two-bit whore," Jake repeated. He staggered to the left. A man put an arm around him.

"Easy, Jake."

"Hell, Frank loved whores. You know that. And you've been there right beside him. Hear you guys got a hell of a case of crabs up at Kellogg one weekend. So why the big change, Jake? Come on, buddy. Take it easy." Sandy lightly shook Jake.

"Listen, buster," Rose said as she moved closer to Jake's flushed face. "You got something to say about a woman? You're gonna have to say it right up here close. Are you sure you weren't some orphan your folks found on the doorstep? I can't see any likeness between you, you little runt, and that beautiful big bald man up there. God I love him! He could feel visions through his body. And he knew what was comin to him. Death by water. He knew it and he went out like a hero." Rose towered over Jake by at last half a foot. As she talked, Herman backed away. He turned to leave the room when Sandy stopped him.

"He won't remember in the morning, Hermy. He's drunk as a skunk and Rose is going to give him something to keep him occupied. Hell, look at Rose go. Jake better start getting diplomatic real soon." Sandy took another swig of beer, his eyes on the woman. "She was real important to Frank. It's how he played football so well and everything else. Her visions made him a star."

"But what about Maxine? Sandy, you remember that day when you and me and Frank and Maxine went to the lake?" Sandy nodded. "I still have my prize. If I had it with me in Boise, the birds would like it. They would like to perch on it when they get out."

"What birds, Hermy?"

"Canaries. I sleep in a room full of canaries with Sonny. Sonny's mother sells them. They sing mostly when the sun goes down and early in the morning. And they're always gettin out. We're supposed to keep the door closed but sometimes we forget and one gets out into the house. Then Sonny's mother gets a towel and flaps it around until the bird goes back."

Sandy smiled. "You're lucky to sleep in a canary room, Hermy."

Herman looked at Sandy. **He must be drunk too.**

Fifteen

Herman got off the bus in Cashmere. He sat on the bench outside the station. He looked down at his book. **Good old Baum. I wish I could write like that.** *Herman runs along the bank of the Cashmere River, stumbles, pitches forward, straightens up, running, running, beautiful loping like the deer in the mountains. He reaches out for the trailing ladder slowly rising from the ground, its last rung at the level of his chest, and he catches it! The ladder gives a lurch upwards and for a moment Herman's toes drag on the ground and then swing free to reveal the snake on his bare arm writhing with the strain. He stretches first his left arm, then his right up the ladder.* **Good thing we did that rope-climbing in gym last year.** *Finally he is able to swing a foot on the bottom rung of the rope ladder and step up. The wind blowing his fine hair back into his blue eyes, hand over hand, the silken braid of the rope soft in his hands, he climbs toward the cloud from which the ladder hangs. Finally, his head enters the cloud, breaks through, and he looks around.*

"Herman. Herman Auerbach?" A small man in his seventies, stooped with curly hair, ivory white, bursting out like a halo underneath a beat-up fedora. **Mr. Beeman.** Herman nodded. "You remember me?"

"Mr. Beeman." **Gramma's manager. The guy who collects the rent, patches up the apartment rows. Mr. Beeman. Like the gum. Licorice. My favorite.**

"You still have that beaver log?" **Oh, yeah.** *He reaches to the ground. The wind blows through the trees above and the sun bounces on the ferns and foxtails about his feet. The river whispers and chats to his left. He picks up the log.* **Something has gnawed at this.**

And the red-winged black grasshoppers. I'd never seen anything like them. I caught maybe fifteen, twenty, and I let them go in Walla Walla. I bet the town's full of them now.

"Not anymore."

"Well, let's go. Mrs. Auerbach's a ways out." They walked to Mr. Beeman's Ford truck. Herman pulled on the door. It creaked, screamed, stuck. "Give 'er a yank, son." Herman did. It popped open so suddenly that he staggered back. He recovered, stepped up on the torn rubber pad of the running board, slid in onto the cracked leather upholstery, and yanked the door shut behind him. **I'd like to ride on that running board. Like Dick Tracy.** He sat in the truck's cab, high off the ground, the cut of coiled and uncoiled springs in his back. The sharp and bitter black smell of oil hung in the hot and heavy air. Along the top of the windshield was a fringe from which bobbed green balls, each on a one-inch string. Like Mrs. Williams' lamp.

He sits by the window across from his grandmother. He picks up a Rye Krisp and looks at the top of her head, which is bent over to read the book she holds. **I didn't know women got bald. Like Uncle Frank.** *"Would you please pass the apple butter, Gramma?" She looks up from her book and smiles. She passes the apple butter.* Outside the cab, Mr. Beeman cranked the engine once and it growled to life. He jumped in and jiggled the choke. "Let er rip!" he shouted. They wheeled from the curb into the street, past a scattering of buildings. "That's the library. Where they'll shelve your gramma's and grampa's books after you finish pickin through them today." He indicated a yellow box on the seat next to Herman. "Want a Cotlet?"

"No thanks."

"They're for your gramma. She's never lost her appetite. Still got her sweet tooth." They drove on in silence. Apple orchards began to appear. "There's McGregor's orchard." Herman looked. "Where your ma met Jake."

"I know."

"I was there, you know. In charge of the thinners. She and Ide. And that Cory. You heard about him?" Herman nodded. **Oh, Tom.** "They were kids and likely to play around. Your dad especially, after he moved out of your gramma's place to live in a little shack with Frank right after Frank moved out, when he and Mrs. Auerbach got in a fight over this woman he was squirin."

"Rose Williams?"

"Yeah, you know her?"

"Yeah, I live with her brother's family."

"Andy?" Herman nodded. "He's a good boy, that Andy." **Boy?** "Sure tamed that Gladys down. She was a heller."

"Mrs. Williams?"

"Bet your life. She was right in the middle of a peck of trouble one day. Seems this Mex thinner took a fancy to that red hair of hers and her flirty ways and was sidling up to her. Well, Willy—that's what we called your Uncle Cory then—saw that Mex talkin to her and saw a rattler at the same time. He scooped up that rattlesnake and jammed it right in that poor man's face. Killed him and nearly went to jail if it hadn't a been for this guy bein from Mexico and not havin any friends here in Cashmere."

"Well, that calmed Gladys down. Right about then she met Andy." Mr. Beeman cleared his throat, spat out the window. "Back to Frank. He sure liked his fun back in those days. Always jokin and laughin. Livin in a thinner's shack with Rose, playin banjo at night with her singing, tryin out the crazy songs kids were singing then. Just outside town about a mile down that road." He pointed at a side road coming up.

"Where?"

"Down there. See?"

"Yeah."

Mr. Beeman cleared his throat again. "Sure gonna miss Frank."

"Me, too."

They rode in silence for a while. Then Mr. Beeman tipped his hat back and wiped his brow. "Warmin up, isn't it?"

Herman nodded. "Yeah." They had moved out of the shadows of the orchards into the harsh summer sunlight.

"Roll down your window. Get some breeze in here." The window squealed as Herman cranked it down. The wind hit the green balls, which danced wildly, colliding with one another and the frame. *"Gonna give you some lunch, boy."* The sweat on Herman's face suddenly grew cold. "We'll be there soon. You only gonna be here for the day?"

"Yeah. Dad just wanted me to say hello and see how she was. I'm goin back tonight."

"Pretty long ride. And Greyhound transfers."

"Dad wrote everything out for me."

"Don't leave till late. You can stay with me and Myra, you know."

"That's okay. Are there many books?"

"A lot. I've got them in crates in the loft above the henhouse. There's a family living in your gramma's place right now."

"What happened to her?"

Mr. Beeman drove in silence for a while. Herman watched him. The muscle in the old man's jaw flexed and bunched. Then he glanced at Herman, then back to the road. "It was the divorce. That started it. The shame of it."

"Shame?"

"Not hardly any divorces in Cashmere. Can't remember a single one. Except Jake's. And remember, she was the principal of the grade school, widow of the Chief of Police, owner of her father's Apple Tree Apartments—an important lady. One that people looked up to. She got real angry when she heard about it. Had her first heart attack. And then the news about Frank…it just did her in." Herman's eyes stung. He looked out at the fields.

The truck swerved, pressing Herman against his door. "Well, here we are." Herman saw before them a large, one-story wooden building, a narrow, long rectangle. **Like an army barracks.** "It's not much of a place. I know Jake's strapped for money and the apartments never met their expenses since his dad died, but still… Well, it's not much of a place. Couldn't she have come to Boise?"

Herman shook his head. "Dad only has a basement room. That's why he boards me with the Williams. I hardly ever see him. He's really busy with the war bond drive now. They even gave him a leave from the newspaper."

Mr. Beeman turned off the motor. "Well. Well, let's go in." The glare of the sun was keen. **Like a knife blade. Something's gonna happen. I don't wanta go in there.** Herman pulled down the bill of his baseball cap so that its rim cut just below the sun. He followed Mr. Beeman into the building. Just inside the door sat a woman at a wooden desk.

"Mrs. Albertson, this is Herman Auerbach. Herman, she'll take you to your gramma." The woman nodded and smiled as she rose. She led Herman from the desk through another doorway into a long, narrow room, both of its sides lined with cots. Old women lay, head to foot, in these cots, their voices a cracked chorus of pleas and complaints. Mrs. Albertson led Herman down an aisle. **Vaseline. And shit. And old. The smell of old. Mold. Piss.** Sun slanted afternoon light through the floating motes before windows, unshaded, uncurtained. "Here." **Gramma.** Herman sat beside the bed and looked at his grandmother. **Uncle Frank's face. She's almost bald.** The woman's eyes were closed but her lips moved. Herman looked at her body, lightly covered with a sheet. She's so fat.

Herman's grandmother sits on the edge of her bed and rocks back and forth, back and forth, her crutches digging into the braided rug at the end of each swing. Suddenly she stands hunched over the crutches, swaying slightly back and forth, her huge body sagging toward the floor. She takes two steps, pivots, and sits in a wheelchair. **Like Lionel Barrymore.** *"Let's have some breakfast, Herman. Do you still like the apple butter?" She wheels toward the breakfast nook. They sit at the small table before the window. Soft light slants in through the branches of the evergreen outside. "I have some books that might interest you. Here, now." She wheels over to the stove and turns the heat on under a kettle of water. "Learn from the teapot, Herman. Even when it's up to its neck in hot water, it still whistles." Herman laughs. "Have you read all of the Billy Whiskers books I sent over?"*

"Yes. And Beautiful Joe. It was sad. I cried at the end. I read it over and over, hoping that he'd be alive again."

"Well, I have a sequel. Didn't I tell you that Beautiful Joe goes to heaven?"

"Can a dog go to heaven?"

"Why not? Would you unscrew this jar for me?"

"My dog, my Blondie, died this year."

"I know. That's why I hunted up this book."

"She wasn't like Beautiful Joe. She wasn't big and ugly and faithful or even obedient. She was little and pretty with floppy ears and she piddled all over the floor every time you touched her. And she'd run off. That's why she ran under the wheels of that truck. Mom carried her back. She hung down off Mom's arms. She was all crooked. And the truck driver was standing there crying as hard as I was. He was the one who bought me Rusty. He looked all over but he could only find a red cocker."

"I'm so sorry."

"I'd never had anything die before. I couldn't stop thinking about Blondie. Wishing that she was alive again. That it hadn't happened. I'd have daydreams about calling her just before the truck hit. It felt like bumping against a wall when you're walking in the night in a room in someone else's house. Bump. You're surprised. So you walk this way instead. Bump. Where are you? Bump. You start to get scared. You can't get out."

"Herman," she put her twisted hand on his. *"Herman."*

"Herman," she was looking at him. Her eyes were pale blue, their whites pink.

"Yes, Gramma."

"Is that you, Herman?"

"Yes."

She looked beside him. "Is that Jake?"

"No, he couldn't come."

"Who is it then?"

"No one, Gramma."

"I know it's you. Who else is here?" She was touching his hand. But her fingers turned in odd ways. **Arthritis. She's really bald.** "Where am I?" **Her voice is so high. It splits. Like Jean Arthur. No, it's higher. When it doesn't crack.**

"Herman?"

"I don't know, Gramma." **She's really bald. Women don't get bald.** "I don't know the name of where we are." She had closed her eyes again and was speaking in a low voice. "What?" The words came rapidly. She began to turn her head to the left. Then to the right. "I can't hear you." Now she smiled. "So pretty, David. So blue." **David. That's the Chief. She thinks the Chief is here.** "Hand me the paintbrush. Look at the kitten. Quickly, dear!" Her words became indistinct again. *"See that picture, the one to the left of my bed? Four kittens climbing an oak sapling. I painted that the first year of my marriage. The mother of those kittens brought David and me together. One night right here in Cashmere. I was out walking in a bad storm, coming back to the Apartments from teaching my class. And I saw a man. Right in front of the Apartments. Right there."* She points out the window.

"By the evergreen?"

She nods. "It was the Chief. Walking his beat. He stopped and bent over above a snowdrift. As I came closer, I saw that he had picked up a kitten, a little, mewing kitten, and he was slipping it into his overcoat. Though I didn't say anything to him—it wouldn't have been proper—I said to myself, 'That's the man that I am going to marry!'" She laughs. "And I did. That kitten was the mother of the kittens up there on the wall. She gave birth to them the first summer of our marriage and I painted them. As a gift to my husband. To David."

"Gramma?"

Suddenly she twisted her head toward him. Her eyes opened. As she turned into the sun, he saw that a film covered her right eye. "Jake?" Herman felt his teeth in his lower lip. **Ouch.** He licked his lip. **She's crazy. It's like Bedlam.** *Boris Karloff stands, head obediently bowed, eyes politely turned away from her and burning with hatred, mouth twisting slightly, "Mistress?"* He looked down the hall. **Where's the lady?** "Herman?" He turned back to her. She pulled her hand from under the sheet. "Herman. I thought you were your father." She pushed at the sheet. "You look so much alike." She sighed. "It's so hot in here. Is the window...?" She twisted to see the window behind her. It was open. The blue gauze curtains were hung, draped, still. "Where's Jake?"

"He couldn't come. Here, he wanted me to give you this." He held out Jake's letter. "And Cotlets from Mr. Beeman."

"Thank you. Jake's a good boy." She heaved herself up. She carefully leaned the letter against a book on the stand on the other side of the bed and set the box next to the book. She settled back, breathing heavily and closed her eyes. *Gramma hands him another rusk. He spreads apple butter on it.* **It sounds like sand paper.** *"Jake loved the Chief so much. Mr. Auerbach was always reading when he wasn't on duty. He read only German—until the First War began. Goethe was his favorite." She laughs at Herman's furrowed brow. "Goethe? He's a German writer. G-O-E-T-H-E. Say, 'Gerta.' We won't try the umlaut yet. Since you enjoy fantasy so much, you'll probably want to read Goethe some day. He wrote a beautiful story about a man named Faust, a man tempted by Satan and...well, you'll read it some day."*

"Tell me more about Dad when he was a little boy."

"He loved to sit on the rug at his father's feet. That little rug over there. The braided circle. It came with your grandfather's family from Dresden. The Auerbachs arrived in this country in 1850. Your grandfather's older brother fought in the Civil War and was a prisoner

in Andersonville. Jochen Stich, my ancestor, came here in 1753. You had seven grandfathers fighting in the Revolution." She moaned. **She's going to sleep again.**

"David. DAVID!" She suddenly screamed and sat upright, her sheet falling away. **Her thigh. Look at the blue veins.** Herman turned his head. He looked at the water glass. **Her teeth.** He looked back at his grandmother. She had closed her mouth, the lips compressed, folding inward, jaw small and fragile, curving into the creases of her neck. Then he looked at her right eye, at the film milky in the sunlight. He retched, the sting of acid at the back of his throat rising. **My God. Gramma.** He stood.

Outside, Mr. Beeman looked out the truck window. "So soon?"

"She wanted to sleep."

"Hmmm."

Sixteen

Herman smelled coffee. **Rich. Like cocoa. I bet it tastes great. Why can't I have any? Dad drinks it all the time. I wonder if anyone's in there?** When he walked into the kitchen, he saw Helen. **We're alone. Together.** She stood in the sunshine splashing through the window above the sink. She watched the coffee pot. She wore a pink chenille bathrobe. **Like Mom's.** A braided yellow chenille rose covered her pocket. **She's beautiful. God, she's so beautiful.** She looked up from the stovetop, brushed curls back from her forehead, and smiled. "Hey, thanks for the honey...honey."

"That's okay." Flush warmed his forehead. **What else can I say? Somethin. Come on, somethin. What?** Helen poured coffee into a blue mug. **Where did that come from? It's not cracked. All our mugs are cracked. It's the color of that eggshell that day.** *Herman sits on the lowest limb of the huge evergreen.* **Where Gramma met the Chief.** *On a mound of drab pine needles is something blue.* **An eggshell.** He looked at the Mexican boy on the oilcloth covering the kitchen table. **The Chief's dead. Gramma's gonna be dead. Uncle Frank's dead. Mom's gone. Dad's runnin the goddamn Seventh War Loan Drive. And Tom...** He looked up at Helen.

"Have you had breakfast?" Herman shook his head. "Well why don't you sit down and have some toast with me?" She began to slice bread. Sitting, Herman watched her move, her quiet flow from bread to butter to jam to table. "There's just Mom's strawberry jam left. I ate all of the honey you and Sonny got from Rose's bees." She laughed. "Honey and Sonny. It's a rhyme. Sonny's a limerick."

She dreamily looked down at the linoleum and then began to chant, at first slowly, then faster:

"There once was a kid named Sonny

Who went out hunting for honey.

The results of his search...."

She paused, then looked up at Herman and laughing, went on in a rush:

"Were bees in a birch

Who made Sonny's nose very FUNNY!"

Herman sputtered into laughter. Grinning, she put a plate of toast and a thick mug of coffee before him, lay her coffee and toast across from him and sat. The grin became a smile. "You probably like your coffee with lots of cream and sugar." He shook his head and gingerly sipped the coffee. **It's bitter.** She took a pack of cigarettes from her pocket. She tapped one out, and struck a kitchen match with a thumb, and drew on the cigarette, her face suddenly taut, sucking. **She looks tough now. Like Joan Crawford.** She looked up, smiled again, and held the pack out to him, framing a question with eyes and brow. He glanced at the doorway into the dining room. **Mr. and Mrs. Williams are gone to the store.** He took the cigarette. **This isn't a Lucky. It's funny shaped.**

"What are these?"

"Ovals. An English cigarette."

Herman inhaled, coughed three times. He coughed again. "They're strong."

"Mmmhmm." Helen spread margarine on her toast. "Why doesn't Mom ever put in the coloring?"

"I guess she gets too busy." Herman spread strawberry jam on his toast. "This is good. Have you tried it?"

Helen grinned. **Like Sonny. "**I'll bet I picked those strawberries. Have you ever seen all the jars she has down in the basement?" Herman nodded. "The summer before I enlisted, Max and I went out with a truckload of Mexicans every day for a month during the strawberry harvest. It's a hell of a way to earn money. Anyway, we came home every night with aching backs and boxes of strawberries. You know Mom. She had to preserve them." She took another bite of toast and then sipped coffee.

Herman took another drag off his cigarette and tried a smoke ring. "I met this funny guy named Al at my Uncle Frank's wake. He taught me a poem. You can sing it to 'Reuben, Reuben,' but I can't sing. It goes like this:

Oysters are prolific bivalves.

Have their babies in the shell.

How they diddle

Is a riddle.

I don't know so what the hell."

Helen sprayed toast and coffee over the table and Herman. **My God.** He looked down at his chest. Wet bread spattered the horizontal green and gray stripes of his pullover. Then he began to laugh. He spilled his coffee mug, hot liquid dousing his crotch, and he jumped back. His chair danced and rattled on the linoleum. Their laughter now soared.

"What are you guys laughin about?" Sonny stood in the doorway, grinning. **Like Helen.** "Hey, Hermy, you're drinkin coffee! And smokin!"

"Yeah, so what?"

"So Mom..."

Helen rose. "Want something to eat, kid brother?"

"Sure, I want some toast. Don't we have anything but Mom's strawberry jam?"

"Tough luck, kid. Don't you know there's a war goin on?" Helen began to slice bread. "Hermy, tell me about the time Rose's bees stung you. They took you to the hospital, huh? That must have been rough. Rose hates hospitals. Says they make people sicker. You got a lot of guts to go after my honey after that."

"I went too, Sis."

Herman's face flushed again. "Rose said when you fall off, get back on. So she showed us where some of her bees hung out and taught us how to make friends."

"Yeah, she taught Hermy and me how to go right up to em. Even pet them. You do it with a finger." Holding up a hand with the little finger stuck out, Sonny smiled as Helen handed him a plate of toast. "I wonder if you can teach bees tricks." He began to spread on strawberry jam. "Herman, how would you know if you got a bee to sit up?"

"When they wash their faces, they look like they're sitting."

"Isn't that the way flies wash their faces?"

Silence. Helen and Sonny crunched into their toast at the same time and, their mouths chewing, looked up at one another. Herman smiled. He asked,

"Have you ever seen bees circle around a person's head? That day, they circled around Rose's head like super fortresses right before I got stung. Then they looked like kamikazes."

"I remember that happened once when I was a little girl. My eyes almost popped out. They flew in formation in that circle for over an hour, and Rose just sitting there and talking like it was nothing. People always talk about her bees when they want somebody to believe that she really does have powers." Helen took a sip of coffee and looked into the cup. "I wonder where she is now. Probably doing tea leaves somewhere. I kinda miss her. I hear you saw her."

"At the wake. Yeah. She was doing good."

"Hey, Hermy, did you hear about your uncle?"

"Uncle Frank?"

"No, your Uncle Cory. He's in the Boise Jail. It was in the newspaper this morning. Mom read it out loud. They caught him. He was camping by the Snake. Out in the wilderness. But they can't prove he killed anybody." **He did.**

"Who is your Uncle Cory, Hermy?"

"His real name is William. William Pillton. Cory is short for Corregidor because he was at the Battle of Corregidor and got captured. He's about the third or fourth husband of my mother's sister, Auntie Ide. He killed some people. Besides Japs. He even shot at me once. That's where I got this." He bared the scar on his neck and rubbed it.

"Oh, honey, how awful. Why would anybody shoot at you?"

"Because I brought Gypsy into the chicken house."

"What gypsy? Rose?"

"Naw, not Rose. Did you know she has a twin sister Mae?"

Helen laughed again. "She's my aunt too, like Rose, remember?"

"Oh, yeah. What a dumbbell. I forgot." Herman's grew hot.

"I just can't see Mae in a chicken house." Helen laughed. **Her teeth are white. Like apple blossoms. And she smells like coffee and honey. Clear honey. Raspberry honey. Apple blossom honey. So many kinds of flowers for bees. Honey smooth and sticky on my fingers. Wax honeycombs to lick. I never thought much about honey before. Before Idaho...** "She loves the carnival. She wanted to be this bareback rider in the circus. Star-struck, Mom said. But it just never happened. When she was young, she had a child a long time ago. No father. No bareback riding. So she just follows the carnival, telling fortunes."

"How'd you know that, sis? I never heard about no Mae."

"You have to listen to the women talking in the kitchen to find these things out. Most men don't have the patience."

Sonny grinned again. **He's proud she called him a man.**

Helen laughed. "Without Mabel, I'd hardly know anything about life. Mabel and Ma say Mae fronts for a lot of young girls. Helps them meet men. For money. Some of them not much older than you, Herman." Helen looked at Sonny. "How's the toast, kid?"

His stomach was on a roller coaster, rushing, plunging, dipping, climbing, slowing, pausing. **Maybe it's the coffee. My stomach won't stop. I hate roller**

coasters. The day Dad made me ride that...what was its name? How old was I? The talk of Helen and Sonny flowed like the soft hush of a river. **The river.** Feelings began to flow, feelings of odd shapes, round or flat, gray, **Tom,** fast and then faster, now warm and smooth like honey, **better than anytime since Mom left,** now hard and jagged and cold. **Feelings. Like a roller coaster.**

Each time that he saw the faces of Corregidor and **Tom,** the roller coaster would plunge and jerk into blur and roar. **And Mom. But I can't see Mom any longer. It's like she's been gone forever. So far away. Like Africa someplace. Mom. Tom.** The wound on his arm ached. **Jesus.** Behind his brow, he felt something crack. Something behind his brow shifted. Two things ground together and came to a rest. **All coppa-whoppa-jaw. I'm getting dizzy. Stop it.** "Stop it," said Herman.

"Did you say something, Hermy?"

"He's just talkin to himself, sis. He's in a daze all the time. Just sits there movin his lips and lookin at somethin that isn't even there."

"Oh, silly, he's not in a daze. His mind was just elsewhere. If anyone here's dizzy, it's you, kid. I was saying, Hermy, our family sprawls all over the country. That's how Rose survives. She visits from place to place. Appears and disappears. Lord, my mother always hated to see her come until she started telling fortunes. Ma's superstitious. She wants to know, but she doesn't." She frowned. "I guess after what happened, Rose won't come around here for a long time. Maybe never." She sighed and began to stir her coffee. "Do you think I look like Rose? People say that. That I have her high cheekbones. And her high forehead. Not Ma's low brow. What do you think, Hermy?"

Herman looked at her as she turned sideways. "You don't look like either of them. You look like you." He looked down at his coffee. "You're beautiful!" he blurted out.

"Why, Hermy, you're sweet. But I don't mean how they look today. Nobody ever looks like their moms or aunts. You have to imagine them twenty-five years ago. Find the bones under the wrinkles and fat. But never mind that. Herman Auerbach, you've let me go all the way around the barn again. Tell me about this Uncle Cory and Gypsy."

"Okay, okay. You win." Helen's eyes flashed as she smiled again. **I wish she'd do that all day.** She pulled on her cigarette, blew a smoke ring, and watched it. Her eyes slid to Herman. "I've heard you before. Once you get going, you can tell a story. It's like you were a bottle and somebody uncorked you." As she rose from the table, she paused and looked down at him. "So tell me. Why'd he do it? Why'd he shoot you?"

"Aw, people say he's just naturally ornery and crazy. Never seen anybody mean as he is. He killed someone. Mr. Beeman—he's from Cashmere—says even before Corregidor. In a fight in an orchard." **Over Mrs. Williams.** "Anyway, he saw my rat Gypsy in his barn and started swearing about rats and chickens. He's wild and he's mean. Then he saw Tom..." **Why'd I say that? I can't talk about that. Tom. No. It's Helen. She makes me feel good. Listens like Mom used to. She understands. That's what happened. But I can't talk about that. I can't tell anybody about Tom. But Helen...** The roller coaster plunged again, now farther down than ever, where what had been was shattered. He heard his own voice far, far up there, but he couldn't make out the words. **Crank up that roller coaster. Get her off the track.**

"Yeah, Hermy's got a scar on his neck. And a tattoo. I wish I had a scar. And a tattoo." **Keep it up, Sonny, old boy. Keep up the chatter.** Herman's stomach began to loosen.

"Sis, can I sit on your lap like I used to when I was little?"

"You're getting a little heavy for this, Sonny, but okay. Nnngh! Sonny! Hey! You can't juggle up here. You'll put your sister's eye out. That's better. How'd you learn to do that anyway?"

"Oh, I just picked it up. I used to try and try to get those balls to stay up there. And they never did. And then one day when I didn't care anymore, they did. It just sorta happened one day. But when I think about them, then they always fall."

"Well, Sonny, you're as good as that clown we saw on stilts at the circus. Remember?" Sonny nodded. "Hermy, I got a proposition for you. Want to come with me to a baseball game next week? I got free tickets. An old friend of mine is playing. I've known him since we were in Lowell in the first grade, but I've never seen him play professional baseball. What do you say—want to be my date?"

"Me too," Sonny said immediately. **Goddamn it, Sonny. Make like a ghost and disappear.**

"Not you, little bud. But I will take you fishing down along the river. If you can stand still and keep your mouth shut while you hold the fishing pole."

"Oh boy! When can we go?"

"Well, what are you doing right now? I am on furlough."

"Hey, Sis! Wow!"

Herman rose from the table, "Come on, Sonny, I'll help you dig up some worms. It's better with flashlights at night but we can unearth something. Get it, Sonny? Unearth? That's one of your jokes." Herman poked Sonny's ribs as the boy wriggled off Helen's lap. **God, I feel good. I don't know when I've felt so good.**

Sonny punched Herman's arm. "Yeah, Hermy. I get it and you can have it right back in your fat face. Helen, do ya think we'll see any thugs down along the river? Hermy figured his Uncle Cory was hiding out down there. And damned if that's where they didn't find the son-of-a-bitch."

"Sonny! If Mom heard you...You sound just like Charlie. He been teaching you to talk like that?"

"Like what?"

"Like a sailor." **Uncle Frank. On the deck of his aircraft carrier, hosing down the fighter planes. He says "I looked over the side. Look at that! Gunners! Gunners! Open fire!"** *The white rat's head still rocks back and forth, back and forth.* **Where's the rest of her? Gypsy?**

"It's a wonder you're not smoking already." Sonny glanced at Herman. *A metallic click.* "Oh, Sonny! You're not old enough to smoke!" *Corregidor reaches into his shirt pocket. He pulls out a shining brass cartridge.*

"Only once. I only tried it once and it was awful. You can ask Hermy. I got real sick." **I'm getting real sick. Tom?** "He's in a daze again. Don't tell Ma about smokin. Please, Helen?"

"Well, go get those worms before I have second thoughts. And Herman, don't you forget about the ball game. Herman?"

"I'm tired of you, kid. Tired of you hanging around, tired of you and your questions, tired of you poppin off that BB gun, tired of you lookin at Iris all the time. So let's get on with this." Tom turns to look at Corregidor. "A Jap? You got a Jap in my barn, too?" Tom stands up. Corregidor smiles. **Tom?** *"Tom?"*

Corregidor slips the bullet into the rifle chamber. **Click.** *Tom bends. He stands again. He holds a pitchfork, prongs pointed at Corregidor. "You're one a them round-eyes sons-a-bitches came to the farm that night..." Tom charges Corregidor. Corregidor clubs the rifle and knocks the pitchfork away to the right, the boy falling to the left. Tom rises to his knees. Corregidor swings the rifle like a baseball bat, bashing in the right side of the boy's head, knocking him back against the wall. Tom lies against a bale of hay, straws on his forehead.* **Like jacksticks.** *His left shoe is gone. The bared big toe twitches once, twice. Corregidor stoops and with* *one hand pulls the boy up by the hair. Blood spills **like a river.** It masks the boy's face. **Like a flood.** He drops the boy back into the hay.*

"Shame on me. I ain't been no kind a host at-all. Gonna give you some lunch, boy." Herman hears the sound of a zipper. He runs. "Herman!"

"Herman!"

"What? Helen." Herman exhaled. The muscles in his shoulders relaxed, sloped. "Helen. I have somethin I wanna tell you."

Seventeen

Playing blackjack with Charlie late that afternoon, shuffling the heavy, sticky cards, Herman looked out the window and saw Sonny and Helen coming back again, sunburned and carrying two fish, rainbow trout, iridescent in the slanting light of late afternoon. They looked as if they were singing. Herman watched the sunlight on Helen's dark shiny curls and the sunlight glinting on the shimmering fish scales. Then he heard the song:

"I'm happy as a lark, be-lee-eev ME as we go rolling, rolling home." He watched Helen laugh and move. **She dances.**

"Deal, schlemiel!" He dealt. **Gotta get some cash for the ball game. Where's Dad now? When's the old allowance gonna kick in? I need some dough.** "Shit!" **Old Charlie's got another stinker.**

"Dealer pays twenty. Tough luck, Charlie." **Better than stealing. Easier on the nerves.** Coins glittered in a heap in front of him. **Dumb luck. When I want something this bad, I never get it. What's going on?**

"You think you're really somethin now, don't you? Big detective or something. Catchin the killer. Just like Tom Sawyer."

"Drop it, Charlie."

"Drop it? I'll drop it on you, schmuck! What you gotta do now? Go to a trial or somethin?"

"It's all over. The cops just asked me some questions and I answered, and it's gonna take care of itself. It's all over." **It's all over. It really is. Thanks. Helen. Thanks, Helen.**

"Herman! We're going to be late!" Helen and Sonny burst into the room shouting, Sonny waving trout. Water splattered onto the card table and, tipping over his chair, Charlie jumped back.

"Goddamn you."

"Charlie! Hey, look at these trout, Hermy! I wonder if they're big enough to enter in the Derby. Maybe I could beat Dad!"

"If a goddamn ranger caught you, you'd be in the pen along with Hermy's uncle. Those are small fry, squirtso—fresh outta the tank."

"You losin at blackjack, Charlie?" Sonny ducked as Charlie swatted him.

"Did you hear, Hermy? We're going to be late. Get a jacket in case it cools off."

"Helen!" Gladys called from the kitchen. "You come right in here and help me set the table. You're gonna eat first."

"I've got tickets to the ball game, Ma. Don't you remember? Get Charlie to help for a change." Helen and Herman went down the hall for his jacket. They looked at each other and laughed as Gladys shouted, "Charlie!" Charlie groaned.

Herman stopped at the hall closet and looked in at his lumberjack jacket. **Mom gave me that.** The pocket was torn and the sleeves too short. **And it's over the hill.** He looked on the top shelf of the closet and found a jacket Gladys had given him that had belonged to Max. He pulled it down and tried it on. The sleeves of the dark blue jacket were the right length. "How's this look, Helen?"

"That used to be Max's, didn't it? I always liked it. But it looks better on you, kid. Matches your eyes."

"Here's lookin at you, kid." He threw his shoulders back. **Throw those shoulders back, soldier. Soldiers, shoulders.** He grinned. **And suck in your gut.** Helen smiled at him. He smiled back. **Now all I need to do is get me a new pair of shoes. And not at Sears.**

"Let's go down the alley, Hermy. So Mom doesn't think this through and remember I never said anything to her about it. Mr. Turner said he was going that way and would give us a lift. We'll eat hot dogs for dinner. On me."

When they got to the ballpark and were standing in the line to go through the turnstiles, Helen said "You did a good thing, Hermy, telling me about your Uncle Cory. I know it was tough on you."

"It's all over with. It's all right." The line moved up slightly toward the ballpark gate. "Who's your old friend on the baseball team?"

"The second baseman, Jay McKee. He used to live next door but I haven't seen him for a long time. I'll introduce you to him afterwards. If I can find him."

"Mmm-hhh." **What about this Donald everybody was talking about? Is she going to marry him? Who the hell is he?** "What about Donald?"

"What about Donald?" Helen asked with a sharp edge Herman hadn't heard in her voice before. She frowned at him.

Herman looked away. "Where is he?" He finally mumbled.

"In Germany. I don't know where. We're not engaged anymore. Is that what you mean? Something happened, but I haven't told the family yet. Why do you want to know all this?"

"Sorry. Dunno."

Helen took two tickets from her pocketbook and handed them to the old man at the turnstile.

"To your right," he said.

When she turned back to Herman, Helen was smiling again. "You're going to like these seats. My friend Jay got them for us. They're right down in front. Box seats. Right off first."

An old man under a baseball cap and wearing a satin jacket with **Pilots** stitched on the chest ushered Helen and Herman to their box seats, produced a large red, white-figured bandanna and elaborately dusted off each of the seats, then bowed to Helen. Laughing, brushing tight black curls back from her forehead, Helen daintily sat and then nodded to him and Herman.

Eyes scanning the field, Herman plopped beside her. "Damn, this is great. I know one of the baseball players too. The catcher. I've known him for a long time. Him and me have the same tattoos like your Aunt Mae's.

"I like your tattoo, Herman. It was the first thing I noticed about you. A rose and a snake, wiggling like our worms did today. Sonny loves it when they wiggle around when he puts them on the hook. I think I'd like a little tattoo someday. Just one little flower where nobody could see it. What do you think, Hermy?"

"Yeah, tattoos are nice. Outside of Mae, I never saw one on a woman. Herman flushed again and felt the scar on his neck tingle.

"So you've been here before, Hermy?'

"Been here, hell. My dad and I used to live here. Before they started playin ball again. It was so quiet around here my dad used to sunbathe naked right out there in the outfield. Made me feel funny." He glanced at Helen and blushed. "Well it did. I never saw him naked before. He wouldn't only close the bathroom door but lock it. My family wasn't like yours. We didn't come and go in the bathroom like it was Main Street. And then he got naked out here. Look." He pointed at the empty third base.

"What?"

"That's where he used to lie." Helen looked at him. "Belly up!" They suddenly burst into laughter. Then the team came out of the dugout and the announcer began to introduce the teams. Helen waved her pink handkerchief at McKee, but the second baseman didn't look up.

After the game got underway, Herman hunched forward in his seat. He watched Sandy's signals and the pitcher's windup. The pitcher was a redhead. "Sandy's gonna have his hands full tonight," Herman said to Helen. "That's Wild Red. He told me about the guy. 'Wild pitcher with wild red hair like on a wild baboon.' Used to be a fielder. He was in trouble with the law so much they wouldn't draft him. Figured he'd be more trouble than a Jap. Sandy says half of these guys learn ball at the State Pen. Has Jay been in prison?"

"Do I look like I would know a convict?"

"Well," Herman looked her up and down. "Let me give that a little thought." He closed his eyes, then opened them and looked at her again. "You got a couple brothers named Max and Sonny? The Williams boys?"

"Oh, you!" Helen punched him on the shoulder. "You're the one with relatives in the hoosegow."

Herman stopped smiling. "They made me call him Uncle. He's no relative of mine. Just some stray my aunt picked up."

Helen looked back at the ball field. "If he's such a wild pitcher, do you think it's safe to sit this close?" Helen asked.

"I can catch almost anything. Sandy taught me." Herman watched intently as the first two batters both hit pop flies. Wild Red hit the third batter who went to first.

"See what you mean." Helen said.

Wild Red walked the next man and Sandy went out to the pitcher's mound. Herman could see him talking and spitting, his mouth moving around words and chewing tobacco, but Herman was too far away to hear what was being said. *"Herman, I want you to develop these pics of Wild Red. We're going to feature them in the upcoming nationwide Red Pouch Chewing Tobacco campaign. Wild Red. Red Pouch. Get it?"*

"Got it, Pop! I'll get on it right away." Torrent of images: developing the pictures, holding the negatives up to dry over the laundry sink in the dark basement where the smell of starch reminds him of his mother. He ponders the action shots, becomes Wild Hermie, chawing, shaking off Sandy's first signals, scratching his crotch, pulling his hat down, spitting on the ball, turning the seams in his hand, feeling the power in his left arm, his pitching arm, the muscles bulging. All these people in the crowd looking at him for the first time, making him feel good. Now the wind up, leg up, arm back, and a fastball right at Sandy, mask back down and crouched behind the plate.

Wild Red worked up to a full count on the batter. Then he threw. Sandy caught the ball, stood up, took his mask off and shouted "Way to go, Red. Another strikeout." He headed for the dugout. The umpire hadn't called anything, but slowly as Sandy firmly walked away, he called "Stee—rike!" and knotted his fist as he motioned the stunned batter out. The batter's jaw dropped open and a stream of obscenities spewed forth, but the umpire held firm, feet planted solidly apart, arms crossed.

"Did you see that?" Helen asked.

"That's why they call him a magician," Herman explained.

"But did you see that?" Helen added, "And he's good looking besides."

"A damned magician, that's what they say."

The next time Sandy walked into the on-deck circle swinging two dark, heavy bats around his head, Herman stood up, cupped his mouth and yelled, "Hey Sandy!" Sandy looked up and waved both bats at him. Herman and Helen grinned at each other, hugged. When Sandy same up to bat, he struck out, swinging.

"Too bad it's not Wild Red pitching against Sandy. Sandy could've tagged that ball and sent it outta here."

"Is he a homerun hitter?"

"Yeah. Well, sometimes."

After the 3-2 win, Helen took Herman to the door of the locker room to wait while the ball players showered. Several boys younger than Herman also waited. Herman recognized the guard, the one who had been there before. The second baseman came out, hair damp and slicked back. Helen called to him, "Jay. Jay!" They hugged. "That was a great hit tonight!"

"Sign this for me, and one for my little brother, will ya Jay?" one of the young boys asked.

While Jay was signing autographs, Sandy came out. "There you are, Herman. I was afraid I'd miss you again. Well, and who is this lady?" Helen blushed.

"Helen, this is Sandy. Helen is on furlough from the war," Herman explained.

Sandy whistled. "One beautiful lady. You two know each other?" Sandy asked Jay, whose arm rested on Helen's shoulders. As the men talked, Helen watched Sandy. Herman watched Helen.

* * *

A week later, Herman and Sonny were playing cards. The game was War. Herman's deck had red roses and Sonny's blue. The game had gone on for a long time, piles of cards growing thicker, only to shrink with the next conflict. No one seemed able to hold an advantage. Finally, a knock at the door brought Sonny to his feet. Herman heard Sandy's voice. "Hi, is Helen Williams here?"

Leaving Sandy standing in the doorway, Sonny went to get her. Before Herman could move away from the card table, Sandy saw and called out "Herman. How's the pitchin arm?"

"Okay," Herman replied. "What's up?"

"What'd you think about the team last week?" Herman shuffled the deck. "Hey, you should come out to more of the games. I can get you tickets. Watchin the game isn't as good as playin but watchin teaches you strategy."

"Yeah." They fell silent. Then Herman asked, "What do you want Helen for?"

"We're goin to a movie tonight." Just then, Helen came down the stairs. Herman stood, shoved his hands into his pockets and balled them into fists. Smiling, Helen reached out a hand to Sandy and, smiling, he held it gently. They said good night and left, still hand-in-hand and smiling.

Herman gathered up the cards, blocked them with sharp raps on the table, looked up at Sonny, squeezed the ends of the deck, and sprayed the cards all over the boy. "Fifty-two Pickup, Sonny." He left the room.

* * *

"Boys," Gladys entered the room. "Helen's almost ready now. Are you? Hermy, go and get the honey." Herman went out to the porch and reached under his cot for the small Mason jar full of honey capped by beeswax. While Helen was packing her things into a duffle bag, the boys came into her room with the gift. Sonny made the presentation. "You liked the last one so well, we went out and got us another one. It'll be good for you," Sonny said. "I heard a doctor say so on the radio." Helen kissed him and wept. Sonny squirmed away and ran to the kitchen. **I wish I had given her the honey.**

As Herman started to speak to Helen, Gladys entered the bedroom. She had sprinkled and steam-pressed her daughter's uniform and now held it out to her. "Herman, give Helen some privacy now." She turned to Helen. "I can't understand why you have to go back. The war in Europe is over."

"Mom, you just can't leave the Army like that. There's lots to be done over there. The German cities are leveled to the ground. People are starving."

"Well, I think they have it coming to them."

"Mom." Helen embraced her mother. Herman left the room.

Max called from the front door. "Hey, come on! I've got Bill's car outside and he's gonna want it back in an hour."

"Mom, I'll just pack the uniform and go this way." Herman left Helen packing and went into the living room. He sat on the davenport staring at Helen's picture on the table before him until Andrew Williams called him to leave.

The Williams family arrived at the Depot Vista just as the train arrived, filled with women, pregnant women, women with babies, and small children in their arms. Helen began to cry, "I'm sorry, Ma, I can't help it. Look at the babies."

Gladys held her. "If you don't stop, honey, I'm gonna start bawling too, and I haven't done that in a public place since 1926."

"What happened in 1926, Ma?"

"You don't even want to know."

That evening, when Charlie and Herman had finished their cigarettes, they walked from the alley around the block to enter the house by the front door. Charlie put a hand on Herman's arm. "Careful now. Don't get too close to her while the smoke's fresh." Then he opened the door. Gladys was weeping, Sonny standing beside his father who was leaning over the large chair in the living room to comfort her. She looked up at the two boys. "Max is gone."

"Gone?"

Sonny grinned. "He's gonna fight the Japs."

Eighteen

The August sun sucked steam from the canoe's sides as Herman steadied it on the sawhorses while Sonny heaved a galvanized pail of water into it and Charlie squatted under it, looking for leaks. Herman pushed his glasses up on his nose. The canoe rocked and Charlie's head popped out. "Goddamn it, hold it steady, Auerbach! If you guys keep diddlin around like this, we're not goin to be ready tomorrow to launch the Sacajawea."

Sonny dropped the pail on the front lawn and squatted beside Charlie. "Leak. There's a leak, Charlie. See? A drip? Right there. Water leakin through. See there? A leak. Charlie. Charlie. What ya lookin at?"

Charlie let out a long wolf whistle. "Will you take a gander at that blonde!"

Herman turned. In the sun and shadows under the umbrellas of maple and elm, two women moved toward the trio of boys. **One young. Blonde. One old. Fat. Silk dress with huge red flowers. Hawaiian. She always said the flowers were Hawaiian.** Now the scar on his neck prickled. **Ide. Ide and Iris. Ide in her church dress, the same one she had worn every Sunday to the Baptist Church.** *Rustle of silk. Drone of the minister's voice.* Ide's nudge. *"Stand up and sing, Hermy." Ide's low voice.* **Alto. Mom calls it alto.** *"We are gathered at the river."* Red *ribbon marking the hymn. Sermon-talk. Eternity. Song again. Nudge.* Ide's whisper *"Watch what's goin to happen."* **Why's that man going up there? He's taking off his coat and his shoes. He's getting into the tank. The minister's pushing his head down.** *"In the name of the Father."*

Again. "*In the name of the Son.*" **Wait. He's coughing. He's choking. He can't breathe. No. He's pushing him down again.**

"*In the name of the Holy Spirit.*" **I hate being under water. Ever since Dad threw me in. I won't breathe until that man comes up.**

Charlie whistled again. Herman gave his good arm a punch. "Cut it out, you sex maniac. That's no dame. That's Iris. My cousin."

"Herman?"

"Auntie Ide." **Auntie. Just like a little kid. Gotta stop hanging around Sonny.** "What're you doin here?"

"Iris and I planned that when the apple-thinnin was over, we'd spend a weekend in Boise to see Cory at the jail and to visit you. We've never been to Boise before."

"I've never been out of Washington. All that desert out there, Hermy. And it's so hot. Worse than the wheat fields." Iris brushed back a strand of damp hair from her forehead. "It's good to see you." Charlie and Sonny grinned. "How you doin?"

"I'm just fine." Herman's eye caught a movement at Iris' breast. From the edge of a small blue pocket trimmed with a white rose a small green head. **Lizard?**

Iris' eyes lowered. She laughed. "Oh. This is Reilly. He's yours Hermy. All yours." She slipped a green ribbon of garter snake from her pocket, held its head over his shirt pocket, and the creature drew itself off her palm into the new darkness. "He likes you." She smiled at him. He smiled back. **She's lovely.**

"Gee, Hermy, I never saw a girl with a snake in her pocket before."

Charlie punched Herman's arm. "Ask the lady to come along tomorrow."

* * *

The next morning, reaching out for the blue juggling ball, Sonny hopped on one foot, then the other. He backed up a step into the porch trellis and his fatigue shirt hung up on thorns studding sprawling canes bent out and blooming with heavy scarlet roses.

"Hermy, help!"

"Don't move! You'll tear it, Sonny. Your mother'll skin you alive. Hold still." Hot sun flat and heavy on his back, lips pressed together in a thin line, Herman snapped off one thorn after the other until the olive drab cloth hung free. "There. Some days, kid, you're more trouble than you're worth. Hey. Look. Now you've dropped your ball. How the hell are you gonna juggle in a canoe?"

"I'm bringin em cause what if I need somethin to do? What if you're all moonin around over Iris and I don't have nothin to do?"

"Sonny, where did you learn how to talk?" Herman lilted in falsetto, "Moonin around?"

"That's what Ma used to say about Max and his girlfriends—there he goes moonin around again. That's what she used to say. But ya know, Hermy, Ma was wrong about somethin. She was wrong about me needin bean bags to juggle. I learned with balls. She's hardly never not right."

"This conversation's makin me dizzy."

"So what if he doesn't come, Hermy? What then?" Sonny had two balls in the air forming perfect arcs. The teeth clenching his protruding tongue tip now began to open, release.

"Worry wart. Max's friend came last time, didn't he?"

"That was before Max left." As Sonny's eyes followed the blue arc of his balls, his face lengthened, drooped under his fatigue cap.

"You miss him, don't ya, kid?"

"He's my big brother. The only one I got left since Matthew was killed."

"Well, most of the time, when he's not teasin you, Max takes pretty good care of you, doesn't he?" Sonny nodded. "So, see? Max's friend will come. Let's see some more of that jugglin. Can you do three balls?"

"Assholes." Legs crossed at the angles, Charlie leaned against the doorsill at the porch's top step. "Good old Max blew it. His friend called. Somethin about a girl and her rich uncle and how he could take us next week but not tomorrow. So I told him about a trip his fancy black coupe could take up his fat ass. Then I hustled us a ride at the pool hall."

"What kinda ride?"

"A truck. And a chauffeur. That's a hell of a lot better than that old Ford coupe. We'd a had to strap the canoe on the roof, and with four of us, one of us'd had to ride on the runnin boards all the way to the river."

"I'd ride on the runnin board." Sonny started juggling again. "Like Dick Tracy."

"So where is this guy?"

"He'll be here at 8:30, Auerbach, old boy. No sweat."

"Wait a minute, Charlie," Sonny began as Charlie lit a cigarette and sat down on the porch step. "How'd you get this guy to be our chauffeur? He didn't just walk up to you and say, 'Charlie, how about if I take ya out to the river tomorrow so ya can try out your new homemade canoe,' did he Charlie?"

"None of your business, squirt." Charlie leaned back against the porch rail. Sonny resumed juggling. Charlie blew a smoke ring into its center. Herman watched the smoke. **What if I fall out of the canoe? How deep is the water?** Sonny asked again. Charlie focused on Sonny. "Well, there was this Basque. Lives over round the river. Truck farmer with a truck. Get it?" Sonny shook his head.

"Truck farmers grow vegetables," Herman explained. "It's a joke." Sonny stuffed the blue balls into his pockets.

"Well, he's a young guy. Big bastard. So he wanders into the pool hall and takes a squint around. And he sees me, sizes me up, and he says, thinkin he's a goddamned comedian, 'When did grade school get out?' He thinks everybody's gonna laugh. And a couple do. The ones who don't know me. I don't say nothin. I just push a ball around with the stick and miss some set-ups. 'Want some lessons, kid?'"

"'Sure mister,' I say. 'What in? Shovelin sheep shit? That's what Basques use for manooer, I hear. Get it from their friends and lovers.' All the regulars laugh and he gets all red-faced and says he's gonna teach me a lesson about my mouth and I say, 'Well, put your money where your mouth is.'"

Sonny laughed. "That's a good one, Charlie." He looked at Herman. Herman yawned and sat on the edge of the canoe. **Where's Iris?**

"'You wanna bet a buck?' he says."

"So I say, 'Bet you? Money on the table, mister. Put your money where your mouth is.'"

"Then he gets real smart-assed and says, 'So how're you gonna play pool, cowboy, with one gimpy arm?'"

"And I say, 'Like a trained seal. Money on the table.'"

"'Easy buck,' he says."

"'Make it two and you got a bet,' I say. Puts a two-spot on the table and says nobody can bluff him. So I pull out the two-spot I'd already won off of Freddy before the spick came in. And while he's settin up the balls, some guy starts raggin him about his new little mackerel snapper bride who thinks it's sinful to gamble. Specially with the tomato money. That's what he's bettin with—his wife's tomato money."

"So who won, Charlie? Ya never said."

"Just hold your goddamn horses, squirt. I'm teachin you about technique here. After ten minutes, he's only gotten two shots in, and the old shark here has cleaned the table and pocketed the dough. Well, old farmer boy he's cussin away when one of the regulars finally gets pissed off and says, 'I think you owe him another two-spot, mister.'"

"And he says, 'How come?'"

"'For the gimpy arm. You know, March of Dimes contribution.' Some other regulars chime in about teachin the Basque a lesson, comin in a white man's pool hall, drunk on Basque wine already and not drinkin any beer, and insultin the boys. Then some guy says he knows the spick's wife—Angela, he says her name is—and says he thinks we oughta give her a little telephone call. Well, old Pancho turns real white and the mastermind here gets a bright idea and says, lookin all innocent, 'I got me a brand new canoe just yearnin for some white water. You got a truck out there?' He nods. 'How about a ride?' He looks at me. I walk over and smile right in his face and tuck the two-spot into his bib overalls. 'And here's little Angela's tomato money. Wouldn't wanna break up a happy marriage.' He still just looks at me. So then I says, 'Or maybe I could give it to Angela herself. Someone here know where this guy lives?'"

"Old Bob says he does. So then the Basque looks around at the other guys. Bob says, 'Your play, Jose.' So you see, squirt? I got him in a corner, and he can't refuse. You see what I mean, about technique?"

"Yeah. Now I know how to blackmail a dumb hick."

"You're learnin, squirt. Well, speak of the devil."

An old gray pickup truck rattling across from them slowed down. Leaning out the front window, the driver scanned houses. Charlie waved and shouted, "Hey Pancho!"

"Is that really his name? Like Cisco's Pancho?"

"Hell, how should I know?"

The truck stopped and out clambered a deeply tanned man well over six feet tall, straight black hair falling in his eyes. He glowered at Charlie. "So that's the goddamn canoe. Well, Sundays ain't no holiday for me. Get that goddamned canoe loaded up. Time I get you where you're goin and git back, half the mornin'll be gone. When I left Angela off at the cathedral, I told her I was gonna pick up a heifer this mornin. She's been wantin a milk cow. My goddamned head ached so much this mornin, the heifer was the only thing I could think to make up as an excuse for missin church. So not only do I have to put up with a goddamn hangover and bein blackmailed by you, you sneaky little bastard, but I have to figure out what to tell Angela when I come home with no heifer." He shook his head and rubbed his neck.

"Hey, mister," Sonny grabbed hold of his wrinkled blue sleeve, "Does your wife like birds?"

"Listen, kid, I don't know how the hell you got mixed up with this bastard, pardon my Spanish, but I got a bitch of a hangover and I don't cotton to bein blackmailed along with bein made a fool of, so shut up and get into the back of the truck."

"Your eyes don't look too good, mister. They're all red around the edges, but all I want to know is does your wife like birds?"

"How the hell should I know?"

"She's your wife, isn't she?"

"In the truck, kid. You're pissin me off."

"Listen, mister, I'm just givin you a cover story. My ma sells canaries. See those yellow birds up there in that tree right above your head? Those are just the extras. They're the ones that don't sing. Ma's been tryin to get rid of them cause we got too many. They won't fly away. We got lots more inside. So you bring your wife a pair of canaries and make her think you were foolin her all along so you could surprise her with a present and she forgets all about the heifer. Lots of people buy canaries for presents."

"Kid, you're not listenin to me. Get in the goddamn truck. Do I look like a walkin birdcage salesman? Where'm I gonna put canaries?"

"Well, how bout that silver pail? We could put somethin over the top."

Herman touched Sonny's elbow. "Sonny, that's your mother's pail for scrubbin floors. You really want to make her that mad?"

"Besides, they'd just fly out of the pail when I got them home. I don't keep birdcages in the barn neither. Get in the truck, kid."

Sonny and Herman both opened their mouths at the same time. "Fred Astaire."

"Hey, mister, we got a cage that's perfect. I'll pick out a couple of real nice ones for ya. As long as I leave her favorites, Ma will never miss them, and will Dad be glad you came. They won't cost nothin. And you can keep the cage, too." Sonny bolted for the cellar door at the back of the house.

"Funny kid," the Basque muttered, rubbing his neck again. "Better make it snappy!" he shouted after Sonny. "We need to get this goddamn show on the road."

Herman turned to Charlie. "But Iris isn't here, yet."

"Listen here." The Basque's voice gathered volume. "Canoe goes in the truck. The minute that kid gets back we shove off. Take it or leave it." He swung into the truck cab and slammed its battered door. Charlie and Herman dropped the tailgate and began to load the canoe onto the bed.

"So, where's Cinderella, Auerbach, old man?"

"I thought she'd be here by now."

"Who is this lovely, anyhoo? You been keepin secrets from Father Charles?"

"Last time I saw her she had freckles all over her and Indian braids. She wore her brother's striped t-shirts, the kind you buy from Sears."

"She's some looker now." Charlie wolf-whistled loudly.

"Leave her alone, Charlie."

"So where is she, Auerbach? You think Cinderella's gonna show?"

"She'll be here. It's better than goin to the jail. She never liked Cory Pillton. I don't know anybody who did, but she had to live around him."

"Well, what's your aunt marry him for anyway, Hermy?" Sonny was scrambling over the back of the truck's tailgate with Fred Astaire's cage filled with fluttering yellow birds. Sonny reached over and banged his hand on the back of the truck's window, waving at the Basque. "Hey mister, I got ya Lana Turner the Third. All the Lana Turners have some black on their wings. And Una Merckle and Charles Coburn."

"Peachy. Just peachy," the Basque shouted back as he started the truck and let out the clutch with a jerk, backing over the curb. They had gone a block when Charlie spotted Iris and Ide. He yanked Herman's sleeve and pointed. The woman and girl walked down the sun-rippled sidewalk, the heat already shimmering around them.

"Stop the truck!" Charlie yelled at the Basque as he banged on the back window. "There's the dame!"

"Shut up, Charlie. She's not a dame. She's my cousin."

Ide handed Iris a brown grocery sack after she had swung up into the truck bed. "Now honey, be careful. Remember my dream. You and your brother were both out in the river's deep water trying to save each other. And then you both drowned." Ide had tears in the corner of her eyes. "If I lost another child…" she choked.

"Ladies, this ain't a tea room."

Iris touched her mother's shoulder. "Ma, that was Ralph who drowned. He didn't know how to swim, and he was drunk. Thomas died cause he fell out of the tree and broke his arm. He was choking on the green apples when he threw up from the ether."

"Say your goodbyes, ladies. This bus is leavin,'" the Basque shouted as the truck began slowly to pull away from the curb, Ide and Iris waving to each other until the truck and the diminishing woman faded from each other.

Sun battered the truck. Shrinking from its heat, Sonny huddled under the canoe. Herman and Iris leaned in the shadow cast by the truck cab. Facing them, Charlie sat with his back against the gate. As the truck lurched over rock and pit in the ancient road leading to the river, Iris had thrown an arm around Herman's shoulders and leaned close to him to talk. **I could love her. She looks like... just like...**

"She always starts to cry when she thinks about my brother. That dream doesn't make any sense. Thomas didn't drown and I'm a good swimmer."

"She thinks I looked like Thomas." **What am I getting into here?**

"You know, she made us some sandwiches. And last night she walked up to a funny little tavern on the corner and bought this green bottle of sparkling wine. She said it's for the christening."

"The christening?"

"You know, like in the 'March of Time'? Some lady always bangs a ship with a bottle of champagne when they launch it from the shipyard."

"How could we forget?" Herman smacked the side of his head in mock disbelief and then grinned. "She's right."

"How come you got a flower for a name?" Sonny asked.

Herman tossed a handful of hay at the canoe. "Sonny, get back under your shell! You're 'how comin' again."

"Did you say hummin, Hermy?" Sonny began humming loudly "Row Row Row your Boat." Iris giggled.

"Kid, I'm losing my patience."

"Yeah, Hermy, I can see the steam comin outta both of your ears. Just like Popeye's before he smacks Bluto a good one."

Herman reached across Iris and swatted at Sonny under the canoe. Iris put her hand on Herman's forearm and said, "He's just a little kid."

"Well, he's gettin bigger and he gets away with a whole lot sometimes." Herman liked the warmth of Iris' hand on his arm.

"He just asked about my name. People do that all the time. My Mom's name starts with an 'I' so she named me Iris, to be like her, but not exactly. I'm her only girl."

"I changed this snake's name from Reilly," Herman said softly, touching his shirt pocket. "It's a girl." He looked into the pocket. "I'm naming her Iris. The Second."

Iris smiled. "You've got her with you?"

"I was gonna put her in the nest in the forsythia bush. We keep adding them, Sonny and me. We're makin a Snake Farm. But I really liked her, so I brought her with me today."

"When you put her in with the others, how will you tell which one is Iris?"

"Oh, I'll be able to tell. There's a little red around one eye."

"Oh, look at that! Ugh!"

"What, Iris?"

"Back there. There was a dead squirrel and these other little squirrels were eating it."

Charlie laughed and shouted across the truck bed. "Gophers, honey, gophers. Hard to find meat out in the sagebrush. We oughta do the same thing—get rid of rationing." He reached out and yanked Sonny's foot. "You'd make a good stew." Sonny yelled and kicked. Grinning, Charlie leaned back against the truck gate. The truck heaved and swayed, creaked and banged, wooden bed and iron frame filling its place in the desert with sound.

Sonny came out from under the canoe and pulled at Iris' sleeve. She looked down. "Do you know my mother?"

"I remember her from a long time ago. She's my aunt," Sonny's eyes widened. "You didn't know we're cousins? One of Mom's husbands was her stepbrother. In fact, she visited once when I was a little girl. I sat on her lap and she braided my hair. I had hair down to there." She pointed to her slender waist.

"Herman said you had braids and ugly old freckles when you was a girl."

"There you go again, shrimp. You made that up. I'm gonna pop you."

"Well, maybe the ugly part I made up. That's cause Darlene has ugly old freckles. She's in my class at school. She wears glasses and she sticks her tongue out at me. I hate Darlene."

"That's cause little boys always hate girls, dummy," Charlie said.

"Oh. So you do talk as well as wolf whistle," Iris' voice was clear but level, her head tilted slightly up as she looked down the length of the of truck at the scowling boy.

Charlie suddenly grinned. "Hey, baby, come on down here and see what it's like to sit next to a man for a change." Charlie held out his good arm.

"Leave her alone, Charlie."

"Butt out, shorty. Whose show is this? Who thought up this canoe? Who got us this ride?"

"Max, Max, and Max. Except if we took his ride, we'd still have our eyeteeth left."

"Charlie, Charlie, and Charlie. Max walked."

Iris' voice cut into Herman's retort. "Who's Max?"

"Max is my big brother," Sonny explained. "Max. Max. Max. Miss Max. He ran away to be a soldier. At least we think he did. Boy, was Ma mad."

"Prolly just ridin the broom that day."

Herman rose to one knee. "Shut up Charlie. Besides, what do you know about it?"

"I know Max."

"Well, I know him better'n you." Sonny stood up with his hands on his hips. The truck swayed and he stumbled. "What broom?"

"You ain't old enough to know. So sit down, squirt. You're gonna fall out of the truck. And we ain't gonna stop. The gophers can have you for lunch."

"I wish Max would come home." Sonny's lip trembled.

"Of course you do, honey. I still miss my twin brother, and he died a long time ago." Iris put her arm around Sonny. She leaned back against Herman again. He felt her cool smooth arm brush his hand. **God.**

"Hey, baby, how come those two are the only ones who get any sympathy? Here you are all over the kid cause he's feelin bad about Max. And you bring Herman presents and moon over him. What does a guy have to do to get some attention from a beautiful dame? Have a brother who enlists?"

Herman rose again, swayed with the truck, staggered and reached for the rail. "Leave her alone, Charlie. She's not a dame and she doesn't need to hear your song and dance."

"You want to see a goddamn song and dance?" Charlie lightly mounted the truck gate and side rail, shifting his feet lightly, falling, falling with the fall, catching his balance, and riding his center again and again as the truck bumped and heaved its crazy path. Iris and Sonny laughed and applauded.

We're getting close to the river. His stomach clenched. **Gotta keep calm. Keep my balance.** He looked back at Charlie, who briefly stood on one foot, the other knee bent. **Like him.** His testicles rose, balled up. He took a deep breath, held it. **Relax. Relax. Nothin's gonna happen. Nothin. And if it does...** Sun slanting through the trees suddenly sparkled on water, shattered the water into dancing bits. He closed his eyes. The shards of sun danced behind them, red, then blue. **Ah. That's what they say in the comics. Aaaah! Cool and wet. Out of the goddamn desert. We're here.**

Nineteen

"Nice day for a canoe launch, ain't it, boys?" Charlie stooped to lift the canoe across the flat bank into the river. He glared under his eyebrows at the others. "One of you 4F's gonna give me a hand?" Then he lifted the bow, grunted.

"Me first!" Sonny shouted, running to the stern of the canoe, feet sinking in the white sand. One of his shoes came off. He stopped to jam his foot back into it. Charlie lowered the canoe and sighed.

"This ain't a contest, Sonny. This is a solemn occasion." He grinned. "We're a-gonna launch this-here beloved canoe," Charlie raised the volume. "THIS HERE CANOE, brethren, into this here river—I SAY UNTO THE RIVER–this 5th day of August IN THE YEAR OF OUR LORD, 1945, a day we will all remember. Now bow your heads and pray."

"Ever thought of bein a preacher, Charlie? You sound like the Baptist preacher givin his John the Baptist story right before he pushes somebody down into the immersh….immersh…the big tank."

"Where do you get this crap, Sonny?" Charlie picked up the canoe again.

"Immersion tank. Ma taught me that word. It's the right word." Sonny grunted as he tried to lift the stern.

"Sonny, don't worry. We're gonna get back home okay." Iris came from behind and bent to help the struggling boy. Herman joined Charlie.

Sonny looked at her and grinned. "Who's worried?"

"Now where's the bottle?"

"In with the peanut butter sandwiches. If you break it, we got nothin to drink."

"Drink the river, stooge. No little kid like you's gonna drink any booze on this trip. Stunt your growth, shorty. We brought the bottle to break." Charlie rummaged among the paper sacks. "It's called a christening. That's a new word you can add to your vocabulary." He rose with the green bottle and walked to Iris. "Takes a lady, a real lady," with his good arm sweeping into a bow and handing the bottle to her, "to christen a boat. And you know what happens if you don't christen the boat?"

"What happens, Charlie?"

"Bad luck. Like when you break a mirror. Bad luck for seven years. Bad like when you step on a crack and break your mother's back. Bad goddamn luck, Sonny." Sonny lowered his eyes. He sniffed.

Herman put his arm on the boy's shoulder. "It's okay, Sonny. Lay off, Charlie. Come on, guys. Let's launch this baby. Get that bottle, Iris, before Charlie changes his mind and chugs it down." Iris took the bottle.

"Fall in, troops!" The boys lined up behind Charlie, stood at attention and saluted with him as Iris swung the bottle like a golf club against the hull of the canoe. The bottle bounced back, intact.

"Not there. Up there on the other end," Herman said.

"Bow, Auerbach. The goddamn bow."

"And hit it harder," Sonny added just as the bottle shattered and liquid foamed over the side. Sonny laughed. Everyone cheered.

Iris tossed the bottle back into a clump of greasewood. She turned to Charlie. "Take Sonny first. Then us." Charlie looked at her, then Herman, but didn't reply as he bent to the canoe and pulled it into the water.

Sonny pointed at Charlie's feet. "Aren't you gonna take off your shoes?"

"Keep em on. If the canoe tips, we may have to wade back over some rock. Get it, shrimpo?"

"Stop callin me shrimpo."

"Now shut up and listen up. I am the captain of this ship and I got some stuff to tell you. When I yell 'port' I mean left and 'stawb'd' means right."

"Hell, Charlie, Sonny doesn't even know what right and left mean."

"I do, too, right is where Kelly chewed up my right pants leg."

"You aren't wearin those pants, shrimpo. It don't make no nevermind. Shrimpo here isn't gonna come within a mile of a paddle. He's just ballast."

"Stop callin me shrimpo. And don't call me ballass either."

"Shut up. Up ahead is forward—and there's the boat bow—and behind is aft, the canoe's stern. The part you hold onto is the gunnel. You gotta know this stuff cause when I shout 'Port' you better go left or we're gonna take a bath. What else? Well, there's the beam, the waterline, thwart, the..."

"Come on, Charlie, stop showin off to Iris and let's get in and go someplace."

"Dammit, Sonny, you gotta do this the right way…"

"Yeah, Charlie, get out there and paddle."

"Yeah, come on."

"Okay, okay." Scowling, Charlie bent and held the canoe firmly by its gunwales while Sonny stepped to the bow. Then he pushed off, stepping in with paddle in hand, sitting in the stern, and dipping the paddle into the river, all in one smooth arc and loop. The canoe glided out into the river, emerald and sky-blue and diamond-scatter cresting and lapping at the canoe's stern, along its waterline as it began to tip and bob into low rocks and a gentle riffle. Herman and Iris sat on the sandy bank, he with legs crossed Indian-style, she with arms wrapped about shins, chin on knees. They rose, laughing as the canoe hit the riffle. Charlie shouted orders and Sonny whooped and cheered. They laughed when they heard Sonny giggle as the canoe bounced in the rapids. When it slid into gentler water, Sonny stood and clenched his hands over his head in a boxer's victory salute as Charlie yelled and splashed water up on him with the paddle.

"Sit down, Sonny," Iris shouted. "It's dangerous." Sonny sat.

Herman looked at Iris' face in the sun. **Auntie Ide. She looks like her mother. Somethin else. Ide and Mom. People always said they look alike, Ide and Mom. Sisters. Two peas in a pod, Mabel says.** Herman flushed when he realized Iris was looking back at him.

"What is it, Hermy?"

"I was just thinkin." He looked down at the sand, saw a small flat rock, picked it up.

"About what?"

"About Iris the Second here." He looked into his shirt pocket. The little snake was coiled upon itself in a tight ball. "Look." Iris leaned forward. Her hair brushed his chin. He pulled back and she looked up. He reached back for another flat stone and crooked his finger around it, leaned back, threw. The rock splashed into the water. "I never could make those damn things skip."

"Thinkin about what?"

"About today." He looked around for another rock. "Today. Today's a sort of funny day."

"Are you worried about the canoe?"

"No." He handed her a rock. "You try it."

She leaned, poised, and arced her arm, the stone leaving the tips of her fingers in a slim angle. The stone kissed the water, rose, touched again, again, another time, disappeared. "What's botherin you?"

"I was thinkin about my mother."

"You haven't been talkin about her."

"I don't think about her."

"Why not? Who doesn't think about their mother? Are you mad about the divorce? Mom says your mother didn't want the divorce. She says your dad was punishing her for dating that New York guy, that sailor…"

"His name is Johnny."

"So, are you mad?"

"No, I'm not mad."

"What happened?"

"You want to hear the story?"

"Hermy!"

"Okay, okay."

"The divorce was in October, here in Boise. Halloween was that week-end and I bought a skull mask, and all day I had been beggin Mom to make me a skeleton suit to go along with it. I was really happy and really sad. I was happy cause now she and Dad were back together—she had left this Johnny she was dating in Walla Walla and had come over to Boise to help me get started in school, and it looked like she was gonna stay with Dad there. And even if Mom and Dad had been fightin some, now it looked like they were getting along really good. And I was sad cause here it was Halloween and Billy and Clarence and Howard and all my friends were back in Walla Walla and I hardly knew anybody in Boise. Have you ever had to leave your home for a while?"

"No. When Mom married Cory, he came out to the orchard to live with us."

"It's sad. To lose all your friends." He looked around for another stone. "I didn't know it could get worse." He found one. Iris reached over and took it gently from his fingers. He looked at her, then away. "Well, that night we all went out to Shelton's Restaurant—that's a really good restaurant downtown—and had dinner. I had the hamburger steak and french fries. I wasn't eatin my green beans and Mom said. 'Eat your green beans, Hermy. Eat your beans or you can't have any...'" He suddenly choked. He closed his eyes. Iris touched his shoulder.

What's she thinking? He breathed deeply, aware of the whisper and hush of the lapping river as it touched the bank. He removed his glasses and pressed his palms against his eyes. **Tears.** He opened his eyes and looked out into the river. The river shimmered, its colors all one now. **It's a blur. Everything's always a blur. Like fog. I wish I could see.** He put his glasses back on and glanced at Iris, then glanced away. "You see, it was one of the happiest meals of my life. My family was back together again. Johnny was gone. Dad was laughin and jokin, and we were both teasin Mom about her new hairdo. Dad said it made her look like she was surprised, and she popped her eyes out at us, and I couldn't stop laughin. Mom can be really funny when she's feelin good." He smiled, then frowned.

"I don't want to tell this story."

"Tell it," Iris said.

"I went to a movie at the Pinney. They were having guests over at the house, a fat guy named Ted and his wife. But when I came home, nobody was there. I could smell cigarette smoke and Ted's cigar and when I looked at the coffee table, there were some empty beer bottles and some glasses. I held the bottles up to the light to see if there was any beer in them. I like beer. Once I sneaked around in the dark during a party and drank so much, Dad had to carry me to bed." Iris smiled. Herman tossed a stone into the river. "Go on, Hermy." Herman lay back on the sand. He laced his fingers across his stomach. He crossed his legs at the ankle. He closed his eyes and frowned.

"What happened then?"

He breathed deeply, held his breath, then expelled it, opened his eyes and rose to a sitting position. "You know, I forgot. I forgot all this. Now how in the hell could I..." He tossed another stone into the river. After it splashed, he began to speak again. "While I was standin by the coffee table, I saw this little scrap of paper. I read everything I can get my hands on. I picked it up.

I read the word 'divorce.' The article said Mom and Dad had got a divorce. I couldn't believe it. I read and reread the article. I just couldn't believe it." He closed his eyes. "Then...Yeah. Then I heard this sound comin out of my mouth and I couldn't believe it either. It was a...a little high sound, like a dog whimpering, like Kelly makes when he's scratching at the door. I was whimpering like a little dog. It surprised me so much I stopped. I looked at the article again. Then it hit me that my name was there, right there in the newspaper." He opened his eyes and turned to Iris. "I remember the exact words just like I had memorized them. 'Custody of their child, Herman Jacob, is yet to be determined.'"

"'Custody.' I didn't know what it meant. So I looked it up in the dictionary. It said somethin about guardians and it said somethin about police. And then I looked up 'guardian' and it said it was somebody 'legally in charge of a minor.' Those were the exact words—'legally in charge of a minor.'" He smiled and looked out into the river. "Well, I thought that meant they were gonna send me to an orphanage and that really scared me. It said 'custody is yet to be determined' and since they had both been in charge of me ever since I had been born, well, it had to mean somebody else. We didn't know anybody in Boise very well, yet, so I figured they were splitting up and givin me to an orphanage." He raised up on one elbow. "I wish they had. Instead Dad gave me to the Schultzes."

"The Schultzes?"

"That's another story. Well, this article didn't have the date on it. It was cut right out of the center of the paper. I went looking all over the house for the paper, but I couldn't find it. I wanted to find out how much time I had before the orphanage came to pick me up. I thought maybe I could run away. Maybe I could go to live with you and your mom." Iris nodded. "So I went to our neighbor's house—we had never spoken to them before—and I knocked on the door until some guy came to it, and I asked him for the paper. He asked me if anything was wrong. I said no. He gave me the paper and I went back home to look through it. I found the article. It had been written that day. I thought to myself, 'Well, that gives me some time.' Then I heard knocking at the front door and…and…well, I just went to pieces. I ran over to the door and locked it and started banging back and yelling, 'Get away, get away, I'm not goin with you, you get away!!!'" Herman had risen to one knee. "There was this little window high up in the door and I could barely see this guy's face in it lookin down and he was shoutin somethin. It scared the hell outta me. It sounded like he was really mad. But it was the guy who lived next door, a guy named Bart. He said he was worried about me, and he had come over to see if he could help."

"I finally let him in. I was sort of embarrassed, and we sat down and talked. I told him everything and showed him the article. He explained about custody and told me that there wasn't any orphanage gonna take me away and even if my folks were dumb enough to send me away, he'd take me himself, by God. He talked on and on and told a couple of jokes, and went back to his house and got us a couple of Milky Ways. It turned out that the house was his folks' house and he was a Marine just back from the South Pacific. He'd even been wounded but was almost okay. He showed me the scar. Anyway, he got me all calmed down, and I ate the Milky Way—I hadn't had one of those for a while but the Marines got them all the time—and then he took me downstairs to the basement where I slept, and he put me to bed. He was surprised at all the books in my bedroom and let me tell him who gave me some of them and what some of them were about. Then he told me to get undressed. I was sort of shy because in my family we never undressed in front of each other, but he said if I went into the Marines, I'd have to get over that crap. And when I picked up my pajamas, he took them away and said, 'Marines sleep in their skivvies.' That means underwear. And I still do sleep in my skivvies." Herman looked over at Iris, who was smiling. He blushed. He looked away. "Well, I do. You know I never saw Bart after he left me that night. I know that he went back to the war. I wonder where he is now. Probably in the South Pacific. I hope he makes it back."

Herman sat back. He dug his hand into the sand. "Then Mom and Dad came back. Bart was upstairs waitin for them and I know he was mad, cause he started shoutin and they didn't shout back. Then I heard the door slam and everything stopped. Then I heard Mom crying. The door to the basement opened and she started down the stairs. When she got to the bottom, she said "Hermy," but I was out on the other side of the bed, and I reached for some books, for my biggest Uncle Wiggly book, and I let her have it."

"You hit your Mom with a book?"

"Yes, and more than one. I was startin on the Hardy Boys when she backed up to the stairs and disappeared. Then everything was quiet for a while, and I heard the door open again. And I heard someone crying. It was my dad." His eyes widening, Herman turned to Iris. "My dad was crying. Can you believe it? When he was spanking me, he used to say that he would hit me only ten times if I didn't cry, but one more for each time that I did. He said that big boys don't cry, and here he was—a man—and crying. I was so surprised I just lay there and let him sit down and talk to me. I don't remember much of what he said, somethin about how it was all goin to be for the best, and how I would find somethin good comin out of this. And to be a man."

"And then I asked him about custody, and he said he was gonna have custody. I couldn't believe it. I wanted to say, 'You! I don't even know who you are. I don't even see you except on weekends when you have a hangover. Why isn't my mother taking me with her? She's the one I know. She's the one who's been around all the time. Where's she going? Where the hell is she going? She's the one I love. I love her, I love...'" Herman's ragged voice broke, and he lay back in the sand, his face buried in the crook of his arm. His words were now muffled. "She never told me why she wasn't taking me with her. I would of done anything to be with her. She left me and never told me why. She never told. Probably went back to Johnny. Or Jack. Why didn't she take me with her? Why?" His shoulders shook, sharply. He wept. He removed his glasses and rubbed his eyes. **God. I**

can't see anything. "Why did she leave me alone. I used to think about that all the time."

"When I woke up the next morning and I finished my Wheaties and went out onto the sidewalk to go to school, I looked around at all the fog and I asked myself, 'Why is she leavin me?' And after she left, I asked it and asked it until I thought I was gonna go crazy. And so I stopped." He stopped weeping. He rubbed his eyes again. "I just stopped. I just stopped thinkin about her. Even when I went to live with her that once. Well, I did say somethin. I asked her if she loved me and she said yes. So I asked her if she loved me more than she did Jack—that's my stepfather. And she said no. That was it. As far as I was concerned, I didn't have a mom any longer. I hardly ever thought about her, never day-dreamed about times with her, not when I lived with Dad or the Schultzes or the Williams. I just couldn't. It's not that I'm mad at her. Nothin like that. I just couldn't understand and I couldn't stop askin and I couldn't get any answers and I was goin crazy. It was killin me." He looked around. "I mean really killin me. I was dying." He looked out at the river.

Twenty

Herman coughed. He stood, brushing off his pants. Iris rose also. "Where'd the canoe go? I can't see it."

Herman polished his glasses. "Charlie's good at maneuverin. Especially with one arm. He cut sideways after the rapids and then drifted a little. I think he and Sonny are carryin it back up the bank but I can't quite see." Herman looked up at the cloudless blue sky.

"Hasn't been a thing hangin up there all summer. No clouds. No planes. You know the Japs never sent their planes to bomb Idaho after I taught Sonny how to spot them. And all that stuff my dad did being an air raid captain didn't amount to a hill of beans."

"My mother says that. 'Doesn't amount to a hill of beans.'"

"Yeah. I remember. I think all mothers say things like that."

"Look, Herman. What's that crawling over by the rock?"

Herman reached down and scooped up a small turtle. "A turtle. Looks like it lives in the river. Here." He held it out to Iris. "My mother sent me a tortoise when she was on her honeymoon. I named him Tank."

Iris set it in the palm of her left hand. "I like having a snake named after me."

He opened his pocket. "Old Iris the Second."

"Who ever heard of a snake named after a girl, for Christsakes?" Charlie came up behind them.

"Yeah, Herman, for Christsakes," Sonny repeated.

Herman swatted at Sonny but he ducked. "You been around Charlie too long, kid. You're beginnin to sound like him. Hey. Where's the canoe?"

"Hermy, the canoe is great. Did ya see us glidin along out there and bumpin into the rapids? Right before that I was signaling to ya. Did ya see?"

"Yeah, yeah, Sonny. Now where's the damn canoe? It's my turn to take Iris out."

"Not without me, pal." Charlie tapped Herman on the chest. "There's only room for three. Sonny can watch."

"I don't wanna stay by myself. What if you go way down the river and you never come back?"

Iris put her arm around the boy. "Sonny's right. He's too little to be left alone."

"Listen, kid. I'm the only one who really knows how to handle that baby. Now I want to take Iris out in the canoe. But Herman here doesn't trust me with Iris. So he thinks he has to come too. Now you want to get in the canoe. Four people and it sinks. Facts of life, Sonny. So what I'm gonna do is take them out for ten minutes. Cut sideways just like I did with you across those little rapids. In spittin distance the whole time. You won't be by yourself. Come on, Herman. Let's go get the canoe and portage it back here."

"Portage?"

"That means carry, jerk."

When they had portaged the canoe back and parked Sonny, and the three had boarded the canoe, the sun glittered on the river as they glided toward its center. Charlie paddled in the stern with his good arm first on one side, then on the other. Herman could feel the shift of the canoe as he moved. **I can feel it. Feel how deep it's getting. Rocks that people never touch. Fish.** He shivered.

Iris trailed her hand in the water. "Water's nice." She waved to Sonny under the leaves of the scrub, blue leaves tinted by sun and sky. **Slanting rays of sun. Sparkling water.** Herman felt muscles loosen, breath slow to an easy rhythm. **This is neat. She really slips through the water. This is the best I've felt for a long time. It was good talking to Iris. Even my neck feels good, bump on my head gone, stomach just there neat and glidin along with the canoe, not all in knots.** He leaned back against the bow and smiled at Iris. She smiled back. "This is a lot better than going to the jail with Mom. If it's like the last time he was in jail, all Cory will do is yell and swear at Mom the whole time. Thanks for askin me to come, Herman."

Charlie dug his oar in sharply. The canoe dipped, rose, and surged ahead. He addressed Iris' back. "Thanks to Herman and Charlie. It was my idea to invite you. Didn't he tell you that?"

"Your idea to invite her and your idea to keep callin her a dame."

"Tryin to make me look bad, Auerbach?" But Charlie resumed paddling smoothly, maneuvering sideways. Sonny had begun walking down the bank, keeping them in sight.

"You know, guys," Iris began, "This river really is something—right in the middle of all this sagebrush. When we came on the bus on Friday, all we saw was desert. Remember Washington, Herman? The apple orchards with blossoms and then apples, and after apple picking when the leftover apples rot on the ground under the trees? You know, this is the first time I've been out of Washington."

"Sometime, Iris, I'll show you California" Charlie said. "Now there's a real state. Not just desert. You should see San Francisco on a Sunday morning, not just river and desert. Ocean, red roofs with slate tiles, fog, Chinese, Mexicans, bars, and the knocked out whores and drunks."

"Aw, quit showing off, Charlie."

Charlie frowned. Then he laid the paddle at his feet and tapped Iris on the shoulder. "Iris, you're next. You said you wanted to paddle. I'm gonna swap seats with you." He rose. The canoe shuddered. Herman's stomach knotted. Charlie stepped past the girl, brushing her body with his hip, and knelt between her and Herman to grasp the gunwale. He grinned at Herman. "Showing off, huh? Makin you nervous, Auerbach?" He rocked suddenly. Herman grasped the gunwale. "Okay, Iris, you move on back. Don't step on the paddle." As she did so, Herman stared at the river. **The water. It's gonna tip. He's gonna do this to me.**

"Auerbach, you're cramping my style. I'm getting goddamned sick of you. Ya wanna see showing off?" Charlie shifted his weight sharply to the left. The canoe heaved.

"Stop it, Char-lie" Sonny shouted from the bank.

Herman watched Charlie. **Is that Sonny? Sounds like he's in a barrel.** "Cut it out, Charlie. You're rocking the boat. Listen to me."

"Why should I listen, buster. Do you listen to me?"

"Leave him alone, Charlie!" Iris moved from the seat to grab Charlie's shoulder. The canoe jumped erratically and began to spin slowly in the river.

"Get your hands off me unless you mean business, honey. I'm gonna teach the competition here a little lesson. Here you go, Cinderella! See how you like talkin to the sailor underwater."

Charlie swung all of his weight to the right. The canoe wavered and spun fully sideways just as the current grabbed it. All three rose. Charlie grabbed the other side of the canoe with his good arm to complete the flip and plunged into the cold river water.

"You bastard! The rocks!" Iris screamed as she fell.

"NO!" Herman shouted.

Suspended. Triangles of blue. "Son-of-a..." "God!" "Shit!" Herman looped into the silver air. **So quiet. Like silver. Silver silence.** Time became space. **So slow. Lazy day. Here I am.** He looked at the river below him, gray and blue, sun-scattered. **I'm gonna die. I can't swim. Not a lick.** He smiled and licked his lips just before water punched up his nose—**ouch**—and he snorted it, sneezed it, coughed, choked. His body went down until his feet went over his head, the soles of his shoes coming flat down in a cracking splash. The current swung his body to the right. **Whoops.** And he broke the surface. He tried to breath again, gagged. He saw Iris' head out of the water. **Hair's all slicked down. Like a seal. Swims like a seal.** He saw her hand catch the canoe. **There. Good.** Off to the right Charlie sprawled, clinging to a great boulder. **Like he just fell from the sun.**

And now the water was next to Herman's face. He felt its flatness. **On my cheeks. Like pavement when I fell skating. My nose.** His nose entered the water again. **Well, I'll just hold my breath, that's all. Faster down there. And I can't stop. I'm late, I'm late for a very important date. Hey, Sonny. I know now! This is what it's like in the tank. In the name of the father....**

Herman tried to open his eyes underwater, saw a rush of shapes spin up, a river of light. **Oh my God, I lost my glasses again. Dad, I couldn't help it about the glasses. I can still throw the ball, Dad. And punch the bag. And old Karl. Even without the glasses. I'll hit him, Dad. Knock the shit out of him. Promise. Scout's honor. Dad. Dad? Suddenly Jake's face before him. I'm afraid. Right in my gut, my balls, I gotta piss, piss my pants. Oh hell, I'm wet anyway. Who'll know. My God. My chest. It's getting big. I'm gonna explode. Now why in the hell didn't I learn to swim? It's gettin darker down here. Sandy! What're you doin here, Sandy? Hey. My cap's gone. How do you keep your mask on? What's that signal? Three fingers up. Now one down. Lucky number. No. Three times. Then dead. Strike three. And I'm out. Hi, Frank. How they hangin? Dad, it's Frank. He's drowning too. And I did hit Karl. See the blood back there? Thin ribbon of blood. Just like this ribbon in Ide's book. Hymnal. "Stand up, Herman. Stand up and sing." I'm comin up, Auntie Ide "Stand up, Herman. Stand!" Ah. Boom Da-daa!!**

Emerging from the water were Herman's fingertips, his hands and arms. Next, water broke about the crown of Herman's head and exploded in a circle outward from his skull, hair plastered flat, his forehead, his open blue eyes, his pressed lips. **It's a miracle. Thanks, God. Thanks Dad. I got another chance! Look at that blue, blue sky.**

"Yow!" Air burst from him and he gasped raggedly, then cleanly filled his lungs. To his left, bobbed the canoe. Iris was hanging on with one hand and reaching out to him with the other. Beyond her, Charlie swam a strong side-stroke with his good arm.

For a moment, Herman lay on his back in the water. His face dipped in and out of the water surface. Lacing thin and supple before his eyes was a ruby snake of blood. **Blood. Charlie's blood. The blood shed for you. The body given for you.**

"There he is, Charlie. Grab him. What's he doin? Oh, Charlie, he's drowning! He can't swim and I can't reach him...he's going under again!"

"Come here, you son-of-a...."

And the Son. Here we go, son. Under again. Number three! You only got three times. Three times a loser and then yer OUT! Dead. D-E-A-D. Dead. Look at the bubbles, silver bubbles. I wonder if I can breathe them. And rocks. Watch it! A jagged rock tore at Herman's shirt and bit into his right shoulder. **Got me. I'll come along without any trouble, sir. So long, sun. So long, Sonny. Sonny! Where's Sonny! Goddamn you, God! Why are you baptizing the Schultz boys? What a waste of time. They're sons-of-bitches. Help Sonny instead. He's my boy, aren't you Sonny? You're gonna make it back to Max. And Helen. And Iris. Hey, wait a minute! That little snake's in my pocket. Little Iris! She's gonna drown. Get her out. Go. Up. Iris. I'll take Iris up. I can't reach the roof of the water. Here, Iris. Here.**

"Damn it, Herman, it's the shoes," **Iris' voice, clear as a silver bell in the sunlight above the water. Sonny running along the bank. Yelling.** "Don't drown, Hermy!" **And Tom. And Charlie. And Max. All running and yelling.** "Don't drown, Hermy! Untie those shoes. Kick them off." **No. Mom bought them for me at Sears. I look out here at Herman Auerbach, his little head bobbing, so small out there in the river, the canoe bobbing nine feet to the right.** "Kick off those shoes, you little son-of-a-bitch and swim over there! Goddamnit, swim over there!!!"

They're ghosts, just ghosts. Tom is dead. He can't be on the shore. I can't be on the shore. I'm dead. We're all ghosts. Like the Holy Ghost. Who's pulling me back under. Blow out the air. "Take off the shoes, Hermy!" **It's the iceman. Not the minister. Look at those muscles! The iceman's face, a skull. Tongs reaching down. They can't touch me. Ice melting around my mother. She's rubbing my arm with ice. My polio arm.**

Take off your shoes, Herman. You can't wear them to bed. Down to the bottom. Are those marbles? Steelies? Green marbles. No that's broken glass down there. Green glass. Christening. Red glass. Broken vase. Ashes for tomatoes. Brown glass. Broken root beer bottles. Exploding. Take off your shoes, Herman. You can't wear them in the bathtub. But there's glass. I'm so tired. Uncle Frank's bald skull. At the bottom. Glass and rocks turning into magic flowers. Iris. Rose.

Pull it together. No. No NO. There go the laces. Damn, that shoe's heavy. I'm sleepy. I could drift and drift. A fish. Look at those whiskers. Ow! That hurt! A goddamn catfish. Ow, Mom, you're pulling too hard when you're cutting. Mom. Mom? Where are you? You can't leave me! Not again! Look at my arm. Hey. Look at that arm. Red eyes. Snake. The scales. They aren't scales. They're feathers! Are those wings? Murph put wings on the snake. Damn you, Murphy, can the snake fly? That Murph. What a character! So the snake can fly. And angels. Is it all over? Heaven. Angels blowing fish bubbles. Angels. Like Auntie Ide said.

"Ow." Pillow? Was this a dream. Hell, it's no pillow—it's a goddamn rock.

"Get his head up. He's choking."

"He's throwing up. He's gonna die!" **Sonny. Will I never escape that little peepy canary voice of his?** They had put him on the riverbank. **Iris, Charlie, somebody pulled me from the river.** Iris was shaking him hard. **Over and over again. And it's making me mad. I wanted to lay down here and sleep. Mad.**

"He's just got a lot of water in his lungs. Look. He's opening his eyes!" **Blue leaves. Bright sky. Spears of light in my eyes. Ow. Oww. Where are my glasses?** "Goddamn you, Herman Auerbach. What were you doing out there drowning? Why did you even go out in a canoe? You can't swim a lick, you little son-of-a-bitch." Herman closed his eyes. **Uncle Cory. Cusses like Uncle Cory. Why's he talking in a girl's voice?** Iris punched him on the shoulder. **Jesus.** "Breathe, dammit. I didn't haul you all the way back here to have you die on me. Breathe!" **Leave me alone. I didn't mean to bring the rat into the barn. Don't send me away. This is my last chance.** Herman squinted at the figures around him. **Just clouds. The cloud people. I'm among the cloud people.** Iris punched him hard on the shoulder again. **No, I'm not. And it isn't heaven. The ground is too hard. The people are too mad. Well, so am I. Goddamn it.**

"Iris, quit whackin him." **Sounds like Charlie.**

"It's what Ma does when I choke. She whacks until it comes back up, and it's comin up."

"Here he goes again. Watch out!"

"No! All over my blouse!"

After vomiting, Herman's head fell back against the hard rock. He moaned. He stared at the misty figures around him, heard their mouths form angry words. **It's Iris and Charlie and Sonny.**

"And you, you screw head," Iris turned toward Charlie, "It's all your fault."

"What'd ya mean 'my fault'?" **He's losing it.** Herman squinted and brought into focus Charlie's face, white under shining wet black hair, white except for the blackening red dried in a jagged wound **like a lightning bolt** into his cheek. **He's marked.** "What about you? You're family." **She's family.** "Didn't you know he couldn't swim?"

"What's the matter with you, Charlie, huh? Why'd you flip the canoe? Jesus!"

Herman squinted at Iris. **Yeah. Why?** She rolled back on her heels and took a breath. Her wet blond hair swung out over her shoulders. Her wild blue eyes centered on Sonny, softened, calmed. **Sonny's crying.**

Iris tried to soothe him. "I tried to throw him up over the canoe, but he slid right off into the current and then down. He doesn't know a goddamn thing about lifesaving. He doesn't even know how to be saved. He left his shoes on and they kept pulling him down. Jesus. I thought he was a goner for sure. I guess he finally heard me and untied them cause he floated back up and the shoes are gone. Look, Sonny. Just socks."

Sorry, Mom. I lost your shoes. Your Sears shoes. Had to think of myself. And it worked. I floated. I floated the deadman's float. Rose was there. Just under the surface. See her? Blowing bubbles. Angel wings fluttering.

Sonny said something. **From far, far away.** "He don't look so good."

"So what are we gonna do now, for Christ sakes?"

"He needs a doctor."

"Don't you think I know that, Sonny? Oh, stop crying. We don't have time. Here, honey. Blow your nose. I'm not mad at you. I'm just scared. Like you."

This chest of mine is heavy. Caving into a cave, dark and dim, back down there. Rushing water, deep down. So heavy. I hear those children again. All those children running along the riverbank. Running and shouting, "Stop! Help! Stop!" Tom and Max. Charlie. Iris. Sonny. "Help. Stop." It doesn't matter, kids. Don't you get it? I already went down three times. See the angels?

"Get him way up in the back with the hay. I'd help you but I got a bad back."

"Watch his head!"

"No. NO." **Why do I keep saying NO? Bright sky. That hurts. Blue leaves. Sun triangles. Yellow feathers. Going down again.** "No. I took the shoes off." **Rose blew a huge silver bubble around Herman.** In the bubble, dark and soft, blanketing him, he floated outside of 1945.

"Dammit, Herman. Stop saying 'no.' You've got to want to live. Or the river will slosh around in your lungs and stay there and you won't make it, Goddamnit. It was hard work saving you. I didn't save you so that you could decide to die. Now you work, damn you!"

"Gotta wanna. Ma always says that. Don't die, Hermy. Please."

"He's gonna make it. Come here, Sonny. Sit on my lap." **It's always okay for Sonny. Somebody always makes the world okay for Sonny.**

"He's gonna make it. He's a fighter." **No. Boxer. Uncle Frank was a boxer. I forgot. Rose said I would be a boxer. And her sister said "The river within. Touch the river within." She didn't say anything about drowning.**

River water in my lungs. That's what killed me. Rose. Her mouth moves, keeping the bubble going. And words are coming in. "You'll find them when you let go." **Life line. She's drawing on my palm. The line falls off. A fishing line into the river. Her mouth moves again.** "Love." **Is she saying love? Or live?** "Something isn't like it seems," **she said.** "Or people aren't who you think they are." **She's saying something. Always saying something.**

Sunset. Clouds. Clouds with faces. The angel Rose rising over the desert. Rose. "Love. Herman, you can't hold on to love. I can't reach you. You have to save yourself, Hermy." **Feathered yellow wings. The smell**

of sagebrush. Beans. A whole hill of beans. Snakes poking their heads out of a hill of beans. Uncle Frank showing Tom how to catch snakes. Bombs exploding into skeletons. Uncle Frank's head. Millions of Franks. Leaping jack rabbits twisting. Jerking. Dying. Get away, Sonny. You're not supposed to be here. Let go of his hand, Sonny. Tom's dead. Frank's dead. You can't come in here. Let go of my hand.

Pop! The pin broke the bubble of night.

"Let go of my hand, Sonny. Let go." **Yellow feathered wings fluttered, settled.**

"He's openin his eyes. I told you he would." **I can't see without my glasses. Sonny and Uncle Frank.** "Get away from him, Sonny." **Little son-of-a-bitch.**

He was back on the sun porch. **And I'm back on the sun porch. Back home. Auntie Ide!** "Herman, Herman. You hear me? You and Charlie are gonna come back with me and pick apples." **Charlie? Aren't I ever gonna get rid of him?** "Iris would like that. You'll stay at the farm. I need some strong young men. Look at this muscle." **Her hands are rough. Patting, patting.**

"This time..." **Oh my God, it's him. My glasses. The damned glasses. Did I lose the keys, too?** The key necklace was gone.

"Dad..."

"It's okay, Herman. You can go back with your aunt and Iris. You need family right now. And I probably need to be alone for a while to get some work done." **Yes. Yes. Huh. Now look at that. I never noticed that. Black hair. Dad. Frank. Charlie. They all have black hair.** Jake's hand touched his cheek. Tears filled his eyes and the people swarmed about him in his vision. **Like fish. Like canaries.**

"Wake up, Hermy. Please wake up. Ya can read about the drownin in your Dad's lousy newspaper. Look at this! Ya came back to life. Ya made the front page." Sonny was tugging on his hand. Herman rolled away and felt a juggling ball roll after him, next to his back. **Sonny, Sonny, those damned balls.... Sonny, Sonny, you should've seen the snakes in the hill of beans in the desert. And the angels. Murphy put feathers on the snake, not scales.**

"Herman. It's Iris." **Iris, not Uncle Cory. And Ide. Iris and Ide. Mom's face in Ide's. And in Iris. They are all there. All three are there. Lucky three.** He opened his eyes. A canary softly fluttered its wings, peeped.

"Hermy, are you awake?" Sonny asked.

"How long have I been asleep?"

"There's somethin else your gonna wanta know. Somethin real big."

"What, Sonny?"

"They dropped a bomb on the Japs! A BIG bomb!! It wiped out a whole city!!!"

"WHAT?"

About the Authors

E dwin Casebeer was born in Boise, Idaho in 1933. He earned graduate degrees at the University of Montana and the University of Washington. He is currently Professor Emeritus, following his career as Professor and English Department Chair at Indiana University Purdue University at Indianapolis (IUPUI). He specialized in popular culture studies. He has published *Herman Hesse*, a definitive work on this author, as well as short stories in *Evergreen Review*. He currently serves as Editor in Chief for Serealities.com, an online new fiction site.

Linda Casebeer was born in 1947 in Boone, Iowa. She and her husband, Edwin, have five children. She earned graduate degrees at The Citadel and Indiana University, and was Associate Professor at the University of Alabama at Birmingham School of Medicine. She is a cofounder of Serealities.com. She has written *The Last Eclipsed Moon*, poems published by Cherry Grove Collections, and *Love Spells*, published as a serial story on serealities.com, and as a novella by Serealities Press.

Serealities™ Press is an imprint of LTLW, LLC. Serealities Press publishes novellas and novels from authors published on the serealities.com website. Serealities.com publishes new fiction weekly, serial stories where readers vote to change the story. For more new fiction published weekly by these authors and others, go to serealities.com

Made in the USA
San Bernardino, CA
28 May 2015